VLADIMIR

Russia on the Pacific, and the Siberian Railway

VLADIMIR

Russia on the Pacific, and the Siberian Railway

ISBN/EAN: 9783337169619

Printed in Europe, USA, Canada, Australia, Japan

Cover: Foto ©Andreas Hilbeck / pixelio.de

More available books at **www.hansebooks.com**

RUSSIA ON THE PACIFIC

AND THE

SIBERIAN RAILWAY

BY

VLADIMIR

AUTHOR OF 'THE CHINA-JAPAN WAR'

8785

'Туда, гдѣ царствовалъ Чингисъ'

'There where Genghiz reigned'

(From the Verses recited in honour of Muravioff on the 9th May, 1854)

WITH MAPS AND ILLUSTRATIONS

LONDON

SAMPSON LOW, MARSTON & COMPANY

(LIMITED)

Publishers to the India Office

1899

TO MY READERS

My last book, on the events which revealed to the world the rising young nation of the Far East, met with such unexpected success, and was so kindly reviewed, that I feel encouraged to publish the results of my studies on the expansion of that European nation which has two centuries of history in the Far East, though the fact has only lately attracted public attention. I have treated at some length ancient history both in Russia and Siberia, but I thought such treatment was necessary to enable the reader to form just notions of present conditions. Great ignorance prevails about Russia, even in the most unexpected quarters, as will appear by the following extract.

In the 'Nineteenth Century' for June 1898, No. 256, in an article by Mr. H. M. Stanley, M.P., 'Splendid Isolation or What?' at p. 873 there is the following passage :—

'Is this picture far-fetched? He who dares say so betrays his ignorance of the rate of Russian progress over Asia. Twenty-eight years ago she had just effected a landing on the eastern shore of the Caspian. During this short interval she has stridden across the continent, and is now at Port Arthur preparing for the locomotive from St. Petersburg.'

Here we have a prominent man upbraiding people for ignoring what is historically false. Russia has not stridden across the continent in the last twenty-eight years ; she did traverse Asia very rapidly—in about half a century— but it was more than two centuries ago.

As I studied the history of Russia and of her expansion in Northern Asia, I had gradually to discard the prejudices and false notions which are generally entertained about Russia in Western Europe. It is my object, therefore, to dispel in the minds of the public the errors which I formerly entertained, and to give a clear idea of Russia's work in the world. It is only at present that, as with Great Britain, the real mission of Russia, her extra-European and world-mission, is appearing before men's minds. For the future history of the world, the conquest of Siberia will be more important than most of the modern history of European Russia.

The subject has been difficult because the Russians themselves have not paid much attention to it, and I fear that, like most Westerners, I have committed many blunders. I have, however, spared no pains to perform my work conscientiously. I have studied the language carefully, and I spent four months in travelling across the Empire, from Vladivostok to the frontier of Galicia. I have also had the kind assistance of a cultured Russian nobleman, both in my travels and in my studies, and I have had thus the opportunity of seeing things from a

Russian point of view—the most important when one wishes to sketch the history of the country.

The critics of my former work paid me the flattering compliment of supposing I was a Japanese, and I wish, though I can hardly hope, that my assiduous study of a little-known subject may lead them to suppose now that I am a Russian.

The following works will be found useful by those who wish to improve their knowledge of the subject :—

RUSSIAN.

SOLOVIEFF : *History of Russia.*

ANDRIEVITCH : *History of Siberia* and *Siberia in the Nineteenth Century.*

SALOVNIKOFF : *Our Colonial Pioneers.*

Lieut.-Col. RAGOZA : *Short Account of the Occupation of the Amur Region.*

ANONYMOUS : *History of the River Amur* (St. Petersburg, 1859).

BARSUKOFF : *Count Muravioff-Amurski* (biographical materials).

MINISTRY OF FINANCE : *Siberia and the Great Siberian Railway.*

MAXIMOFF : *Our Problems on the Pacific.*

KRAEFSKI : *World Transit and the Siberian Railway.*

FRENCH.

DU HAILLY : *Revue des Deux Mondes,* August 1, September 1, 1858 (account of the war in the Pacific).

ENGLISH.

ATKINSON's book on the Amur.

Prince WOLKONSKI : *Pictures of Russian History and Russian Literature* (Lamson, Wolffe & Co., Boston, New York, and London).

This last work will be invaluable to persons desirous of forming clear general views about Russia.

CONTENTS

a

ILLUSTRATIONS

PLATES

MAPS

RUSSIA ON THE PACIFIC

CHAPTER I

THE EXPANSION TO THE URAL

THE northern part of the old continent forms an almost continuous plain from the Pacific Ocean to the shores of the Baltic and Black Sea. This striking geographical similarity has affected the whole history of the races that have dwelt there at different periods. The few mountain chains such as the Ural and the Yablonoi are of such inconsiderable height that they form no permanent obstacle to men accustomed to roam for hundreds and thousands of miles on the boundless prairies. This absence of natural boundaries has led the nomad races of a primitive state of society to wander almost along the whole length of the ancient continent, while it has facilitated the formation of huge empires when the genius of a conqueror like Genghis Khan or the powerful political organisation of Moscow has appeared on the field of history. The same causes have produced these various effects, and the present division of European and Asiatic Russia is only a modern counterpart of the European and Asiatic Scythia of Herodotus. The whole region offers such a sameness of features that it forms a geographical unit, and its inhabitants are bound either by identity of life and customs or by a common political power.

B

In the early ages, when, through scarcity of population and absence of cultivation of the soil, nomadic habits prevailed, almost the whole region was overrun by Asiatic races which, pressing westwards in successive waves, constituted those terrible invaders known in European history as the Huns, the Magyars, and the Mongols, besides others only known to Russian history. In modern times the process has been reversed ; a single race, Christian and civilised, of sedentary habits, has slowly but steadily pushed westwards, conquering as much by its policy and culture as by the sword its former conquerors—the Asiatic nomads which destroyed the Roman empires of the East and West.[1] This has been accomplished by the principal branch of that great Slav race which is still so young that it may be said to have only lately made its appearance in history.

Before examining how this long march of conquest was accomplished, it will be necessary to briefly sketch the origin and early vicissitudes of the race. By this method the following events will stand in their true light, not as accidental enterprises of bold adventurers, but as necessary consequences of a whole series of historical antecedents. These consequences were doubtless hastened by the character of the men who had a hand in their accomplishment, but their advent had already been fatally indicated far back in the past.

Our earliest knowledge of the Slav races only goes back to the ninth century, when they occupied a tract of country extending from the Balkans and the Adriatic to the Baltic, and from the Elbe to Lake Ladoga, the upper course of the Volga and Oka, and the course of the Dnieper. They thus occupied the greater part of Prussia,

---

[1] Though Rome was destroyed by the Germans, its fall was indirectly due to the pressure of the Asiatic hordes and to the conquests of Attila.

Austria, and the Balkan peninsula, but only a small portion of modern European Russia: the modern cities of St. Petersburg and Moscow indicate approximately their extreme northern and western frontiers. The Slavs are supposed to have come from the banks of the Danube [1]: an origin which would show that in prehistoric times the direction of their migrations had been north and east. This tendency has continued in later times, as we now find the Slavs pushed back from the Elbe on the west, and struggling for independence on the south, while they have extended over the whole northern part of the continent, far away east up to the Pacific.

It will not be necessary to pay much attention to the political development of the western and southern Slavs, as it does not concern the subject we are treating; and indeed later the political power of the Poles had rather an adverse influence. The north-eastern Slavs, or the ancestors of the present Russians, were at a very early age divided into many independent tribes or races [2] who lived in constant discord. Their mutual warfare rendered them an easy prey to their neighbours, whom their united strength could have easily vanquished. This fact should be borne in mind, as therein lies, as we shall see, the explanation of the modern political organisation of the present Russian empire.

In the ninth century the scattered, disunited Russian races were subject to attacks from southern and northern enemies. The southern invaders, the Kozari, a nomadic race dwelling on the Don and the Volga, in that steppa region which was the bane of early Russia, were so successful that they imposed a tribute [3] on the southern

---

[1] Solovieff, *History of Russia.*

[2] Ilmenski, Krivichi, Polochane, Radimichi, Viatichi, Sieveriane, Drevliane, Poliane, Volynane, Uglichi.

[3] A squirrel from each hearth.

Russians. The northern foes, called the Varaghi by the Russians, were the Normans or Northmen of western history. They plundered and conquered the Russians and also the Finnish tribes, who then occupied the whole of North Russia up to St. Petersburg. For a short time the Russians united, and drove away the Scandinavian invaders; but as soon as the foreign enemy had ceased to be dangerous, the usual internal troubles broke out. The confusion was so great that at last the Ilmenski and Krivichi sent ambassadors to their former foes—the Varaghi—to search for princes to govern them. The envoys said, according to the ancient chronicles: 'Our country is large and abundant, but there is no order; come over and be our princes, and govern us.' In response to this invitation (A.D. 862) Ruric and two other Scandinavian chieftains came over; the former reigned in Novgorod to the south of St. Petersburg, the present capital of Russia; the two others ruled the country around Lake Onega,[1] and part of the present government of Pskof. By the early death of his fellow princes, Ruric remained sole lord of the northern Slavs, and he left the throne to his descendants, from whom most of the noble Russian families claim their descent.

The route selected by Ruric for effecting his conquests was similar to that chosen by his brethren, the dreaded sea-kings of Western Europe; he followed the natural water-ways, passing from the Baltic to Lake Ladoga, and to the river Volkhof, where he halted at the town of Novgorod. His successors extended their conquests in the same direction, passing from Lake Ilmen to the river Lovat, whence they crossed the water-shed and descended by the Dnieper, taking in succession Smolensk and Kief. This latter town, which had been already occupied by

---

[1] Then inhabited by Finnish races (Solovieff, *History of Russia*).

some Varaghian adventurers styled usurpers by their more powerful brethren of Novgorod, now (A.D. 882) became the capital of the embryo Russian state.

This change of capital was of the greatest importance for the whole future history of the people. Novgorod was in water communication with the Baltic, the sea of the wild heathen Scandinavians, while Kief, by the Dnieper, communicated with the Black Sea, at whose outlet lay Constantinople, the only centre of civilisation in Europe at that dark period. The immediate results which followed in quick succession were : first piratical attacks on the Greek empire ; then a series of wars and treaties, which gradually established commercial and diplomatic relations between the two states, culminating in the marriage of a Russian sovereign with a Greek princess.

Oleg, the immediate successor of Ruric (A.D. 879–912), led an expedition of 2,000 boats against Constantinople. The Russians at that period employed canoes formed of a single huge trunk dug out, with the sides raised by planks. In these rude craft they boldly navigated the Dnieper and the Black Sea, beaching their boats and dragging them overland whenever necessary. Sviatoslav (957–972) had a long series of wars with the Greeks in consequence of his conquests in Bulgaria. His object was to extend the Russian dominions southwards, and to transfer the capital to a city on the Danube. But the Byzantine empire still possessed too much power, and the Russians, notwithstanding their reckless bravery, were obliged to retreat. The next sovereign, Vladimir, also warred with the Greeks until he married the Grecian princess, Anna. This marriage brought about the most important event in the ancient history of the country : the conversion to Christianity (A.D. 988) of Vladimir and his people.

In little over a century the successors of Ruric had gradually extended their sway over the country along the great water-ways between the Baltic and Black Sea, which had already been used as the great commercial route of Eastern Europe.[1]   Their expansion was from north to south, and was only stopped by the Byzantine empire.   Their contact with the only polished people of Europe not only brought Christianity, but a certain degree of culture : reading, writing, and a knowledge of architecture, necessary for the construction of the churches erected in all the towns, were derived from the Greeks.   As the Russians received Christianity from Constantinople they adopted the Orthodox creed; this fact was of great consequence to their future history.   The final separation and bitter hostility of the Greek and Latin Churches created a barrier, almost impassable in the Dark Ages, between Russia and the rest of Europe, which had received its Christianity from Rome.   The isolation of Russia was increased by later events, which cut off her communications even with Constantinople, and she was left to develop her national life under almost exclusively Asiatic influences.

The united state which Ruric and his successors had created by their valour and wisdom, and which had put an end to dissensions and the shameful tribute to the hordes of the steppes, was unfortunately of short duration. The kingdom declined into a form of feudalism peculiar to Russian history.   At the death of the sovereign, Yaroslav the Wise (A.D. 1054), his lands were divided among his children, and this system was continued by

---

[1] Nearly along the line of the recently projected canal between the Baltic and Black Sea.

all the new princes, who at death bequeathed appanages to their several descendants. The only check on this indefinite subdivision of the country lay in the ambition of the petty princes: the weaker states being often absorbed by the stronger. These feeble attempts at reunion of the country were dearly paid for by the evils of incessant warfare and malevolent intriguing between the petty feudatories.

The history of Russia went back two centuries: the renewed dissensions brought back the old attacks from north and south, from the Scandinavians and nomads of the steppes. The latter had never desisted from their pillaging raids on the Russians, inflicting severe losses even when the country was united under the Varaghian sovereigns; but after long struggles they had been repulsed and they vanished from history, never to appear again, as was the fate of the Pechenegs. But their place was taken by fresh hordes from Asia.

The broad plain which extends from the Ural mountains to the Caspian Sea has been always the open gate through which Asiatic invasions have poured into Europe. In the second half of the eleventh century the Polovtsy penetrated into Europe through this highway, overwhelmed the Pechenegs, and spread over the whole of Southern Russia. The vast plain which forms the eastern part of Europe was covered by dense forests in the north at that period, and offered considerable natural difficulties to the raids of the nomads; but the southern part, the steppe, was covered only by thick vegetation of tall grass and wild flowers (so picturesquely described by Gogol[1]) which served only to hide in their 'green embrace' the advancing swarms of predatory horsemen.

The Polovtsy, following the custom of their prede-

---

[1] **Tarass Bulba.**

cessors, the Pechenegs, made annual incursions among
the Russians, destroying, pillaging, and carrying into
captivity the unfortunate peasants.   This new and
formidable enemy did not awaken the warring Russian
princes to the dangers of their country and prompt them
to united action.   Some even forgot the ties of blood, of
Christianity, and nationality, and allied themselves to the
nomads for the petty object of their personal aggrandisement.   The sufferings of the Russian people during this
period of internal discord and foreign invasion are
touchingly rendered in the words of an old Russian song :
' Sorrow grew on the Russian soil.'

For some time, Kief, the mother of Russian towns,
continued to be the most important political centre.   The
eldest of the reigning family, recognised as lord paramount with the title of Grand Duke, always chose it as his
capital.   But during one of the civil wars Kief was
besieged, taken, and pillaged (A.D. 1169) ; the conqueror,
George Bogolinbski, instead of remaining in the conquered town, returned to his beloved residence in the
north, where he established the new capital of the disordered country.   From that time the centre of political
life shifted permanently to the north-east, passing successively to Rostof, Vladimir, and later, as we shall see, to
Moscow.

This event was of great importance, greater than
could be foreseen at the time.   National ambition was
no longer directed regretfully towards that Byzantine
empire, now separated by a wide zone of triumphant
nomadism, but tended eastwards to the wide unknown
lands either uninhabited or occupied by scanty, unwarlike
tribes.   A slow process of colonisation began in the
region, which in its present geographical denomination
bears the trace of the historical rôle it has played.   The

Russia of ancient times, the Russia of Ruric, now became Little Russia, while the vast region slowly colonised, which bore the same relation to the former state that Magna Grecia bore to Hellas, now assumed the name of Great Russia. The expansion checked on the south tended for some centuries eastwards, under the immediate guidance of the new capitals situated in a region almost surrounded and intersected by the upper waters of the Volga and its affluents, the Oka, the Moskva, and the Kostroma. The geographical features of this region resemble that 'Ile de France' which about the same time constituted the kernel from which the following centuries were to evolve the monarchy of France.

The same causes which had necessitated a transfer of the political centre to the north-east brought about a change in the commercial field. Kief and the adjoining cities, which had grown rich and flourishing with the southern trade down the Dnieper to the Black Sea, languished in poverty when their river trade-route was commanded by the victorious and predatory Polovtsy. Novgorod—the city which, by calling in Ruric and his Scandinavians, had laid the basis of a powerful state— now became the great emporium of trade in Russia. The water-way by the river Volkhof, Lake Ladoga, and river Neva into the Gulf of Finland and the Baltic was free ; while the regions of Northern Russia, along the banks of the North Dvina, Petchora, and Kama, were then rich in rare and precious furs. The enterprising citizens of Novgorod sent expeditions to the north, levying tribute of furs from the Finnish aborigines, and distributed the produce throughout Europe. The city became the richest in Russia, and was called Novgorod the Great, and, as its republican constitution did not give it sufficient status in an age rife with feudal notions, it received a kind of collective nobility, and was officially styled ' Sir Novgorod.'

The wealth and prosperity of the inhabitants of Novgorod attracted the hostility of their neighbours. The Swedes endeavoured to drive them away from the Neva and Ladoga, closing all free access to the Baltic. They also tried to destroy the Greek Christianity which had been introduced by the Russians among the Finnish races dwelling on the Gulf of Finland. The Latin form of Christianity adopted by the Scandinavians and Germans formed everywhere a convenient pretext for wars of conquest on the Slavs of the Greek Church.

German Catholic missionaries endeavoured to convert the pagan Livonians, but as their persuasive powers were found insufficient to overcome the resolute opposition of the natives, the third Bishop of Riga, Albert, founded in 1201 the Sword-bearing or Livonian Order. The ostensible object, the conversion of the heathen, soon gave way to the more congenial task of conquering and enslaving him. The success of the knights brought them into immediate contact with the weak Russian princes, the suzerains of the pagan Livonians they had been unable to defend against the German incursions.

Thus, while Kief and the southern principalities were exposed to the raids of the Polovtsy, Novgorod and its territory were menaced from the north and west by Sweden and the Livonian knights. The only states enjoying comparative security from foreign invasion were those of the north-east. But a new and more formidable foe now approached to deal a crushing blow on the weak and divided Russian people.

Nearly eight centuries had passed since Attila had swept over Europe, spreading destruction wherever he went. Now a similar man, Genghis Khan, had given unity and strength to the scattered nomads. Having conquered the centre and east of Asia, he had left to his successors the task of extending the Mongol sway to the south and west. The first appearance in Europe of these new terrible conquerors was in 1224, when they advanced to impose tribute on the Polovtsy. Mongol ambassadors were sent to the Russian princes, explaining that the war would not affect their cities, but was only directed against the Polovtsy, 'the slaves and horse-grooms' of the Mongols. The Russian princes unwisely resolved to assist their former foes, the Polovtsy, and advanced under the guidance of Mstislav of Galicia, a kind of knight-errant who was always ready to engage in any war of a hazardous and romantic nature. The battle took place near the river Kalka. The Mongols, with the thoroughness characteristic of their warlike operations, completely destroyed the allied forces. The captured Russian princes were treated with the brutal indignities usual to those triumphant barbarians. They were bound to the ground, planks were laid upon them, and the conquerors feasted on the prostrate prisoners.

After their victory the Mongols soon returned to Asia, and Russia was left in peace for twelve years. This brief truce was followed by a more terrible invasion. In 1236 Batu started with 300,000 men on his famous raid, which was to bring destruction on the whole of Eastern Europe as far as Silesia and the Adriatic. He first conquered the Bulgars on the Volga, and the following year marched on Riazan, summoning the inhabitants to deliver a tenth of their property. 'When none of us shall remain, all will be yours,' was the heroic answer of the townsmen, and, though a mere handful, they boldly advanced against the overwhelming Mongol host.

They were defeated, Riazan was pillaged and burnt,

and the few remaining inhabitants crucified or enslaved. Batu pushed on north to Kolumna, where he met the army of George, Grand Duke of Vladimir. The Russians were again defeated, and the town burnt ; the Grand Duke fled beyond the Volga to gather a new army. The Mongols destroyed Moscow, then a very small place, and on February 3, 1238, they besieged the city of Vladimir, which was taken on February 17. The town was sacked, the inhabitants killed, even the family of the Grand Duke George being burnt in the cathedral, where they had fled for refuge. The victorious Mongols spread all over the country in various detachments, and captured fourteen towns in the month of February, killing or enslaving all the inhabitants. On March 4, on the river Sita, Batu met the Grand Duke George with his new levied army, which was completely routed, the Grand Duke himself being killed in the battle. The Mongols now pushed on east, took the town of Torjok, and advanced to within a hundred versts of Novgorod ; but the forests presented great natural difficulties, and the approach of spring threatened them with the dangers of swollen rivers and thawing swamps. Batu retreated southwards towards the steppes. The small town of Kozelsk boldly resisted and detained him for seven weeks. The Mongols, as usual, took the town, destroying all its inhabitants.

This first campaign had destroyed the power of all the new north-eastern principalities of Russia ; in the following year (1239) the Tartars issued from the steppes and commenced the conquest of the south-western districts. Tchernigof was taken and burnt, and the atrocities of the Mongols spread such terror that all the inhabitants of the villages fled into the woods, or even killed themselves, rather than fall alive into the hands of the enemy. In 1240 Batu himself led his army against Kief, which, though no longer the political capital, still was venerated as the old centre of Russian Christianity. The beautiful situation of the city, the many-coloured tiles of the princely palaces, the gilt domes of the churches, produced an impression of wonder on the rough, ignorant horsemen of the steppes. Far different were the feelings of the unfortunate besieged ; the old chroniclers say that the noise produced by the vast host, the shouting of the Tartars, the creaking of the carts, the roaring of the camels, the neighing of the horses, was so great that the people of Kief could not hear each other's voices. Notwithstanding a brave and obstinate resistance, the city was taken, and the inhabitants massacred ; but by a singular trait of generosity the Mongols spared the commander Demetrius, whose heroism won recognition even from these relentless enemies.

After the conquest of Russia, Batu advanced further east, ravaging Poland, Moravia, and Silesia. At Wahlstadt he met the united forces of the Poles, Silesians, and Teutonic knights ; but the Germans were not more successful than the Slavs., They were completely routed, and Duke Henry himself was killed in the battle. Batu, after ravaging Hungary, returned to the steppes between the lower Danube and the river Ural, establishing his capital near the Caspian Sea at Sarai, on one of the branches of the Volga. This new Tartar power, under the name of the Golden Horde, ruled Russia with an iron hand ; heavy tributes were levied, and the Russian princes were obliged to appear at the Horde, kneel before the Khan, and suffer other humiliations. Michael of Tchernigof, who, even in that time of national disaster, would not submit to such indignities, was massacred with all his boyars.

The Tartar domination oppressed Russia for over two

centuries. The only nation in Europe that has passed through a similar ordeal is Spain. But the conditions of Russia were far worse. The uniform flatness of the country offered no refuge, like the Asturian mountains, where the remnant of the unsubdued could safely brave the power of the conquerors and train itself by secular wars for the final work of liberation. The Arabs worshipped the same God, and their religion had a broad, common basis with Christianity; they cultivated the arts and sciences, while Western Europe was plunged in intellectual darkness. The Tartars were Pagans when they entered Russia, and the acquisition of wealth and power never developed any taste for science or literature. Spain, moreover, in her long struggle, was encouraged by all the neighbouring nations, and occasionally even assisted by the chivalry of Christendom, while Russia in her darkest hour found in the west enemies, relentless through race hatred and theological rancour, who readily seized the opportunity to attempt her complete destruction.

Novgorod and its territory was the only part of Russia which had escaped the ravages of the Mongols, but it sustained the attacks of other enemies on the west. We have seen that the Sword-bearing or Livonian Order had advanced to the Russian borders; in 1224, the year when the Tartars made their first desultory attack, the Germans took the Russian town Yurief, which they christened Dorpt,[1] and began to threaten Novgorod. When Batu with his campaigns, in the years 1237–40, had destroyed the remainder of Russia, the Swedes, the Livonian knights, and the Lithuanians prepared to accomplish the ruin of Novgorod. It appeared as if the Russian race were destined to be overwhelmed under these numerous enemies, and had to disappear from history, when in the hour of

[1] It has been lately renamed Yurief.

utmost need the nation was saved by a man gifted with varied and exceptional qualities.

The people of Novgorod, though attached to their republican freedom, often elected princes to govern them ; these elections were often capriciously revoked, and the prince who had not satisfied the unruly citizens was dismissed with scant ceremony, though with no personal violence. 'We do not want you ; go where you like,' was the usual notice to quit.

At that time Novgorod was ruled by Alexander, a son of the Grand Duke of Vladimir. In 1240, the year when Kief was taken by Batu, the King of Sweden, under the pretext of converting to the Catholic faith the followers of the Greek Church, advanced to attack Novgorod. Alexander had only a small force to oppose to the invader, but he encouraged his soldiers with words inspired by the heroism necessary at such a moment : ' We are few, but God sides with right, not with might.' He attacked the Swedes on the Neva (July 15, 1240), winning a glorious victory, and his name has gone down to posterity as Alexander Nevski.[1] The Novgorodians, with the usual fickleness of popular government, dismissed their heroic prince, but democratic caprice had to give way to the necessities of national existence. The Livonian knights conquered Pskof and threatened Novgorod ; merchants could not pass safely even at thirty versts from the city. Alexander Nevski was recalled to face the new enemy, drove the Germans out of Pskof, and invaded Livonia. A terrible battle was fought on the frozen Lake Peipus, known in Russian history as the Battle on the Ice (April 5, 1241). It lasted the whole day, but the superior generalship of Alexander prevailed, and the Livonian knights were completely routed. The Lithuanians also

[1] Of the Neva.

attacked the Novgorodians, but Alexander Nevski defeated them in three engagements. These successive victories raised the spirit of the Russian nation, which had been almost crushed by the dreadful Mongol invasion.

An occasion now arose which showed that, besides the qualities of an able general, Alexander Nevski possessed also those of a wise statesman. Batu heard of his victories and resolved to assert his superiority ; he haughtily summoned him to appear, declaring that ' All people are subject to me : if thou wishest to save thy land, come and pay homage.' Alexander sacrificed all feeling of vanity and personal dignity for the good of his country ; he justly realised that, though valour and skill had proved sufficient to defeat Swedes and Germans, they were inadequate to cope with the overwhelming power of the Mongols. He went to the Horde, offered his submission, winning the esteem and favour of Batu by his wisdom. Alexander Nevski, elected Grand Duke of Vladimir on account of his merits, continued to display tact in his endeavours to shield his country from the excesses of the Mongols. He prevailed on the Novgorodians to pay tribute to the Golden Horde. When the Russian people of many cities, maddened by the exactions of the Tartar tax-collectors, rose, killing and driving them away, he hastened with great personal danger to Sarai, and by his intercession saved Russia from a second invasion. On his return from this expedition he died on November 14, 1263. To show the place he held in the hearts of his people, it will be sufficient to quote the words of the Metropolitan of Kief on hearing the news : ' The sun of the Russian land is set.' The first twenty-five years of the Tartar domination were the severest : a heavy poll-tax was levied, and exacted so rigorously that twice within that short period a general census was taken of the Russian people. As the Tartars were unaccustomed to business, most of the tax-collectors were Jews and Armenians, who abused their authority by often exacting more than the legal rate; their extortions were enforced by detachments of Tartar troops that marched through the country committing every kind of wanton violence. The general distress of the country, however, had no effect in calming the animosity of the rival princes; they continued their wars and intrigues, invoking the decision of the Khan of the Golden Horde in favour of their claims.

This intestine warfare was favoured by the geographical features of the country and its social conditions. No mountain chain divides the land into natural provinces, offering convenient bases for separate political organisations in a feudal age; even the huge rivers are converted by the rigour of the climate into commodious highways. No permanent distinction, such as the formation of dialects,[1] could exist among the people. The retainers and feudatories of the princes, the *drujina* and *boyars* of Russian history, were attached simply to the person of their chief, and their fidelity was voluntary and temporary. They were always free to change masters, and no taint of disloyalty attended such transfer of allegiance. These fluctuating conditions of a race exempt from territorial restrictions facilitated the work of personal ambition; an able prince could always attract a numerous following and extend his dominions. These conditions, though favourable to dissensions in the period of the *appanages*, also contributed to political unity when the men required for that work arose at the proper time.

Another fruitful source of disorder lay in the strange, almost oriental, order of succession. At the death of the

---

[1] Throughout the greater part of the Russian empire, from Moscow and St. Petersburg to Vladivostok, the same language is spoken.

Grand Duke the eldest male of the line, generally a brother, was the legal heir, thus stimulating the rivalry of the younger and more restless descendants.

The Mongol invasion and the attacks from the west increased the tendency to shift the centre of political activity to the north-east. Kief, after its capture, was reduced to an insignificant town with only about two hundred houses; the neighbouring country became a wilderness strewn with skulls and human bones. Lithuania, which had failed in its attacks on Novgorod through the valour and skill of Alexander Nevski, thanks to a succession of able monarchs, gradually absorbed the whole of South-west Russia, and formed a huge state extending from the Black Sea almost to the Baltic, from which it was separated only by a narrow coast line belonging to the Teutonic knights. In 1386 the Lithuanian Grand Duke, by consenting to embrace Christianity, still further extended his power and ascended the throne of Poland.

In the north-east, in the region where the new Great Russia was being slowly formed, Vladimir was the principal city, where the eldest prince with the title of Grand Duke resided. Its importance was also increased when the Metropolitan, the head of the Russian Church, recognising the altered conditions of the country, transferred (A.D. 1299) his see from Kief to Vladimir. But a new city began to aspire to pre-eminence in the region which was destined to give birth to the hugest continental empire of modern times.

The first historical mention of Moscow occurs in 1147; according to a tradition, its site was originally occupied by the summer residence of a small feudal lord who was executed for some crime by George Dolgoruki. The beautiful situation pleased the latter, who built a town surrounded with palisades.

The river Moskva winds in great bends, somewhat like the Seine at Paris, and passes under the steep sides of a hill. Here now we find the Kremlin, that assemblage of churches and palaces which with their historical associations constitute the palladium of Russia. This small space contained the original town of Dolgoruki. Around this town a state gradually rose, which, from being the smallest appanage of the Grand Dukedom of Vladimir, has become the empire of Russia.

While still a place of very small importance, Moscow, with the presumption of youth, displayed an ambition not unworthy of its future fortunes. Even at the time of Alexander Nevski the lord of Moscow had the presumption to claim the grand-ducal title, although neither by birth nor extraordinary merit could he justify his extravagant pretensions. He was defeated and killed in the attempt, but his premature aspirations were kept in mind and slowly realised at the proper time by the princes of another race, who succeeded in the fief of Moscow.

At the death of Alexander Nevski, Moscow, as the pettiest appanage, was given to his youngest son Daniel. The successors of Alexander Nevski in the Grand Dukedom of Vladimir were his brothers, and then his sons, according to the law of succession prevalent in Russia, that the eldest male of the race should reign. But this inconvenient system gradually began to decline before the rough and ready methods of powerful and ambitious princes, who purchased their investiture from the Tartar khans, the exclusive dispensers of all sovereignty at that time in Russia.

War broke out between the two eldest sons of Alexander Nevski ; the younger went to the Golden Horde, bought his investiture, and with the assistance of a Tartar army was installed as Grand Duke of Vladimir. But on the departure of the Tartars the elder returned with an army of mercenaries from the Baltic. After a long struggle he was finally obliged to renounce his claims to the Grand Dukedom. Daniel of Moscow was very active during all this period, siding alternately with his two brothers, supporting always the one in distress, probably through fear of the excessive aggrandisement of the other. He succeeded by his successful wars in adding several small towns to his dominions.

About this time the Russian appanages underwent a transformation. Hitherto the whole state had been considered the patrimony of the reigning house, to whose various members different towns and districts were allotted temporarily, a fresh distribution taking place at the death of the eldest member of the race, even as at present the lands of a Russian village are distributed periodically among the families of the villagers. But gradually the petty princes began to consider themselves as absolute sovereigns of their appanages, and to dispose of them at pleasure, without consulting the other members of the reigning race. An example of this was given by the lord of Pereyaslav, who, dying childless, left his lands to the lord of Moscow. Daniel of Moscow died in 1303, and was succeeded by his son George, who kept Pereyaslav and extended his dominions, which now comprised the whole course of the river Moskva.

In the following year, 1304, the Grand Duke of Vladimir died. The eldest of the race was Michael of Tver, but George of Moscow also claimed the Grand Dukedom. The two candidates hastened to the Horde to obtain a fresh investiture, but Michael outbid his rival, and was appointed Grand Duke. This rivalry, and the retention of Pereyaslav by George, were the source of continual warfare between the two princes. George encouraged the citizens of Novgorod in their opposition to the governors appointed by Michael, and when the latter in 1313 was obliged to go to the Horde to obtain a fresh investiture from the new Khan, George hastened to Novgorod, where he was received with joy by the unruly populace. But their triumph was of short duration, as George was summoned to the Horde to justify his disorderly conduct.

He not only succeeded in clearing himself from the accusations of the Grand Duke, but won the favour of the Khan, and even married his sister. Strengthened by this alliance, he returned with a Tartar embassy and made war on Michael, but was entirely routed, and obliged to fly to Novgorod, his wife, the Tartar princess, being made a prisoner. This success, however, was fatal to Michael, as the princess died in captivity, and a report was spread that she had been poisoned. He was therefore summoned to the Horde and barbarously executed. George, who had brought his complaints to the Khan, was now appointed Grand Duke. But the eldest son of Michael accused George at the Horde, and, when he appeared to defend himself, killed him. The Khan ordered the execution of the murderer, but granted the Grand Dukedom to another son of Michael. Thus Moscow was again foiled in its attempt to secure supremacy.

These disgraceful scenes are given in detail to show the bitter hatred prevailing among the rival Russian princes, and the abject degradation to which they had been reduced by the Tartar domination. George was succeeded by his brother Ivan, surnamed Kalita, ' the Purse,' on account of his wealth. During the troubles of the preceding reign he had been often left in charge of Moscow, while his warlike brother proceeded to Novgorod and to the Khan; and on each occasion he had given proof of ability.   He possessed qualities rare in his time and his country; he resembled those sovereigns, Ferdinand of Castile, Henry VII. of England, and Louis XI. of France, who, two centuries later, consolidated the monarchies of Western Europe.   He was far-seeing, hard-working, and so thrifty that with the poor revenues of the smallest appanage he became the wealthiest prince of Russia.   His political sagacity succeeded where the wars and intrigues of his predecessors had failed.   His cool judgment perceived the great factors of the political history of that time.   In the collapse of the Russian state, consequent upon Batu's invasion, the Church alone had remained unsubmerged and uncontaminated; it constituted the only bond among the scattered inhabitants, and the only link with the civilisation of the west which prevented Russia relapsing into complete eastern barbarism. By the side of this moral power, bearing the promise_ of the future empire, there was the hateful Tartar Horde, whose irresistible domination also offered the opportunity to the genius of a subtle, far-sighted politician of effecting the long-needed unity of the nation.   On these facts Ivan Kalita based his policy, and he achieved success without effort.

In 1299 the Metropolitan of Kief, the head of the Russian Church, had transferred his see to Vladimir; his successor, Peter (a saint of the Russian Church), in the exercise of his ministry, often visited Moscow.   The gracious reception afforded him gradually induced him to prolong his residence, until Vladimir was almost entirely neglected.   Ivan Kalita built a stone [1] church at his instigation, and Peter chose a spot for his grave, where shortly after he was buried.   His successor would not

---

[1] Stone buildings were then rare in Russia, as even now they are in remote villages.

forsake the spot hallowed by the mortal remains of the holy Churchman, and Moscow thus became the permanent see of the Metropolitan. This event not only raised the importance of the new city as the religious centre of Russia, but gave Ivan Kalita the means of exerting immense influence. We have seen that, in the national collapse consequent on the Mongol invasion, the Church alone had preserved its power: it enjoyed an immense advantage, due to the fact that while the princes were many and acted independently, the authority of the Metropolitan was unique and uncontested. Now, this unquestioned power was skilfully, though indirectly, wielded by Ivan Kalita.

An opportunity soon presented itself to the skilful Prince of Moscow to enlist in his service the other important factor: the dreaded power of the Golden Horde. In 1327 a Tartar embassy came to Tver, and committed such outrages that it was massacred by the infuriated inhabitants. Ivan Kalita at once started for Sarai, and won such favour that he returned with an army of 50,000 Tartars, devastated Tver, and was named Grand Duke. The former Grand Duke, Alexander, fled to Pskof, where the generous inhabitants protected him. When he declared his intention of going to the Horde to avert their threatened danger, they said, 'Whatever may happen we shall die together with thee.' Ivan Kalita then prevailed upon his friend the Metropolitan to excommunicate the inhabitants of Pskof because they sheltered Alexander.

In these events Ivan Kalita had only shown the common ambition and rancour of the Russian feudatory of that age, who was always ready to invoke Tartar aid against his private enemies. In the long struggle for supremacy between Tver and Moscow, he had secured victory for the latter. The use he made of his authority showed, however, that, more than his personal aggrandisement, he had in view the permanent prosperity of his people. Peace reigned in the country ; rich and powerful boyars were attracted to Moscow by his just government ; by wise economy he had always the means to bribe the Tartars ; and he extended his dominions, not by conquest, but by purchasing cities and villages from the extravagant and needy princes. The tribute due to the Tartars was no longer collected by their rapacious tax-collectors, but paid by Ivan Kalita, who thus farmed the revenue of the Khan. This arrangement satisfied both parties : the Russian princes and people were delighted in being delivered from the hateful intrusion of their oppressors, and the Khan was pleased at the simple and ready payment. Neither saw what the following centuries showed, that they were contributing to form a power which would conquer and rule all. Ivan Kalita - has received the name of the First Collector of Russian land : he was in fact the founder of the empire, and his methods have been curiously followed even by his remote successors.

Ivan Kalita was succeeded by his son Simon, who obtained the investiture from the Tartars. He followed his father's policy ; made frequent visits to the Horde, where he was always received with honour. The friendship of the Khan was adroitly used to curb the growing power of Lithuania, which gradually absorbed Southwest Russia, and even threatened Moscow. This danger from the west menaced the young Russian state for several centuries.

Simon died in 1353 of the ' black death ; ' he left no children, and, another brother dying about the same time, all the territory of Moscow devolved on the remaining brother, Ivan II. This circumstance was of great importance, as the rising state required that its forces should not be scattered. Ivan II. was a quiet prince, who secured for the exhausted Russian people a few more years of much-needed peace.

He died in 1359. His eldest son, Demetrius, was a child, unable to go to the Horde, and the Prince of Suzdal seized the opportunity to obtain the investiture of Grand Duke; but the rich and powerful boyars of Moscow could not suffer such a humiliation for their city; they took the young Demetrius to the Horde and purchased his investiture. After a brief struggle Suzdal was obliged to yield.

Under Demetrius the Kremlin was surrounded with stone walls and towers. Before his time Moscow, like all Russian towns, with the exception of Novgorod and Pskof, had been defended only by a stockade. The new fortifications and the advantages of its position rendered the Kremlin the strongest fortress in the country. This was of great advantage to Demetrius, who sustained long wars with Lithuania, the new rising power on the west. When he was unable to hold the field against the overwhelming force of the enemy he retired behind the strong walls of the Kremlin, waited until the storm passed, and then sallied forth to prolong the contest. Demetrius stands forth in marked contrast to his grandfather, father, and uncle, who had preserved and expanded their dominions by prudence and policy. He was the warrior prince who gained his object by force of arms, and in this respect he surpassed his successors as well as his predecessors.

His wars with Lithuania, successful in their final results, were of a defensive nature, and had for their object to arrest the expansion of a state which threatened to absorb the Russian nation, then feebly struggling for life. He understood the true future mission of Russia, and was the first, after the Tartar conquest, to inaugurate an aggressive policy in the east. He advanced against the Bulgarian races beyond the Volga and against Kazan, forcing the chieftains to pay tribute. These aggressions provoked a conflict with the Tartars, and in 1377 the troops of Moscow, through the rashness of their commander, were routed by the Tartars. A Russian historian[1] justly remarks that this over-confident rashness was a proof of the new spirit animating the nation at that period. The peaceable reigns of Kalita and his successors, the gradual disappearance of the Tartar tax-gatherers and their marauding escorts, had formed a new generation, who knew the foreign conquerors only by tradition and could not understand the trembling fear which possessed their fathers at the bare mention of the Tartar name. Demetrius, in the full vigour of youth (he was born in 1350), was the fit representative of this new generation.

In 1378 a Tartar army was defeated by the Russians, and it became evident that the small but compact state of Moscow was a dangerous enemy to the Golden Horde, now rent by factions and often governed by imbecile khans. In 1380 the Khan Mamai resolved to advance against Demetrius; Yagaila, the King of Lithuania, promised his assistance to defeat Moscow. Against this formidable alliance Demetrius could only oppose a part of the forces of the Russian nation. The Prince of Riazan, on account of his frontier position, dared not join Moscow in the unequal contest; the Prince of Tver and the popular Diet of Novgorod, through jealousy, refused to co-operate in the struggle for freedom. Demetrius, undismayed, gathered 150,000 men, the largest army that

[1] Solovieff.

Russia had ever placed in the field, and with the blessings of the holy Abbot St. Sergius he boldly advanced against the Tartars. To attack was the most prudent course, as on the defensive he would have been crushed between the Tartars on the east and the Lithuanians on the west.

On September 8, 1380, the armies met on the plain of Kulikovo, near the upper waters of the Don, where a battle was fought which is celebrated in the annals of Russia and deserves to be chronicled as one of the most hardly contested in universal history. The carnage was terrific, the Russians, it is said, losing 100,000 men, the enemy still more. Victory was long doubtful, and then seemed inclining to the Tartars, when the Russian reserve, which had been held in ambush up to the last, rushed on the enemy and decided the day.

This great victory, which earned Demetrius the title of Donskoi, gave very slight immediate results. The first news of the unexpected success of the Russians frightened Yagaila, who was advancing on Kulikovo, and he hastened back to Lithuania. But the losses had been very heavy; almost all the fighting strength of Moscow had been sacrificed to obtain the victory, and little was left to prosecute the war. Mamai gathered another army to revenge his defeat, but he was killed by Toktomysh, a chief of the Tartars beyond the Ural, who now prosecuted the war against Russia. In 1382 he advanced so rapidly that, before Demetrius could gather another army in the exhausted country, he surprised and devastated Moscow. This misfortune encouraged the Prince of Tver to intrigue with Toktomysh for the investiture of the Grand Dukedom of Vladimir. Demetrius was obliged to send his son with an envoy of boyars to the Horde and consent to pay a heavy tribute. The Tartar suzerainty was thus re-established, and lasted for another century.

Though the brilliant valour of Demetrius Donskoi had secured no immediate results, and had shown itself inferior in practical utility to the prudent policy of his predecessors, it bore moral consequences of a far-reaching nature. The charm of Tartar invincibility was broken; the Tartars now had to employ surprise and stratagem to insure even partial success. Confident hope in a final day of deliverance began to rise dimly in the mind of the oppressed Russian people; and to this hope was attached faith in the city of Moscow, which had boldly stood forth among the craven, treacherous princes to battle for religion and national freedom against the enemies of the east and west. On the field of Kulikovo Moscow won the leadership of the Russian people.

Demetrius Donskoi died in 1389, naming as his successor his son Vassil, who proceeded to the Horde and obtained the investiture. During his long reign (thirty-six years) he continued to gather the Russian lands and to strengthen the power of Moscow. Taking advantage of the growing weakness of the Tartars, he discontinued the visits to the Khan and the humiliating homage; he even neglected sending embassies, and retained for the use of his treasury the tribute collected for the Horde. He had more dangerous enemies on the west; Yagaila was constantly encroaching on Russian territory and extending the frontiers of Lithuania. His marriage with the heiress of the Polish throne augmented his power and gave him the support of the civilisation of Western Europe. In 1386 Lithuania had been converted to Christianity, but, unfortunately for Russia, adopted the Latin rite, thus creating an insuperable barrier between the two peoples. Vitofit, his successor, continued the aggressions on Russian land; he took Smolensk, and even coveted Novgorod the Great and Moscow. Vassil, however, opposed him with a large army, and succeeded in fixing the river Ugra as the eastern frontier of Lithuania. It was dangerously near to Moscow, but it marked the farthest eastern expansion of Lithuania. A glance at the political map of Eastern Europe at the end of the fourteenth century shows a vast disproportion between the two states, and it is very remarkable that the smaller should have expanded to its present extent and converted the larger into a provincial dependency.

Vassil I. died in 1425, leaving an infant son, Vassil II. Hitherto Moscow, either by the death or renunciation of collateral heirs, or by the choice of prince and nobles, had maintained an almost regular succession in the direct line. But the youth of Vassil II. was the occasion for an attempt to revive the old system of inheritance by seniority; the eldest male claiming the throne according to Oriental notions. George, the brother of Vassil I. and uncle of Vassil II., claimed the Grand Dukedom of Vladimir, and after his death the claim was taken up by his sons. To settle these rival claims appeals were made to the khans, thus strengthening the vanishing Tartar suzerainty. Vassil II. was several times obliged to fly from Moscow, but at last, with the assistance of the clergy, succeeded in overthrowing his enemies. This long civil war was not entirely unfavourable to the country; the relations of Vassil II., by their rebellion and constant intrigues, forfeited their right to appanages which by the then prevailing Russian custom were bestowed on all members of the reigning family; thus the power of Moscow was in the end strengthened. It also showed the necessity of adopting measures to prevent the recurrence of disputes about the succession. Demetrius Donskoi, before dying, had named his eldest son Grand Duke of Vladimir. Vassil II. went a step further, and towards the end of his reign appointed his eldest son Grand Duke—all official acts bearing the names of both princes. By this wise and timely measure Russia was saved from a fresh relapse into those disorders which had rendered her an easy prey to foreign invasion.

In 1462 Vassil II. died, and was succeeded by Ivan III., who first assumed the title of Autocrat of all Russia. He possessed all the qualities of the race of Kalita; he was thrifty, slow, prudent, averse to decisive and risky measures, but gifted with unrelaxing perseverance in the accomplishment of his plans. His reign, perhaps the most important in Russian history, is a lucid example of the methods which have formed the Russian empire. He was faced with the same difficulties and dangers as his predecessors: the powerful Lithuanian state on the west, dynastically united with Poland, and the Tartars on the east. By a series of fortunate circumstances which he skilfully adapted to his ends he was able to achieve signal success. The King of Poland and Grand Duke of Lithuania was occupied by the feuds of his two states, and with the affairs of Prussia, Bohemia, and Hungary, and could only give passing casual attention to his eastern frontier. The Tartars were now split up into several khanates, Kazan and the Crimea being almost independent and hostile to the Golden Horde of Sarai. During the two centuries of interaction between the two races, Russia had gradually acquired unity and peace under the strong government of Moscow, while the Tartars were now rent by those bitter persistent feuds which had been the ruin of Russia at the time of Batu's raid.

Ivan III. first directed his conquests against Novgorod, the republican town of the north-west, which had hitherto, by occasional tribute to Moscow or by alliance with Lithuania, escaped subjection and extended its trade and

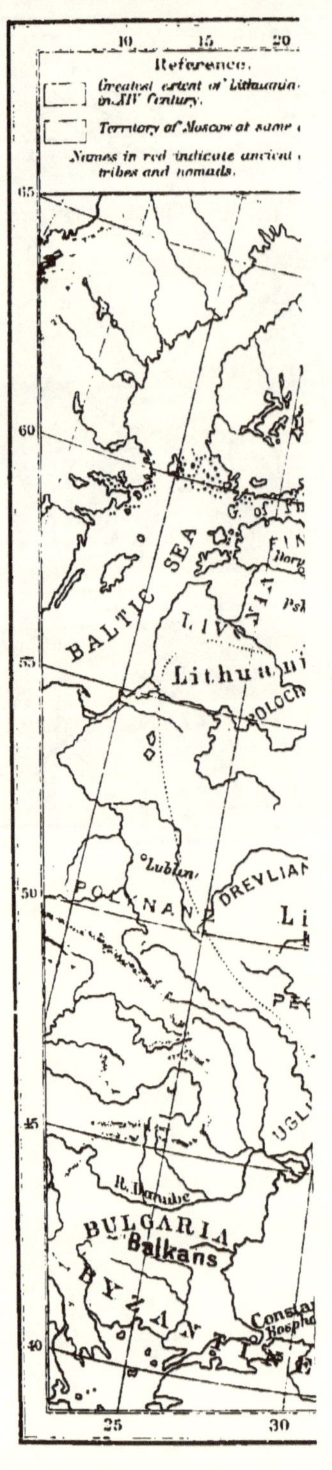

Reference.
Greatest extent of Lithuania in XIV Century.
Territory of Moscow at same
Names in red indicate ancient tribes and nomads.
BALTIC SEA
G. of FIN
FINLAND
LIVONIA
Lithuani
BOLOCH
POZNAN
DREVLIAN
Lublin
PE
UGL
R. Danube
BULGARIA
Balkans
BYZ
Constan
Bosph

London: Sampson Low, Marston & Co. Limited

influence over the whole of North Russia. The Grand Duke accomplished his purpose with the slowness and obstinacy characteristic of his policy. In 1471 the army of Novgorod was totally routed, and the citizens, abandoned by Lithuania, were obliged to sue for peace, pay a heavy ransom, and promise to receive their princes and archbishops from Moscow and not from Lithuania. Ivan III. seized every opportunity to tighten his hold on his prey and, finally, in 1478 Novgorod was incorporated in the Muscovite state. To prevent future trouble a large number of influential families were transplanted to the towns of Eastern Russia, and a colony of boyars and merchants were sent from Moscow to fill up the vacancies in Novgorod. Thus disappeared that democratic government which had only served to encourage the tendency to discord and faction prevalent in ancient Russia. The conquest of Novgorod, besides removing a troublesome neighbour which was always intriguing with the dangerous Polish-Lithuanian state, increased enormously the territory of Moscow ; it now extended over the vast half-unknown lands of the north and east up to the Arctic Ocean and the Ural mountains. As early as 1472 Ivan III had also advanced eastwards, conquering Perm.

Ivan III. had been left early a widower (1467), but he soon contracted a new alliance (1472), which had important results both in the internal affairs of the state and in foreign policy. After the capture of Constantinople by the Turks, the brother of the emperor fled with his family to Rome. Pope Paul II., interested in the unfortunate refugees, succeeded in effecting the marriage of the daughter, Sophia Paleologus, with the Grand Duke of Moscow. This was a brilliant connection for a prince hardly known in Western Europe, and it brought about a transformation in the simple court of Moscow. Hitherto the Grand Duke had lived in great familiarity with the rough boyars, who considered themselves as his equals by birth ; but this simplicity was repugnant to a princess whose ancestors had occupied the throne of the Cæsars. Gradually some kind of court etiquette was established, and Ivan III. began to assume those outward signs of majesty which are necessary to inspire awe in the minds of the people.[1] A feeling of dynastic respect now hovered round the house of Kalita, which had risen from such humble origins ; nearly five centuries before, Vladimir had married the Byzantine princess Anna and introduced Christianity into the land. This new alliance with the now fallen power of Constantinople seemed to evoke the past greatness of the house of Ruric. It also gave Russia the opportunity to preserve the sequence of historical tradition ; the conquest of Constantinople, the subsequent destruction of the Christian states of the Balkan peninsula, left her the sole unconquered representative of the Greek Church. Popular hopes throughout Eastern Europe considered the marriage of Sophia Paleologus as the material pledge that henceforth Russia would stand forth as the champion of Christianity, destined at some future day to bring back the triumph of the Cross on the shores of the Bosphorus.

These hopes are yet unrealised, but the influence of Sophia Paleologus contributed to bring about far more important immediate results. Her royal pride could not suffer that her husband should be a tributary of the Tartar khans. Ivan III., cautious and practical, would probably have deferred the dangers of an overt refusal of a purely formal homage, and would have remained satisfied with his growing power and the increasing weakness

---

[1] He also adopted the Byzantine double-headed eagle as the arms of Russia.

of the Horde, but he had to yield to popular pressure and the expostulations of his wife. In 1480, just a hundred years after the battle of Kulikovo, Ivan III. finally shook off the Tartar yoke.

The political conditions were precisely the same as in the time of Demetrius Donskoi. The Tartars formed an alliance with Casimir, King of Poland and Lithuania, and their Khan Akhmat advanced with a large army to the river Ugra on the frontier of Lithuania. Ivan III. was forced to advance to prevent a junction of his enemies. But the subsequent events were totally different ; though the Russian army was more numerous, the prudent Grand Duke would not risk a battle. Perhaps the memory of the dreadful slaughter of Kulikovo, which had left Russia defenceless, deterred him from risking what might prove a dear-bought victory like that of Demetrius Donskoi. The Tartars, inferior in numbers, and always hoping for the arrival of their Lithuanian allies, naturally avoided an engagement. The protracted war gave Ivan III. leisure to leave his army and return to Moscow, where the infuriated people openly accused him of poltroonery. Bassian, the Archbishop of Rostof, violently expostulated with him, saying, " Why dost thou fear death ? Art thou immortal? Give me, dotard, thy army, and thou shalt see if I turn my back to the Tartars ! " Ivan III. returned to his army, but doggedly refused to engage the enemy, notwithstanding a violent letter from the vehement Churchman, Bassian. The course of events finally justified his prudence ; the terrible Russian winter, which three centuries later was to save the country from the greatest warrior of modern times, now began in grim earnest. The lightly clad Tartars could not bear it, and, after severe sufferings, Akhmat, on November 16,[1] 1480,

[1] On November 26, 1812, commenced the terrible passage of the Beresina,

retired from the Russian frontier, and with him vanished for ever the domination of his race.

Ivan III., by judicious temporising, had delivered his country from the hateful foreign yoke without striking a blow. This bloodless close of a domination of 240 years, which commenced with the terrible raids of Batu, was almost synchronous with the expulsion of the Moors from Spain. Grenada was taken in 1492, and Sophia Paleologus may be said to have played in Eastern Europe the part of Isabel of Castile. But while Spain achieved her liberation by centuries of warfare, Russia effected her purpose by a quite different process ; there was only one important battle, that of Kulikovo, and it had no immediate influence on the question at issue; the Tartars were slowly but irresistibly crowded out by the sedentary Slav race, which expanded and probably also absorbed the best elements of the nomads. In this silent work Moscow furnished the element which had been always wanting in the Russian nation—a strong hereditary government and the set purpose of unifying the country. The shrewd descendants of Kalita took to heart the severe lessons of the Tartar invasion ; unable, with their scanty resources, to undertake a war of deliverance, and convinced of the impossibility of securing the sincere co-operation of the other Russian princes, they employed the only means left at their disposal. They quietly supplanted the autocratic power of the Golden Horde, and the substitution was so gradual that the final overthrow of the Tartar suzerainty took place without a struggle, like a pangless death at an advanced age. The spectacle of Ivan III. quietly waiting with his army on the banks of the Oka for winter to disperse the powerless Tartar

which marked the final collapse of the remainder of Napoleon's ' Grande Armée.'

force is typical of the whole process. His obstinate refusal to yield to the bold suggestions of his people is an instance of the uniform conduct of the Russian Government, which has always acted as a moderating check on the impetuous tendencies of the young expansive Slav race.

Ivan III. improved his victory by extending his authority over Kazan. Desultory war, without important results, had been carried on since the commencement of the reign, but a fortunate feud between two rival candidates to the khanate enabled the Grand Duke to send an army to Kazan (1487) and put on the throne a khan who acknowledged the suzerainty of Moscow. The expansion to the north-east continued, and in 1489 Viatka, a colony of Novgorod, was also incorporated in the state of Moscow.

A series of wars with Sweden and Lithuania produced unimportant results, and the death of Ivan III. in 1505 closed a long useful reign, which raised Russia to the rank of a nation. But, though independent, she could hardly be considered a European power ; the long Tartar domination had profoundly affected the whole people ; the dress of the boyars, the seclusion of the women, were entirely Oriental, and it required the genius of Peter the Great, two centuries later, to remove the deep traces of Asiatic influence, and give Russia her right place in the world.

Vassil III., the son of Sophia Paleologus, succeeded his father, and added slightly to his work. The vassal khan of Kazan had rebelled towards the end of the reign of Ivan III., and two parties were formed in Kazan—one favourable to Moscow, the other to the khanate of Crimea. This became an important question for Russia, because a union between the two khanates would have reconstituted the Tartar power, which now threatened to be supported by the formidable Turkish Sultan, who had enforced his suzerainty on the Crimean Tartars. The Grand Duke secured victory for the Moscow party in Kazan. To diminish the importance of this Tartar town as a trade centre, in 1524 an annual fair was established at the mouth of the Sura (right affluent of the Volga), to which Russian merchants were ordered to repair instead of Kazan.[1] On the west, a long war with Lithuania ended in the conquest of the important city of Smolensk, which now returned to Russia. The process of unification of the country was finally accomplished by the incorporation of the free town of Pskof, of the principality of Riazan, besides minor feudal states. Vassil III. is styled by Solovieff the Last Collector of Russian lands.

Vassil III. was succeeded (1533) by his infant son Ivan IV., known as Ivan the Terrible, the most dramatic figure in Russian history, and one of the most extraordinary men that ever occupied a throne. He was only three years old at his father's death, and ambitious nobles began to intrigue for the regency; five years later his mother died, and the poor child was left in the worst of solitudes, that of a palace haunted by factious parties. Rival families disputed the regency, and the jealous holders of power inflicted exile and torture on those who showed kindness to the infant autocrat. At last the pent-up sufferings and vindictiveness of the boy exploded, and at thirteen years of age he assumed power, and his first act was to execute Prince Shinski, who, despite his tears, had deprived him of his favourite. The

[1] In 1641 the fair was transported up river to Makarief, and in 1817 this celebrated fair was again transferred further up to Nijni Novgorod, with whose name it is associated in Western minds.

precocity developed by his stormy childhood endowed him with a far-reaching ambition, and at his coronation in 1547 he assumed the title of Tsar, indicating with this corruption of the name of the Cæsars the world-wide mission which history destined to the Russian empire.

A period of domestic peace now influenced the life of Ivan IV. He was blessed with a good wife, Anastasia Romanoff, and through the good counsels of a holy Churchman, Sylvester, he acquired habits of diligence in the despatch of business and acquisition of knowledge; he became the most learned man of his country, and the greatest monarch of the house of Kalita. In 1550 a new code of laws was compiled, more explicit in its sanctions than the one of Ivan III. In 1552 Kazan was besieged, taken, and incorporated in the Russian empire. Though this conquest was an insignificant military feat, as the Tsar, with an army of 150,000 men and 150 guns, was held in check for seven weeks by 30,000 Tartars and a mere palisaded town, yet it caused great rejoicings in Moscow. At last the House of Ruric had produced a sovereign who, by attacking the Tartars in their strongholds, showed how to prevent all future recurrence of their invasions. It required, however, five years of desultory warfare to conquer the different Finnish or Tartar races dwelling on the banks of the lower Volga.

The conquest was facilitated by the fact that, as we have seen, for sixty years there had been in Kazan a party favourable to the Russians: the quieter elements, tired of the tyranny and continued feuds of the khans, being attracted towards the strong, just government of Moscow. This feeling now spread. In 1553 another Tartar prince applied for assistance against the Khan of Astrakhan, and, in 1554, 30,000 Russians took the town and installed their ally on the throne. The new Khan, with barbarian fickleness, ungratefully revolted, but he was punished, and in 1556 Astrakhan was incorporated into the Russian state. Thus the whole course of the Volga, then already a great commercial highway, of which the Russians hitherto had only occupied the upper waters, fell into the hands of the Tsar. Russia had now the way opened to the Caspian.

After Ivan IV. had extended his dominions to the Ural and to the Caspian, all these vast territories became gradually developed by merchants and agriculturists. The young sovereign had raised the power of his country to a height never before attained, when a change came over him and altered the character of his reign. In 1553 he fell sick, and was thought to be dying; he called his faithful counsellors, and told them to swear fealty to his son; amidst the sufferings of his illness his feeble senses caught the sound of the wrangling of the ambitious courtiers in the next room. Regardless of the Tsar, whom they thought past recovery, the proud nobles, who all claimed descent from Ruric, loudly proclaimed their unwillingness to accept as sovereign a son of the new family of the Romanoffs. When Ivan IV. recovered, the vision of the posthumous treason which had been planned so close to his sick-bed roused all the suspicion and cruelty which had crept into his nature during the bitter years of his childhood, and had only been kept dormant by the good influence of Anastasia Romanoff and Sylvester.

The Tsar gradually withdrew his confidence from his counsellors, and they, perceiving his coldness, appeared less frequently at Court. The Muscovite autocracy, which had always been tempered by the influence of the boyars, now assumed a despotic character. A partisan of the fallen Sylvester, Prince Kurbski, one of the most learned men of the country, fled to Lithuania, where he was well received by King Sigismund Augustus; from his exile he wrote a letter full of reproaches to the Tsar, who, vain of his learning, promptly answered. A long correspondence followed, which exhibits the strange political opinions of Russia at that time. Prince Kurbski sustained the old theory that the dependence of the boyars on the Tsar was voluntary and temporary; they were always free to enter the service of another sovereign. Ivan IV. had to pay dearly for the venomous correspondence, as the exiled prince became an active inciter of the Polish wars against Russia.

The Tsar, growing gradually more suspicious of the discontented boyars, at last left Moscow and shut himself up at Alexandrofska; he formed a special corps of adherents, the dreaded *oprichniki*, who rode with a dog's head and a broom attached to their saddle to indicate their mission of sweeping away treason. Abandoning father and mother, they took an oath to obey only the Tsar, and were ever ready to execute his worst wishes, even those he dared not formulate in words. Special towns and even whole streets of Moscow were allotted for their use; they thus formed a dominant class in the nation, spreading terror with their ruthless crimes.

Ivan IV. had achieved the most brilliant successes in the east, while accomplishing the true mission of his country and following the lines of the natural expansion of the people; but he soon changed his policy and directed his conquests to the west. In a century when knowledge was spreading rapidly in Europe, Russia, owing to her seclusion and the Tartar invasion, was still in the darkest ignorance. The Tsar attempted to remedy this deficiency, and sent an envoy to Germany, who in 1547 obtained the permission of the Emperor Charles V. to recruit learned and skilled men for the service of the Tsar. But the Teutonic knights and the Poles, who even then dimly foresaw the coming power of their neighbour, prevented the passage of the artisans engaged for the work of civilising Russia. The Teutonic knights even executed one who had attempted to escape to Moscow. In 1554 and 1555 Chancellor arrived at Moscow by the White Sea, but the northern route was too long and difficult, and the bold enterprise of the English navigators only increased the Russian desire for communication with the outside world without affording practical means for obtaining it.

Ivan IV. in 1558 began a war in Livonia with the Teutonic knights, who had not only shut him off from the Baltic but prevented even the access of simple artisans. The war was very successful, Livonia was overrun, and had to recognise the suzerainty of Poland to escape complete destruction. The Tsar, however, still continued to be victorious until, in 1570, a truce was concluded for three years.

In 1569 two important events took place which threatened the expansion and even the existence of Russia. The Turkish power was then at its height (the battle of Lepanto took place two years later), and the Sultan viewed with disfavour the Christian domination of Moscow over the Mahometans of Kazan and Astrakhan. A bold project was conceived to overthrow the power of the Tsar in his newly conquered eastern territories. An expedition of 17,000 Turks with 50,000 Crimean Tartars was to proceed to the Don where its course bends towards the Volga, and where a 'portage' existed, and dig a canal between the two rivers; then, having established regular water communication, Astrakhan and Kazan were to be conquered. The Turks began digging the canal, but before finishing their work they proceeded to Astrakhan for winter quarters, where the troops mutinied and dispersed at the approach of a Russian army.

If the Turks in the pride of their power could have foreseen the dangers from the great northern empire, and the future development of the fertile lands of South-east Russia, instead of wasting their strength for centuries in vain struggles against the nations of Southern Europe, they might have extended their empire in the valley of the Volga, retarding the expansion of Russia for centuries.

In 1569 also was concluded the celebrated Liublin union. Before that event Poland and Lithuania had been only dynastically united, the same sovereign being King of Poland and Grand Duke of Lithuania, but the approaching extinction of the House of Yagaila now required a closer bond. With much difficulty the Polish nobles succeeded in effecting the complete union of Lithuania to their kingdom ; the consolidation of the powerful western neighbour became a great danger to the very existence of Russia in the following reigns, especially as Poland had the advantage of contact with Central and Western Europe, whose science and civilisation she was able to adopt without allowing it to pass on to Russia. Probably religious differences alone prevented her absorbing Moscow as she had absorbed Lithuania.

The last years of the long reign of Ivan IV. were marked by a series of disasters. In 1571 the Khan of Crimea with an army of 120,000 men suddenly invaded the Muscovite frontier, and, attacking Moscow, burnt the whole town except the Kremlin ; it is said that 800,000 people were destroyed, and 130,000 carried into captivity. The following year a Russian army was assembled, which repulsed with great loss a new invasion of the Khan. Matters were no better on the western frontier. In the sixteenth century great progress had been made in military science in Western Europe; the appearance first of the Swiss and then of the Spanish infantry had transformed tactics; great improvements had been made in artillery; while professional mercenary troops everywhere supplanted the raw untrained militia of feudal times. Russia had only partly adopted these improvements, and was no match for Sweden and Poland. In 1575 Stephan Batory, Prince of Transylvania, had been chosen King of Poland; with a fine army of German and Hungarian mercenaries well provided with artillery he vigorously prosecuted the war against the Tsar. The Russians were repeatedly defeated by the Swedes and Poles, and in 1582 Ivan IV. was obliged to ask the intervention of Pope Gregory XIII., by whose good offices a truce of ten years was concluded.

The disasters and humiliation of his declining years increased the violence of the Tsar's evil passions; in 1581, for some slight offence, he struck his eldest son with his iron staff so savagely that the unfortunate youth died. The inhuman father did not long survive his crime; he died in 1584, and a few years after the House of Ruric became extinct and Russia was a prey to the worst disorders.

The character of Ivan the Terrible resembles that of Henry VIII. of England by its mixture of lust, cruelty, and bigotry. This Tsar had seven wives, was always occupied with the study of theology and the rigid observance of religious practices. The political cruelty of Ivan the Terrible must be judged by the standard of the times; his methods were not worse than those employed by Louis XI. to establish the monarchy of France. The severity of the first Tsar finally crushed that Russian feudalism which had ruined the country. He abolished the absurd hereditary seniority which the feudal notions of the boyars had introduced into the army, and which forbade any nobleman to serve under the descendants of men who at any time had served under his ancestors.[1] He organised the first regular army—the celebrated Strielitz or archers —and established garrisons and watch towers to guard the frontiers against the nomads of the steppes.

The development of the power of Moscow had been facilitated by the length of the last reigns, thus securing continuity of purpose. Vassil I. commenced his reign in 1389, and Ivan IV. died in 1584. Nearly two centuries were covered by only five sovereigns. After seven centuries the House of Ruric had extended its sway over the territory comprised in modern European Russia, with the exception of the shores of the Black Sea and the Baltic and the western provinces. Ivan IV., at first, following the historical tendency of the race, had advanced eastwards, conquering the lower valley of the Volga and the lands at the foot of the Ural mountains ; but at an early date, abandoning this policy, he wasted his strength against his powerful western neighbours. The people, however, took up the work laid down by their sovereign, and in 1582, the year when the proud Tsar had to invoke the intercession of the Pope, an outlawed peasant had commenced the conquest of Siberia.

---

[1] Special genealogical books were compiled which registered the past military rank of different families and served for fixing the seniority of their descendants.

CHAPTER II

THE CONQUEST OF SIBERIA

THE enterprising merchants of Novgorod, in their keen search after furs for the European markets, pushed their expeditions eastwards over the whole of Northern Russia, and at a very early date reached a mountain chain which seemed very high to men accustomed to the dead level of the Russian plains. It was called by some the Yugra chain, by others the Stony Girdle, because it was supposed to mark the limits of the world; the modern name is the Tartar equivalent of the latter, as Ural means 'girdle' in the language of the natives. A little experience soon showed that the chain was not difficult to cross, and the Novgorodians reached the lands beyond, which they called Yugra. It is said that the first knowledge of Yugra reaches back to the eleventh century. Extravagant accounts of the distant land were told by the rare travellers: the inhabitants were said to be speechless, and to live close to cannibal nations, just as the Greeks of Homer peopled with Lestrigones and Cyclopes the land which was to become the Magna Græcia of their descendants. The Novgorodians never attempted to settle on either side of the Ural, but were content to send parties to collect tribute and barter with the natives. Even this was sufficiently dangerous, and many of these early pioneers were massacred.

Far different were the methods employed by the people of Moscow. Their advance was much slower, but more permanent. In their expansion to the north-east they did not send expeditions to collect tribute or barter, but colonists to build log-huts and cultivate the land. The two currents of emigration were bound to meet, and after about a century the Muscovite settlers intercepted and stopped the trading parties of Novgorod. This happened during the reign of Ivan III., who, as we have seen, shortly after conquered Novgorod, and annexed its possessions in Viatka. He had already occupied Perm some time before.

Having reached the Ural mountains, the Muscovites, as the Novgorodians before, were induced to cross the chain, and send an expedition into the mysterious land of Yugra. In 1499 an armed force was sent to conquer the lands on the river Ob; it returned with many prisoners, and the name of a new province is mentioned by historians which, from its name Obdorsk (Obdor in the Zyrian language means 'mouth of the Ob'), was probably situated far in the north, near the shores of the Arctic Ocean. It was probably visited by Russian ships, which, as we shall see later, were often met by English navigators in the high latitudes in the following century.

This expedition led to no practical results, as the government did not keep a hold on its distant possessions; but it brought back a fresh stock of wonderful stories. The inhabitants were said to fall asleep in autumn, and to wake up only in spring. For bartering, they left their goods at a fixed spot and retired, when the merchants came and replaced them by equivalent articles. The practice was said to lead to strife, as sometimes the goods found were much inferior in value to those left. As the latter story had been told of the Chinese centuries before, it only shows the wonderful vitality of geographical legends.

The Ostiaks and other aborigines of Yugra lived in constant strife, and were therefore exposed to the raids of the Tartars issuing from the southern steppes. Hard pressed by these enemies, they appealed for aid to Ivan III., promising to pay tribute on condition of being defended from the southern nomads. Only the first part of the contract was carried out; tax-collectors were occasionally sent, but Moscow was too far to afford effective protection. Later, when Ivan the Terrible, the grandson of Ivan III., conquered Kazan and Astrakhan, news of these important victories, which extended the power of Moscow to the Ural, reached Ediger, a chieftain in Yugra, and inspired hopes of timely assistance. Ediger promised to pay tribute on the same condition of receiving protection, but the power of the Tsar was still insufficient on his new distant frontier, and the Tartars killed Ediger and took his lands.

As tribute was always pleasant to collect, Ivan IV. attempted to exact it from the Tartar conquerors, whose only answer was the murder of his envoy. They also made frequent raids across the Ural into the province of Perm. The centralised government of Moscow, whose object for centuries had been the gradual establishment of order and suppression of crime, was unfitted for the task of undertaking the adventurous conquest of unknown regions peopled by wild races. This object could only be achieved by men fashioned by the peculiar circumstances of Russian border-life, by men who had escaped from and even revolted against the influences of autocracy.

When the Golden Horde was losing its power and ferocity, Russian adventurers began to roam in the southern borderland, in those steppes overrun by the nomads. They were mostly lawless characters; and the distance from Moscow, the immunity from law, the liberty of the boundless plains, the constant contact with the Tartars converted them into marauders like their Asiatic neighbours. These people without home and family were called Cossacks to distinguish them from the settled Russian population. History, which was probably late in recording the new phenomenon, first mentions the Cossacks of Riazan about the middle of the fifteenth century, but the most celebrated were the Zaporoghians,[1] who lived in the islands of the Dnieper around its rapids.

Close to the old original Russia of Ruric's successors, which had become Little Russia, and had fallen into the hands of Lithuania, when emigration had formed Great Russia, the Zaporoghians were admirably situated for sallying forth in their marauding raids, and for collecting the outcasts of the neighbouring regions. The lower course of the Dnieper was the boundary between Lithuania and the Tartar steppes, while the upper course flowed through Little Russia. The Polish supremacy, distasteful even in Lithuania, was more so in the conquered Russian provinces. The boldest among the Russians were tempted to fly from the oppression of the Polish nobles, hateful both on account of their religion and their nationality. The Zaporoghian Cossacks offered a refuge to all. No questions were asked about the past life of the newcomers. The only conditions for admission in the rough community were: belief in the orthodox faith, a strong body, and a stout heart. It is said that, as a test of courage, the candidates were required to swim across the rapids, buffeting the strong current. Complete equality reigned among the Cossacks, and all except arms and clothing was held in common; important measures were decided by a general council of the whole community, and the government was entrusted to elective *atamans*, whose orders were implicitly

---

[1] Za-porog = beyond the cataracts in Russian.

obeyed. The remembrance of past wrongs, the general hostility of their neighbours developed a strong feeling of comradeship, which bound fast together the members of this military republic.

The chief occupation of the Zaporoghians was war against the Tartars and Turks. They built rough boats like their ancestors centuries before, often consisting of a single huge trunk scooped out, with the sides raised by planking; and with these primitive craft they descended the Dnieper, and boldly roved in the Black Sea, attacking and plundering the Turkish ships. The reappearance in the Black Sea of the daring adventurous Russian race long smothered by the Asiatic invasions seemed like a return to the time of Oleg, the half-legendary conqueror of Constantinople. On land the Cossacks in their incessant warfare with the Tartars adopted the desultory tactics of their enemies, and became wild horsemen of the steppes. They spread out like a fan on the waste borderland of Russia, ever advancing and driving back the nomads refractory to civilisation, smoothing the way for the settlement of a sedentary population. Their mission in the East was similar to that of the trappers and backwoodsmen of the West, who, struggling with the Red Indians hundreds of miles ahead of the American settlements, rendered possible the wonderful expansion of the United States. Like the pioneers of the Far West, the Cossacks, through necessity of war and frequent intercourse with an inferior race, were obliged to conform to the rough life and half-civilised customs of their enemies. But these defects were useful and indispensable in a population which was to serve as an intermediate stage between Asiatic nomadism and European civilisation. They have been everywhere the advance guard of Russian conquest. From the Dnieper they passed to the Don and the Volga, and then to the great

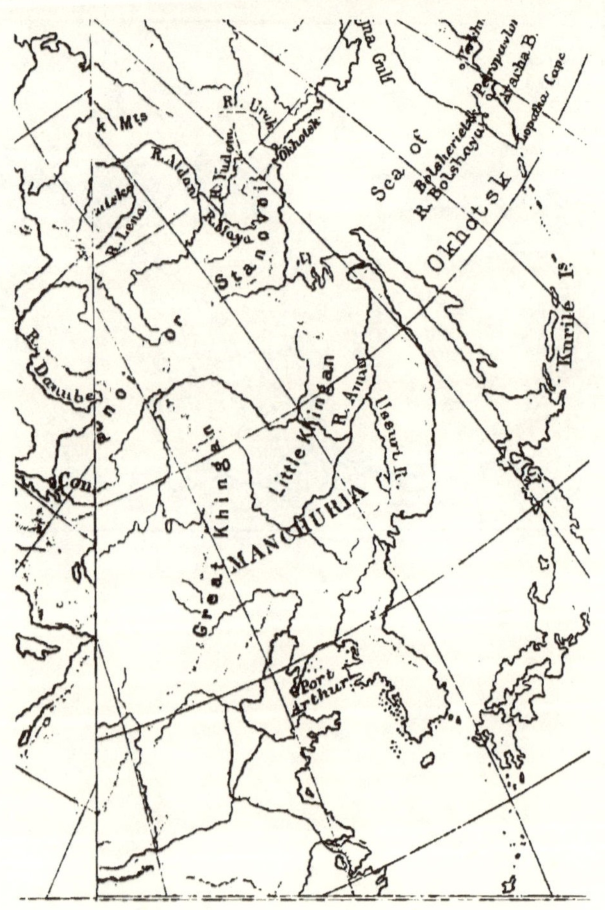
k Mts
R. Uruk
R.Aldan
R.Yudoma
Okhotsk
ulek
R.Lena
R.Maya
Stanovoi
or
R.Danube
Little Khingan
R.Amur
Great Khingan
MANCHURIA
Ussuri R.
Sea of
Okhotsk
Bolsheretsk
R. Bolshayaya
Petropavlv
Avacha B.
Lopatka Cape
Kurile Is
Con
Port
Arthur
na Gulf

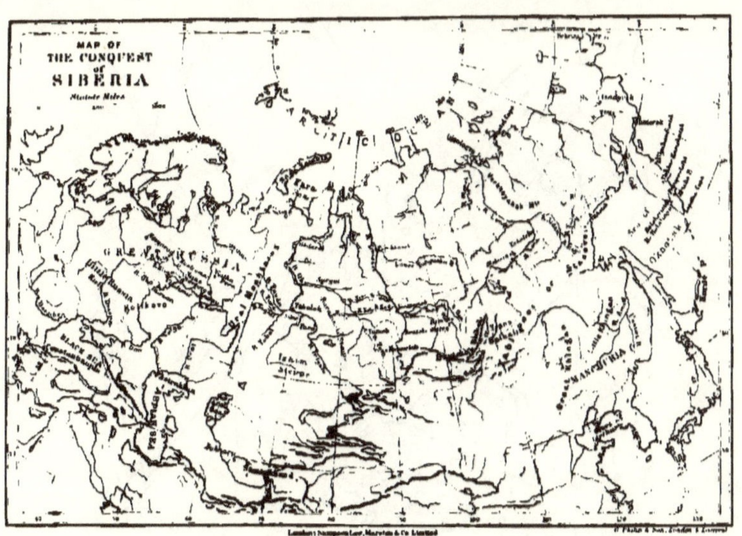

London: Sampson Low, Marston & Co. Limited

Siberian rivers flowing into the Arctic Ocean, and now we find them on the Amur and the Usuri, on the shores of the Pacific. Whenever the aborigines have been conquered, the Cossacks have become settlers, but they have kept the essential traits of their origin; the members of the village community decide on all matters of importance, and they elect their *atamans* or village chiefs; they are only bound to military service in requital of the lands bestowed by the Tsar.

The notion held on the continent of Europe that they are a special body of irregular cavalry formed by a despotic government, of whom they are the dreaded symbol, is wrong. They started as river pirates, and only became the wild horsemen of the steppes to meet the nomads with their own tactics; their home has always been on the banks of the great northern rivers; their military organisation is only a recent development. Far from being the willing instruments of despotism, they were the outposts of national independence, whether against the Poles or the Tartars. They were the vigorous offshoots of a young race ever eager to find wider fields for the enjoyment of their boundless individual freedom. Their frequent revolts under Mazeppa Pugacheff prove how difficult it has been for the government to curb their unruly character, averse to all restraint.

The advantages derived from the individual enterprise of the Cossacks could not escape the sovereigns of Moscow; and, though their object was to suppress violence and establish order throughout Russia, they were forced by circumstances to encourage private enterprise in the newly conquered northern territories, and to supplement the weak action of the central government by delegating its powers to private persons fit for the purpose. When, by the conquest of Perm and Viatka, the Muscovites reached the frontiers of the mysterious land of Yugra, among the scanty settlers the Stroganoffs (now one of the great families of the Russian aristocracy) acquired great wealth and influence. It is supposed they were of Tartar origin, being descended from a ' Murza,' or prince of that race, probably another instance of the attraction by which the strong orderly government of Moscow enlisted in its service the best elements even from among the hostile races. At the time of Ivan the Terrible they added to their possessions 150 versts of land around the Kama (the largest tributary of the Volga), and by a charter of the Tsar they were authorised to cut forests, colonise waste lands, establish salt·works, and engage workmen ; they were also granted exemption from taxes for a period of twenty years. In exchange for these privileges they were obliged to defend Russia from the incursions of the wild races beyond the Ural, and at their own expense build block-houses, purchase guns, and keep a sufficient armed force. The arrangement was convenient for both parties, and during three generations the Stroganoffs accumulated great wealth while defending the border. The third Stroganoff far surpassed the modest conditions of his contract; he furnished the means for commencing the greatest conquest of Russia, and deserves, therefore, a conspicuous place in the history of his country.

We now must glance at three generations of another family in far different circumstances—a family struggling against great poverty, but destined by fortune to come across the path of the Stroganoffs and assist them in their great enterprise. This family was destined to produce one of those few men who mark an epoch in the history of the world—one who is the greatest popular hero of Russia, though, strange to say, he is hardly known beyond the frontiers of his country.

The grandfather of this hero was called Athanasius Alenin, and lived in great poverty in the suburbs of Suzdal. Want of work obliged him to remove to Vladimir, where he became a carter. At that time the dense forests of Murom, situated between the Oka and its affluent, the Kliasma, in the neighbourhood of Vladimir, were infested by bandits, and Athanasius Alenin often transported them with his horses, being well paid for his valuable assistance. But this profitable business was of short duration. The complaisant carter was arrested with a party of brigands and put in prison, whence he, however, soon contrived to escape, and fled to Yurievetz Povolski, a place on the Volga about halfway between Kostroma and Nijni Novgorod, where he died. His death plunged the widow and children into worse poverty. They heard of the flourishing business of the Stroganoffs on the river Kama, of their demand for labour, and of the good earnings of the new settlers, and emigrated, settling on one of the affluents of the river Kama, the Tchusavaya, whose upper course runs almost parallel to the Ural mountains. The sons took the name of Povolski from that of their last residence, married, and had children.

Among the grandsons of Athanasius, the carter of Vladimir, the smartest was Vassil, the son of Timothy. From his early years he was remarkable for strength and fluent speech, and when he attained manhood, though not tall, his thickset, broad-shouldered frame, his quick bright eyes, pitch-black hair, and thick curly beard attracted attention in a community where physical qualities were the only marks of distinction. His first occupation was that of a tracker on the Kama and Volga.[1] In that rough life he often had to cook food for his comrades, who

---

[1] Until the introduction of steam, vessels were constantly towed up stream by gangs of trackers.

bestowed on him the nickname of Yermak (the millstone of a handmill), a name which he rendered famous, and by which only he is known in history. The tame drudgery of the tracker's life soon disgusted the bold adventurous Yermak, and he joined the Cossacks of the Don, who, struck by his daring, soon selected him chief of one of their small settlements.

This first success showed Yermak that he had found his calling, and he decided to choose a larger field for his activity. He led his Cossacks to the Volga, where he gathered a large band of robbers. His local knowledge now was invaluable ; the slow, monotonous work of the tracker had given opportunities for his keen eye and quick intellect to reconnoitre the shores of the river, and to learn the habits of the trading vessels ; it was, therefore, an easy task for him—perhaps not devoid of a certain grim pleasure—to plunder the ships he had towed in- his youth. The Volga had been always a great commercial route, and it had grown in importance since the conquest of Kazan and Astrakhan had given to Russia the whole course of the river. There was, therefore, plenty of booty, and under a clever leader like Yermak piracy flourished to the terror and confusion of the traders. Matters grew so bad that complaints even reached Moscow, and Ivan the Terrible ordered the pirates should be seized and hanged, an army being sent to carry out the order.

This unpleasant news obliged Yermak to relinquish his profitable occupation and seek safety in some distant region out of the reach of the law. The huge river which offered such opportunities for plunder also afforded ready means of escape. The pirates ascended the Volga, and then by the river Kama reached those wild thinly peopled districts where Yermak had passed his childhood. The Cossacks arrived in a favourable moment.

Some years before, as early as 1573, the Stroganoffs, enriched by their possessions on the Kama, had cast covetous eyes over the Ural to the mysterious land of Yugra, rich in valuable furs, aspiring to extend in an easterly direction their profitable work of colonisation. They applied to Ivan the Terrible for a charter, similar to the one they had already received for the land on the Kama, authorising them to cross the Ural, to cultivate the land, build block-houses, and purchase guns. They also added artfully that the Ostiaks were ready to pay tribute to the Tsar if they were protected. The latter clause was especially agreeable to Ivan the Terrible, for, as we have seen, repeated attempts had been made by Moscow to collect regular tribute from Yugra, and they had persistently failed, because the distant Tsar could not afford the protection the natives required in exchange for their furs. The proposal of the Stroganoffs solved the difficulty, and the charter demanded was granted. Now, however, the Stroganoffs were faced by their greatest difficulties. The experience acquired on the Kama and the armed force at their disposal would have sufficed to collect tribute from the Ostiaks and other aborigines; but lately the Tartars from the south had pushed northwards and conquered the country. The Stroganoffs dared not risk a war against these fierce nomads, whose power was magnified by distance and mystery.

The daring spirit of Yermak was not deterred by dangers either real or imaginary, and, with the directness of genius, he saw that the slow advance of the Muscovite settlers was inadequate for the new project of the Stroganoffs—the subjection of Yugra could only be achieved by rapid conquest.

It was a century marked by the wonderful expansion of Western Europe. India and China had been rediscovered by Portuguese navigators ; a new world had been found where Spanish adventurers had conquered empires. Though Russia had little intercourse with the West, still some vague report of these astonishing events must have reached her. English navigators, in their attempts to find a north-east passage to China,[1] opened commercial relations with Russia. Less than thirty years before Yermak's proposal, in 1553, Chancellor had traversed the whole northern part of the country on his way to Moscow. The consequent creation of the Muscovy Company had given English traders the monopoly of the commerce of the White Sea. In 1556 Burrough had met numerous Russian vessels near Nova Zembla. In 1557 an agent of the Muscovy Company, starting from the White Sea, had traversed the Dvina, the Volga, the Caspian, and had reached Samarkhand. A year before, in 1580, Pot and Jackman penetrated into the Kara Sea. A restless spirit of discovery pervaded all the nations of Europe, and this vague feeling would act powerfully on the quick intelligence of a man like Yermak.

The proposal to conquer Yugra was readily approved by the Stroganoffs, whose wealth enabled them to furnish the necessary arms and provisions for the distant and difficult expedition. Yermak had brought with him his trusty lieutenants, the famous Volga pirates, Ivan Koltzo, Iakob Mikhailowitel, Nikita Pan, Matvien Meshtcheriak, and a body of the boldest Cossacks. Their numbers were now swollen by a motley crowd of Russians, Tartars, Germans, and Lithuanians, whom the Stroganoffs had ransomed from the Nogai Tartars of the south. The whole force amounted to 800 men, and was well equipped with the best arms of the period (light cannon, muskets, and arquebuses). A large stock of provisions was pro-

---

[1] First proposed by Robert Thorne in 1527.

vided for the long journey in an unknown and probably barren country. Interpreters were engaged, and even spiritual wants were not neglected, three popes and a runaway monk being attached to the party. Yermak started on September 1, 1581,[1] amidst loud flourishes of trumpets, as the Stroganoffs wished to mark with great pomp the departure of the expedition.

The Stroganoffs risked paying dearly for the assistance given to Yermak. The same day he started, the Vogulichi, a tribe beyond the Ural, made a raid, burning and robbing several Russian settlements. This disaster could not be concealed from Ivan the Terrible, who also was informed that outlawed Cossacks had been sheltered by the Stroganoffs, and allowed to organise an armed invasion of Yugra. The two events got mixed up in the mind of the distant Tsar, whose only vague notion of Yugra was that of a land whence occasionally valuable furs could be obtained at the cheap price of a perfunctory promise of protection. The rash act of a few pirates seemed to imperil a profitable transaction. He wrote severely to the Stroganoffs, upbraiding them for harbouring dangerous robbers, who, instead of being employed at least for the protection of the settlements, were allowed to attack tribes willing to pay tribute. The advance of the Cossacks threatened to ruin the whole business, and they were ordered to be recalled.

The Tsar showed himself a worthy descendant of those first Grand Dukes of Moscow whose virtues, a Russian historian[2] sneeringly remarks, were less valorous than lucrative. When we compare his reluctance to risk the loss of a few sables with the fearlessness of Yermak,

---

[1] Up to the time of Peter the Great the Russian year commenced on September 1 : so Yermak started on New Year's day.

[2] Kuchewsky, *Course of Russian History*.

ready to face death and endless privations in an unknown land, we must recognise that the late tracker of the Volga had a more kingly soul than the terrible Tsar, the descendant of the long line of Ruric.

The severe orders of the Tsar, however, produced no effect. At that time it took more than a month for news to travel from Moscow to the Kama, and when the Stroganoffs received the command to recall Yermak he was far away. He had already won his first victories.

Yermak led his men, in true Cossack fashion, by river in a fleet of boats. At first their course was up the Tchussavaya, on whose banks his father and uncles had settled, and where he had passed his childhood. They made slow progress, as they had to row against the strong current flowing between steep rocky banks. From the Tchussavaya they passed to its tributary, the Serebrianka. The Ural mountains now appeared quite close, while the current grew stronger and the banks steeper. At last the water grew too shallow for the heavily laden boats, when, it is said, Yermak dammed the stream with sails. The increased depth obtained by the accumulation of intercepted water allowed the flotilla to proceed a little further. But at last all the resources of Yermak's local knowledge, and of his varied experience acquired as a boatman and tracker, were of no avail; the boats had to be taken out of the water and dragged to the next stream.

The central part of the Urals (the Ural of Goroblahodat) where Yermak effected his passage is of slight elevation, only three peaks rising above 2,000 feet, and even this slight height is attained by such a gentle slope along the extended Russian plain that the passage from the European to the Asiatic watershed is quite imperceptible. On the road from Perm to Yekaterinburg a post, with the

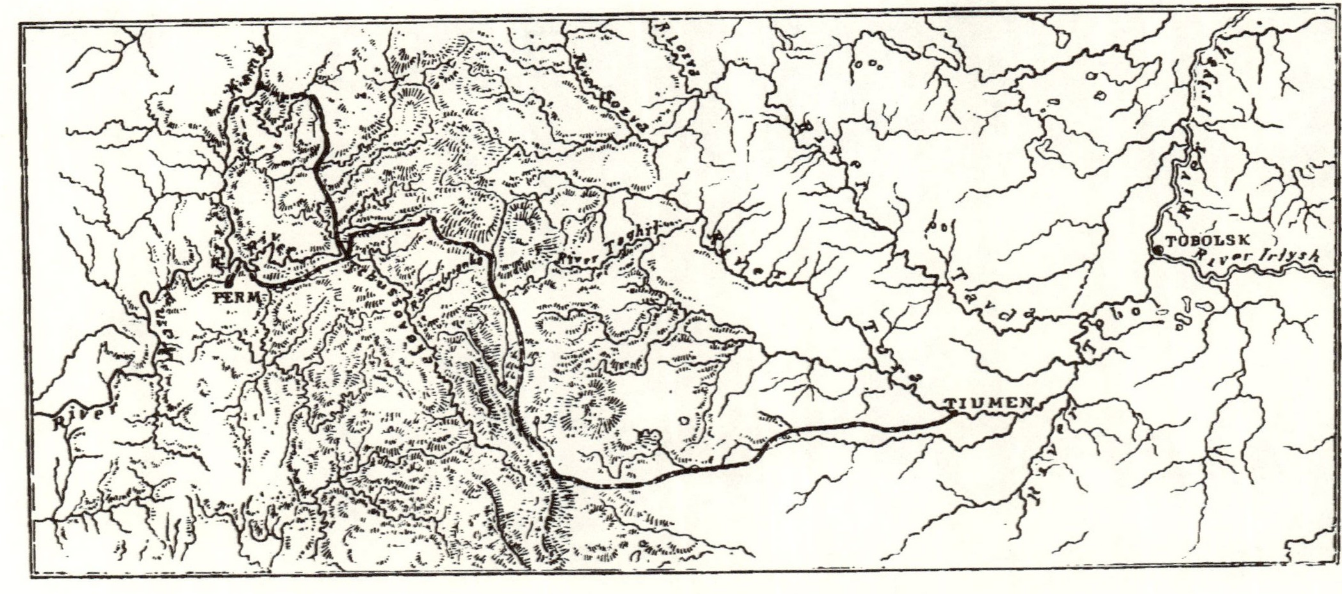

MAP SHOWING THE COUNTRY TRAVERSED BY YERMAK

(The railway from Perm to Tiumen is also marked)

words Europe on one side and Asia on the other, indicates the fact to the traveller.

An easy 'portage' therefore brought Yermak's boats to the small stream Jaravli, on which they floated down to the larger Taghil, and thence to the still larger river Tura, all forming part of the basin of the Ob. On the river Tura the Cossacks were attacked by the aborigines, who shot arrows from the banks; but when the Russians discharged their firearms they fled in great terror, imagining that thunder and lightning were directed against them. The Cossacks then landed and sacked several villages, but were unable to capture any prisoners, as the whole population had escaped. They were more fortunate later when they reached the river Tavda, where they succeeded in seizing a Tartar. Yermak, perceiving the impression produced by firearms, determined to show the terrible effects of his weapons. A musket was fired at a coat of mail, which was pierced by the bullet. When the terror of the Tartar had subsided, he was questioned about the land and its inhabitants. The whole country belonged to Kutchum, the Tartar chief who had invaded Yugra and conquered the aborigines; the same who had put to death the envoy sent by Ivan the Terrible to demand tribute. His capital, Isker, or Sibir, was situated on the Irtysh, the largest affluent of the Ob, and could be reached by following the Tobol. Kutchum, though old and blind, was full of energy, and was assisted by a young kinsman, Makhmetkul, the most daring warrior of the whole region. All the surrounding tribes were tributaries to the Tartars, who were, however, unpopular, because they tried to convert to Mahometanism the pagan natives.

Yermak was in somewhat similar conditions to those of Cortez when he undertook his daring conquest of

Mexico. His followers, though few, had firearms and defensive armour, while his numerous enemies fought with spears and bows and arrows. A rapid victory was sure to break the power of the Tartars, as the disaffected natives were ready to change when they found a stronger master.

The prisoner was released, and, as expected, reported to Kutchum the arrival of strangers with wonderful bows which shot flames and pierced iron mail. The old chief, undismayed, hastened preparations to stop the enemy on the Tobol. In a place where the river narrows, iron chains were thrown across the stream to stop the boats, and a large force was stationed on the bank to attack and destroy the Russians. A stratagem of Yermak's fertile mind outwitted the simple Tartars. Bundles of sticks and brushwood were dressed up as Cossacks and placed in boats, with a few men to steer, while the bulk of the expedition landed and resolutely attacked the enemy on the banks. The Tartars, frightened by the numbers of the Russians advancing on all sides, fled without resistance.

This defeat obliged Kutchum to gather another larger army to stop the invaders. It was divided into two corps. Kutchum with the bulk of his force entrenched himself at a short distance from the capital, while the cavalry, commanded by the renowned Makhmetkul, advanced against the Russians. The Cossacks were at first disheartened by the superiority of the enemy, who was thirty times more numerous; but Yermak encouraged them by his example, and a desperate engagement took place. Despite their numbers the Tartars could not stand against firearms and were routed; but the victory was dearly bought, as Yermak lost some of his bravest followers.

The Cossacks continued to descend the river Tobol, harassed continually by parties of Tartars shooting arrows from their hiding-places on the banks. At last the Russians landed, and, driving away the enemy, resumed their route on the river Irtysh. Now they were near Isker, and close to Kutchum, who had collected all his forces in defence of his capital. Yermak halted in a Tartar village to give his men a night's rest before the battle. The Cossacks, in their usual fashion, assembled in a circle to discuss and take counsel. The long fatiguing journey in an unknown country, the hard-won victories, the expectation of a doubtful battle against a still more numerous enemy produced a feeling of despondency, and it was proposed to return. Yermak used all his eloquence to dissuade his followers; he said such thoughts were unworthy of them, and pointed out that retreat now was impossible—long ere they could reach their homes all the rivers would be frozen.[1] After a long consultation the Cossacks recognised that their only chance lay in victory, and consented to remain.

On the morning of October 23, 1581, the Russians boldly attacked the enemy, entrenched behind an abattis of felled trees. A fierce struggle ensued; the Tartars rushed out, surrounding the assailants on all sides; but the Cossacks, encouraged by Yermak and his lieutenant, Ivan Koltzo, who were everywhere in the thickest of the fight, resolved to sell their lives dearly. A lucky shot struck Makhmetkul, who had to be removed to the other bank of the Irtysh, and the Tartars, now leaderless, were put to flight. Old blind Kutchum, hearing of the defeat, abandoned his capital in despair and fled south to the

---

[1] The Irtysh at Tobolsk freezes generally about November 7, though sometimes as early as October 22, or as late as December 1 (*Russki Kalendar*, 1899. Suvorina).

steppes of Ishim. This victory, the most important they had won, gave the Russians the whole country from the Ural to the rivers Tobol and Ob, but it cost the lives of many Cossacks. Yermak, by successive desertions and casualties, had now but few men left.

On October 26 Yermak reaped the firstfruits of his victory by occupying the abandoned capital of Kutchum, the town of Sibir. This name, applied also to the surrounding country, was adopted by the Russians to denote their possessions beyond the Ural, and as these gradually grew until they reached the Pacific, so by a common extension of geographical terms the same word was used to indicate the dominions of the Tsar in Northern Asia. Thus the name of a small Tartar town, the headquarters of an obscure chieftain, has become the collective geographical designation of the largest region on the earth.

The town of Isker or Sibir was strongly protected on two sides by the steep banks of the Irtysh and of a small stream, the Sibirka, and on the other sides by a triple earthen rampart and ditch. It is said the Cossacks found rich booty in silks, furs, and even gold, which was equally divided, but their newly acquired wealth could not purchase what they wanted most. Their provisions were almost exhausted, and no food was found in the town; the near approach of the rigorous northern winter rendered their position very dangerous.

The news of the great victory, of the flight of Kutchum, of the occupation of his capital spread rapidly, and on October 30 the Ostiaks came, as Yermak had expected, to offer allegiance to their new masters. They also brought presents and much-needed provisions. The peace which now reigned over the country gave the Cossacks leisure to start fishing and hunting to collect a sufficient stock of food for the long winter. But their enemies now appeared again, and in the beginning of December Makhmetkul, recovered from his wound, fell upon a party of twenty Cossacks, who were all massacred. Yermak had to leave Sibir in pursuit of Makhmetkul, who was again severely defeated.

The long winter, with the rigid weather of the region, precluded all possibility of military operations; but in April 1582 Yermak was informed that Makhmetkul was not far distant with a very small force. An expedition of ten Cossacks was promptly organised, which proceeded so rapidly and secretly that the Tartars were surprised, dispersed, and their chief captured.

Now was the brightest period of Yermak's life. The power of Kutchum was completely broken, as he had lost the service of his valiant kinsman, and was attacked by another Tartar prince whose father he had killed. The Russians descended the Irtysh and the Ob, enforcing the submission of the different tribes and collecting tribute.

Having completed the first part of his work, Yermak thought the moment had come to inform the Stroganoffs of the result of his undertaking. He probably also felt the want of reinforcements, as in his last expedition one of the *atamans*, Nikita Pan, with several Cossacks, had been killed, and every slight loss told heavily on the dwindling band of adventurers. The acute mind of Yermak realised the importance of his position and of the extraordinary work he had accomplished. He not only wrote to the Stroganoffs informing them of his victories and of the capture of Makhmetkul, but he also wrote to Ivan the Terrible. After asking pardon for his past misdeeds, Yermak added that the Russian empire had now a new territory—the land of Sibir, which only needed the laws and the *voivodes* of the Tsar. The messenger charged with the delivery of this letter and of the prisoner

Makhmetkul was the trusty lieutenant Ivan Koltzo, the robber chief of the Volga, who had been condemned to death by a proclamation of Ivan the Terrible.

The arrival of this strange embassy filled Moscow with wonder and pleasure; a handful of Cossacks had conquered the mysterious land of Yugra, and the wealth they had found was evinced by the valuable presents they had sent and the rich dresses of their envoys. The Tsar, who had shown such displeasure at the departure of Yermak, was now soothed by the report of his success and by the fine sables brought by Ivan Koltzo. He gave money and presents to the Cossacks and sent Yermak a fur mantle which had covered the imperial shoulders. What was still more acceptable to Yermak was the despatch of a *voivode* with 500 *strieletz*.

The conquest of Siberia, even in the limited sense in which the expression was understood at that time, was far from accomplished. The forces at the disposal of Yermak were inadequate for the purpose, as soon as the natives began to recover from the astonishment produced by the arrival of the strangers with their wonderful weapons. The powerful reinforcement sent from Moscow was of little use at first, because the *strielitz* were less fit to endure privations than the Cossacks; the cold and moisture of the winter, the want of fresh food caused a violent outbreak of scurvy. The *voivode* himself and many of his soldiers fell victims to the disease, which raged until spring brought warmth and a supply of bread.

A crafty chief, Karatcho, had won the confidence of Yermak by a specious show of friendship, and under pretence of seeking assistance he inveigled a party of Russians into his power, when he treacherously murdered them; the famous Ivan Koltzo was killed on this occasion. The news of this massacre caused a general revolt of all the subject tribes, who besieged Sibir, surrounding the place with a long line of wagons, which prevented the exit of the Russians and afforded protection from their firearms.

The courage and enterprise of the Cossacks extricated them from this perilous position. On a dark night,[1] June 12, 1584, led by Matvien Meshtcheriak, they stealthily penetrated through the line of wagons and fiercely attacked the surprised Tartars, who were slaughtered in great numbers while asleep. The desperate struggle continued until the following midday, when Karatcho, finding he could not drive away the Cossacks from his train of wagons, fled to Kutchum in the steppes of Ishim.

Yermak was now indefatigable in punishing the scattered rebel tribes and revenging the death of his men. His task was now more laborious, as almost all his brother *atamans* had perished ; Yakof Mikhailoff had been killed with a scouting party, and only Meshtcheriak was left of the old Volga pirate chiefs. Having pacified the country, he returned to Sibir, but only for a short time ; rest was denied to him even in the last months of his adventurous life.

During the two years the Russians had been established in Sibir, commercial intercourse had been opened with distant regions of Asia, merchants coming even from Bokhara to barter their goods. A party of these traders had been long expected by the Russians, but now they were informed that Kutchum, their old enemy, prevented the passage of the Bokharians. Yermak, with his usual prompt resolution, started with a party of fifty Cossacks to meet the caravan, but after a day of fruitless search he

---

[1] It must have been very cloudy, because in that latitude and season twilight lasts all night.

was unable to find either the merchants or Kutchum. An encampment was chosen for the night with the deep rapid stream of the Irtysh on one side, and a shallow ditch filled with water on the other; the boats were moored to the bank, the tents were pitched, and the tired Cossacks fell asleep; all were so exhausted that no watch was kept. Unfortunately, Kutchum was near.

It was August 5, 1584; the night was very stormy; the furious waves of the Irtysh tore away the boats from their moorings and floated them down the river; the noise of the howling wind and pelting rain drowned the sound of the hoofs of the advancing Tartars. Old blind Kutchum had been informed that the Russians were sleeping, but would not credit the report, fearing an ambush. A scout was sent with orders to find a ford across the ditch, to stealthily enter the camp, and bring back proof of the report. He returned with three muskets. The delighted Kutchum could no longer doubt that chance had given him at last an opportunity to have his revenge and destroy the terrible enemy who had deprived him of his dominions. Amid the roaring of the storm the Tartar cavalry rushed into the camp and commenced the butchery of the slumbering Russians. Only two were able to get to their feet: a Cossack, who escaped to convey the sad news, and Yermak. He fought valiantly for his life, cutting down the Tartars who approached; but at a glance he saw he was alone and had no chance. He rushed to the river bank to find a boat, but the boats had all drifted away. Driven to bay, he plunged into the deep river in the vain hope of swimming to the boats, but the weight of his armour dragged him to the bottom.

A few days afterwards a Tartar discovered in the river the corpse of Yermak, conspicuous by its rich coat of mail with a golden eagle on the breast. It is stated to have

YERMAK

(From the Statue by Antokolsky)

been subject to great indignities, though finally buried with great honours. The sword and the armour of the renowned *ataman* were divided among the Tartar chiefs ; but after seventy years, by chance, the coat of mail fell again into the hands of the Russians.

Such was the end of the founder of the Russian Asiatic empire. His career was one of the most remarkable in history ; from the humblest origin, from the meanest occupations and unlawful pursuits, he rose to a position of wealth and power, where he had free scope to show that his abilities were far above those of the common freebooter.

The bold raid into Siberia might have occurred to the mind of any daring adventurer, but the persevering struggle against difficulties, the severe discipline he enforced, the organisation he attempted to establish in the new country, were the work of no ordinary man. It would be wrong to consider that chance alone ; the general European expansion of the century, the Russian conquest of Kazan and Astrakhan, had raised him to eminence. A century before, a Russian expedition had crossed the Ural, but failed to realise what it had achieved. Yermak himself created the importance of his position, and forced its recognition by boldly writing directly to the Tsar. While, as a loyal Russian, he asked forgiveness for his past crimes, he clearly showed that an empire was offered as his atonement : an empire whose future value was discernible to the keen insight of his genius.

In the last glorious years of his life his pride was gratified by high honours ; it is said he received the title of Siberian prince ; he, the tracker and pirate of the Volga, wore the mantle of the Tsar, sent by the imperious Ivan the Terrible ; but the greatest consolation amid privations, fatigues, and sufferings must have been the proud consciousness that he had done for Russia what no other man ever had done. Demetrius Donskoi, at Kulikovo, had only defended the independence of his country with 150,000 men at his back ; Ivan III. and Ivan IV. with their powerful armies had only encroached on the decaying Tartar khanates ; while he, with the scanty resources he had been enabled to obtain in the hard struggle of his life, with the rough companions gathered on the banks of the Volga, had conquered the land across the Ural, which extended far away to the east beyond the knowledge of his time. He was the founder of that Greater Russia which promises to be in the future to the Great Russia of Moscow what the latter was to the Little Russia of Kief. After many centuries of subjection to the Tartars, of the prudent, shuffling policy of the Grand Dukes of Moscow, he was the first to reveal to the Russian race what daring deeds it could accomplish, and to restore that feeling of self-confidence which is the first element of national greatness.

It is difficult to find in Russian history men possessing higher qualities than those of this rough peasant : we must go back to Alexander Nevsky, who by his valour and wisdom averted destruction from his race, or we must look forward to Peter the Great, whose genius and incessant work removed the dross left by the Tartar conquest, and secured for his country her right place in Europe. The memory of Yermak is revered all over Siberia ; his name and exploits are the subject of innumerable songs and legends, and even in the houses of the peasants we find rough pictures of the popular hero.

The personal influence of Yermak can be measured by the effects that immediately followed his death. The Cossacks, decimated by cold, sickness, and wounds, had not the courage to continue the work of their beloved leader, and resolved to return to Russia. They abandoned the town of Sibir and commenced their retreat, but on their way they met the *voivode* Mansuroff, who had been sent with 100 men by Theodore, the son and successor of Ivan the Terrible. Thus reinforced, the Russians returned to Sibir, but were unable to enter the town, as it had been already occupied by the Tartars.

The work accomplished by Yermak had been of such importance that it could not be permanently effaced even by his untimely death. The defeated Tartars had lost cohesion, and Kutchum, who had reoccupied his old capital Sibir, abandoned by the Cossacks, was quickly driven out by another chieftain. A Russian *voivode*, Tchulkoff, arrived with a fresh reinforcement of 300 men, but, deeming it unwise to attack Sibir, built another town, Tobolsk (1587), at sixteen[1] versts distance. All attempts to live at peace with the Tartars, however, proved ineffectual; the chieftains plotted to destroy the Russians by treachery, but were discovered and captured by Tchulkoff. Old blind Kutchum, the relentless enemy of Yermak, wrote to the Tsar, and for some time lived under his protection, but his pride refused to accept a dependent position, and he fled to the Tartars in the south, where he was murdered. His old capital, Sibir, the glorious conquest of Yermak, which has given a name to the whole north of Asia, gradually vanished before the growing importance of the neighbouring Tobolsk; the ramparts, ditches, and a few ruins still indicate its past glory.[2]

The government of Moscow soon tried to develop the territory it had so unexpectedly acquired through the boldness of the Cossack adventurers. As early as 1586

---

[1] Nineteen versts according to the *Guide to Siberia* (W. A. Bolgorukoff).

[2] It is said that in May and September the local Tartars assemble here to commemorate their ancestors of the Irtysh (W. A. Bolgorukoff).

peasants were sent with horses, cows, and ploughs to colonise and cultivate the land. But the agricultural development of the country was very slow, for few persons were willing to engage in a risky occupation in the troubled region, with prospects of relatively small profits. Almost all the settlers were either soldiers occupied in collecting tribute and subduing the natives, or merchants trafficking in furs.

The Russians in Western Siberia found themselves in similar conditions, and exposed to the same enemies as their ancestors in European Russia : on the south there was a region of steppes which, extending through a gap in the mountains, bounding the rest of Siberia on the east and south, reaches to the shores of the Aral and the Caspian ; from these plains the Tartars were always ready to make raids northward when there were hopes of plunder. Forts had to be constructed, and troops were stationed in the south to stop the inroads of the nomad horsemen. The *ostrogs*, or forts, built by the Cossacks, were similar to the block-houses of the early settlers in the United States who dwelt in the vicinity of the Red Indians. A rough but strong palisade of pointed beams surrounded sufficient space for the log-huts of the soldiers and peasants. These *ostrogs* were in some places merely military outposts, while in others they formed the defence of a settlement which often became a town when favourably situated. In the latter case an inner enclosure was formed with wooden walls and towers.

The town of Tara on the Irtysh, founded in 1594, is an instance of these early fortified settlements, and details are given to show their small size. The inner enclosure of wooden walls and towers was a square of ninety-eight yards a side, and contained the church, the residence of the *voivode*, the powder magazine, and government storehouses; around this there was the *ostrog*, whose palisade formed a rectangle 1,400 feet long and 1,050 wide; the log-huts were situated in the intermediate space between the two enclosures. Tara was a place of great importance in the early times, and, together with Kuznetsk on the upper waters of the Tom, founded more than twenty years later, formed the southern line of defence against the nomads. But the scanty numbers of the Russians were quite inadequate to guard the immense Siberian plains : it is sufficient to note that at Tara a detachment of sixty Cossacks was supposed to defend the fertile Barabinski steppe, situated between the upper courses of the Irtysh and Ob, which has a breadth varying from 250 to 400 miles.

The numerical weakness of the Russians, and the terrifying effects produced by firearms on the natives, led to the wide use of cannon. Almost every *ostrog* had several small guns, and the official documents of the time contain full details about the serving out of ammunition, and the appointment of gunners for firing and peasants for handling the guns. The terrors of artillery, however, were insufficient to stop the inroads of the southern nomads, especially when the Kirghizes and Kalmucks also joined in the raids : the outlying *ostrogs* were often burnt, and Tobolsk itself, though situated so far north, was exposed to attacks even up to sixty years after the invasion of Yermak.

The fierce aggressive races of the south prevented the early expansion in that direction of the few scattered Russian adventurers, who were therefore obliged to undertake the conquest of less warlike races in more inhospitable regions. These circumstances produced the strange result that the Russians settled first in the cold northern plains, and only slowly advanced later towards warmer regions. Thus Berezof (1593), towards the mouth of the Ob (N. lat. 63° 55'), was founded before Tara, Surgut, Narym, and eleven years before Tomsk. This was also due to the hydrographical conditions of the country, and to the means of conveyance employed by the Cossacks. The course of the Ob and Irtysh flows from south to north, and the Russians, who always proceeded in boats, preferred to drift down the rivers from their head-quarters at Tobolsk, avoiding the laborious work of rowing and tracking against the stream. In their navigation the Cossacks used rafts, and one-masted decked vessels 84 feet long. These craft were of the roughest kind, without any iron; even the anchors were of wood weighted with stones to make them sink. The ropes were made of twisted strips of reindeer skins, and the sails of tanned hides of the same animals.

The hereditary skill of the Cossacks as river sailors, derived from the practice of their ancestors dwelling on the banks of the Dnieper, Don, and Volga, handled these primitive vessels with such effect that the whole central part of the basin of the Ob and Irtysh, with their tributaries, became a network of communications for the scattered Russian settlements and outposts. These, in consequence, were all situated on the rivers, either near the confluence of two streams or where an easy portage led from the upper waters of one river to those of another. The inundations of the Siberian rivers, caused by the great increase of water in the spring, were a source of great distress to the early settlers, until they learnt to choose appropriate places for the *ostrogs* on steep banks or on elevated ground.[1]

The northern part of Siberia, to which the Russians

---

[1] The town of Tara, in consequence of the inundation of 1669, had to be removed.

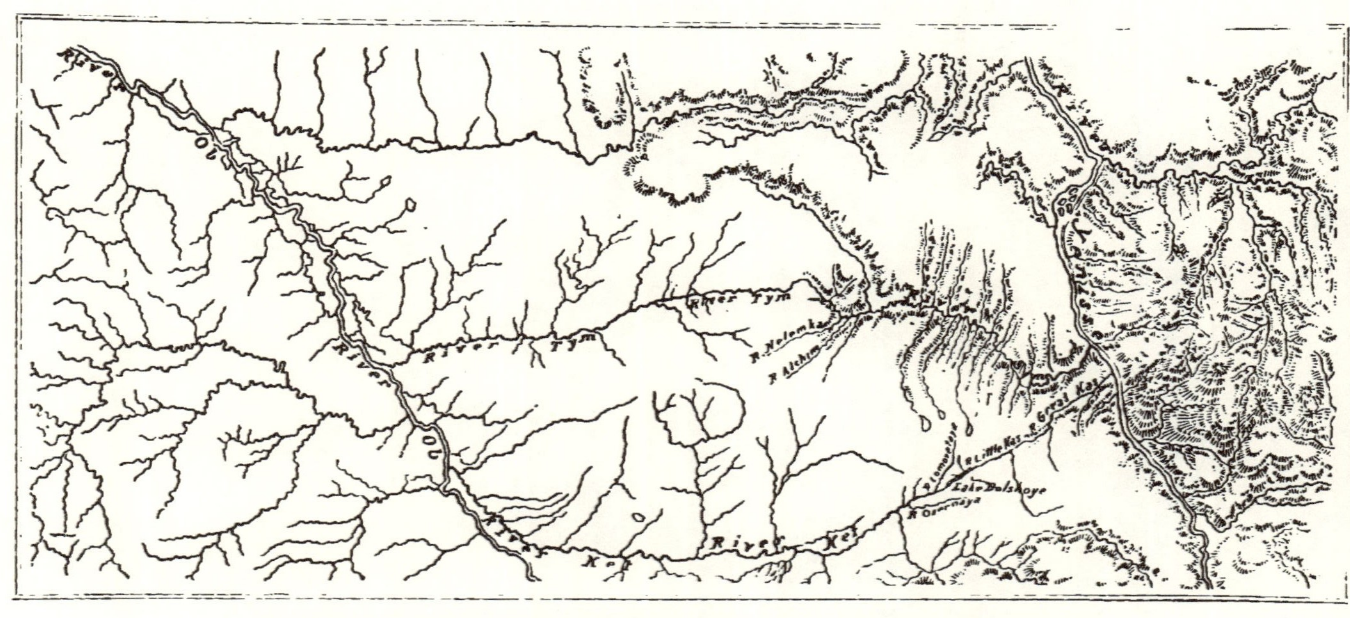

MAP SHOWING THE COMMUNICATIONS BETWEEN THE OB AND YENISSEI RIVERS

were confined by the hostility of the warlike southern tribes, was rich in those valuable furs which had been abundant in European Russia in early times, and had constituted the principal trade of Novgorod the Great. These articles, representing a great value with slight volume and weight, were especially adapted to the necessities of the Cossacks, obliged to wander over extensive tracts of country with slow, laborious means of conveyance. The fur trade in Siberia corresponded to the keen search for the precious metals, which attracted the Spanish adventurers to America.

The subject tribes of Ostiaks and Samoyedes were obliged to pay tribute, which was levied in furs, parties of Cossacks being sent all over the country for collection. Traders soon followed, and in some cases even boldly preceded the official expeditions, bartering with the natives for the precious commodities. The trade increased so enormously that in 1640 no less than 6,800 sables were collected; there was such abundance that even simple Cossacks had sometimes coats lined with sables. The search was so keen, and the Cossacks spread around so actively from every *ostrog*, that often rival parties starting from different quarters met to collect in the same locality, causing sometimes quarrels. The ever increasing demand, the growing numbers of the immigrants all eager to acquire rapid affluence, together with the diminishing numbers of the hard-pressed animals, obliged the Russians to search constantly for new unexhausted regions.

As expansion was checked on the south, the Cossacks had to move eastward. The advance in this direction was also facilitated by the course of the rivers and the configuration of the country. Though the great Siberian rivers flow from south to north, the numerous affluents, all considerable navigable streams, spread out east and west. The trifling elevation of the vast northern plains, through which flow the lower courses of the rivers, offers no obstacle to pass from one basin to another. The Cossacks, accustomed to patient labour, were thus able to drag their boats from the right affluents of the Ob to the left ones of the Yenissei.[1] The establishment of the Russians on the second great river of Siberia took place about 1620, though the first explorers must have reached it somewhat earlier. Some give the foundation of Yenisseisk in 1618, and of Turukhansk, further north, even earlier (in 1607).

In this new region the Russians fou. 1 a more rigorous climate, and extensive forests and swamps. The hardships of the bold pioneers increased, especially as the further they went from the Ural the more difficult it was to get stores and to secure numerous recruits for the distant expeditions in the unknown districts. Small parties of soldiers and traders wandered over the country, navigating the rivers in spring and summer, and retiring in the cold

---

[1] At present water communication between the two rivers is thus effected according to Strelbitski * :—

    305 miles on the Ket, right tributary of the Ob.
    36 miles on the Lomovataya, tributary of the Ket.
    19 miles on the Yazevaya, tributary of the Lomovataya.
    4 miles on Lake Bolshoye, whence issues the Yazevaya.
    5 miles on a canal from the lake to the Little Kas, left tributary of the Great Kas.
    30 miles on the Little Kas.
    100 miles on the Great Kas.

From the above itinerary it appears that only five miles separate the nearest waters of the two rivers. There is also another portage between the two basins of the Ob and Yenissei, somewhat lower down, to the north of the above. The Nelemka, an affluent of the Tym (a tributary on the right of the Ob), approaches to within three miles of the Alchim, an affluent of the Sym, which falls into the Yenissei.

* The official work *Siberia and the Great Siberian Railway* gives a slightly different description ; between the Ket and the Lomovataya there are nearly ten miles on the river Ozernaya, and the distances on the Little and Great Kas are respectively 59 and 127 miles.

season to winter quarters. These, called *zimovie* by the Russians, played a great part in the early history of the country. They were often the first kernel of an *ostrog*, and then, in succession, of a town. A simple peasant's hut of roughly squared logs, with an earthen stove, the windows closed with panes of mica, or even of transparent ice, formed the refuge of as many human beings as could huddle together without being suffocated by the noxious confined air. During the terrible snow-storms [1]— the terror of the Siberian winter—the *zimovie* was often completely hidden by snow-drifts, a thin cloud of smoke alone revealing its existence on the desert white plain ; a rough wooden cross distinguished it from the habitations of the aborigines.

Yenisseisk became the centre of trade in the region on the banks of the newly discovered river Yenissei : natives and Russians congregated there to barter, and it was chosen as the site for the central government store, where the tribute collected among the surrounding tribes was deposited previous to being despatched to Moscow. Reports from the different expeditions in the unexplored country were also sent to the capital, and the news of fresh discoveries gave an impulse to emigration.

In 1630, 100 men and 150 women with girls were forwarded to Tobolsk. Besides these large official expeditions there was, of course, a constant flow of individual emigrants, escaped serfs, and adventurers in search of wealth in the new country. Fresh supplies of colonists were required to prevent the old settlers from sinking into complete barbarism.[2] As they advanced eastward, the

---

[1] Called ' purgas ' in Siberia.

[2] Bybowski, who visited Kamchatka in 1879-80, says that the descendants of the Russian settlers in that sequestered region have degenerated almost to the level of the Kamchadales, among whom they have lived for nearly two centuries ; they can neither till, spin, nor sew, and it is

distance from the mother country, the terrible privations, and the constant intercourse with the aborigines lowered the originally not very high moral standard of the adventurers. In 1662 the patriarch Philacete had written to the Archbishop of Tobolsk, complaining that the Cossacks in Siberia did not even wear the cross, and contracted irregular unions with native women, whom they sold and exchanged with great freedom. The treatment of the subject tribes also was often cruel and oppressive, far different from the humane methods of Yermak. All the orders from Moscow concerning the collection of tribute enjoined strict justice and humanity, but the Tsar was too far to secure faithful execution of his instructions.

On the Yenissei the Russians had found a different race of aborigines, the Tunguses, from whom they collected tribute; but as they ascended the river they found another powerful race, the Bratskis (now called Buriats), a branch of the Mongol race. This tribe was warlike, with a strong love of independence, and obliged the scanty Russian pioneers to defer all ideas of conquest, and to turn again eastward in search of new lands.

About ten years after the discovery of the Yenissei, reports came of the existence of a third river also flowing north—the Lena. Another race lived on its banks—the Yakutes. The boldest pioneers hurried to the new region, and already, in 1630, 2,000 sables were collected. In 1632 a rough *ostrog* was built, which became the town of Yakutsk. The new river, with its numerous tributaries, became the highway of a great trade : from the *ostrogs* and towns on its banks, containing the largest part of the settlers, small parties of Cossack tribute collectors, of

amusing to watch their painful efforts in attempting to sew with thread only twisted with the fingers.

trappers and traders in search of furs, irradiated in all directions through the swamps and dense forests. Difficulties and hardships increased all the time ; the enormous distances were no longer measured by versts, but by day's journey ; the nearest settlers were often a hundred versts apart, and provisions had sometimes to be brought from an *ostrog* a thousand miles away. No man could venture to advance a step in the forest without his axe ; the scanty population,[1] spread over such a vast territory, was exposed to great dangers from the savage natives.

To show the conditions of life of the early settlers, it will be sufficient to describe at some length an incident which was of no uncommon occurrence.

Thedka Nedostriel and Vaski Karetin were engaged in the fur trade on the Lena, near the Tchetchinski portage. In autumn, deciding to make preparations for the severe winter, they floated down the river to an old abandoned *zimovie*, moored their raft, and discharged their provisions. While they were busy storing their goods in the log-hut, a party of six Yakutes, armed with spears and bows, entered and sat down. Thedka, wishing to propitiate the unwelcome guests, offered them two loaves and some fish, but, after tasting the bread, they threw it away with disgust. Thedka, fearing that mischief was meant, went out of the hut to secure the provisions that were lying about. As soon as he left, the Yakutes seized and bound his companion Vaski ; then, sallying forth, they dragged in Thedka, and tied him to a post near the stove.

Rendered utterly powerless, the Russians were tortured and mocked by the Yakutes, Thedka being wounded in the shoulder with a knife. Then the savages went forth to pillage, and from their talk it seemed they were dis-

---

[1] Many years later, in 1662, it was estimated that the total Russian population in Siberia did not exceed 70,000 souls.

cussing about killing their prisoners. They re-entered, pulled the hair of Vaski, and cut him on the head with an axe. Thedka had been carelessly bound, and with his teeth he managed to free his hands. He seized a knife, and, brandishing it wildly, rushed on the savages with the courage of despair. They fled, and Thedka pursued them to the door, where he perceived that they had already set fire to the hut on the outside. He freed his companion, but the Yakutes shot arrows through the windows, and Vaski fell wounded on the floor. Thedka was now left alone in the burning hut; flames broke out in every direction, and the roof commenced to fall through. He rushed out, fled to the river side, unmoored the raft, and floated down the stream. But the Yakutes ran to the banks and showered arrows. Thedka, wounded in four places, fainted through loss of blood, and drifted helplessly down the Lena.

The raft with the wounded Thedka floated down past another *zimovie*, where eight Russians were preparing for the winter. They rescued their countryman, and dragged him into the log-hut. But on the following day news came that the Yakutes had pillaged one *zimovie* and massacred the inmates of another. The traders had to fly for their lives, and abandoned the still unconscious Thedka in the hut. There he remained a whole week, alone in the forest, until he regained consciousness and was able to reach another *zimovie*, where he was taken in and sent to the hut of a farmer, who sheltered him for the winter.

Communications between the Yenissei and Lena were effected principally through the Ibinski portage, where now a road from Ilimsk[1] leads to Mukskaya.[2] The dis-

---

[1] On the river Ilim, right affluent of the upper Tunguska (Angara), which falls into the Yenissei.

[2] On the river Muka, affluent of the Kuta, which falls into the Lena.

tance between the two places is 56 versts (about 37 miles) by road, but there are smaller streams, probably used by the Cossacks, which shorten the distance to about ten miles from the waters of one basin to the other. Lower down, further north, there was another, the Tchetchinski portage, where the upper waters of the lower Tunguska approach to within about ten miles of the Lena itself. The intervening ground is of slight elevation.

But the difficulties of these communications were enormous. The upper Tunguska and the Ilim had numerous rapids, which rendered tracking slow and laborious; the small rivers were rocky, and had often insufficient water; boats could not pass in the latter, while rafts were often capsized in the former. At the portage it required seventy or eighty men with cables to drag a boat to the nearest stream, which sometimes was too shallow to float it. The Cossacks had to imitate Yermak, damming the streams with sails to collect sufficient water to float their vessels. Provisions were often dragged across the portage in sledges by the soldiers, but each sledge could contain at most four poods.[1]

The Russians, in the early times, were generally disinclined to attack the warlike southern races, preferring to defer their subjugation to a time when the increasing numbers of the settlers would render the task easier. But the situation of the important Ilimski portage between the basins of the Yenissei and Lena, far south, in the vicinity of the Bratski (Buriats), obliged them to engage these fierce tribes. Before the foundation of Yakutsk the two important Ilimski and Bratski *ostrogs* had been established, to protect this important communication from the attacks of the natives; but later,

---

[1] 144 pounds.

in 1641, an expedition under the command of Vassil Vlasieff was sent to conquer the Buriats. It met the most determined resistance. A chieftain, Chepchugui, while besieged in his stronghold, answered the Russian intimation to surrender with a dogged refusal: 'Cossacks, you shall never take me alive.' And he kept his word, preferring to be burnt alive with his son rather than surrender.

The war was long and ferocious. Vassil Bugor, with 130 Cossacks, undertook another expedition, and inflicted a severe defeat on the obstinate Buriats. In his report he says: 'By the grace of God and the good luck of the Emperor, the imperial soldiers stood firm, and the Bratski (they were 500) were all destroyed to a man.' The long contact with cruel savages produced the usual deteriorating effects, and no quarter was given even to the wounded.

The progress of the Russians around Lake Baikal, near which are situated the head waters of the Yenissei and Lena, was much retarded by the stubborn resistance of the Buriats. Irkutsk, now the most important town in Siberia, which has far outstripped its rivals on the three great rivers, was founded in 1651, much later even than Yakutsk.

The Russians had now stretched almost across the northern part of the continent. Tobolsk, Yenisseisk, and Yakutsk marked the main stations in the long route traversing the three great rivers; but there was no halt in the rapid advance; the sea alone could stop their impetuous progress.

The Cossacks, who had established their head-quarters at Yakutsk, proceeded to explore the upper tributary on the right, the Aldan, with its affluents, the Maya and Yudom. This brought them, about 1630, to the chain of

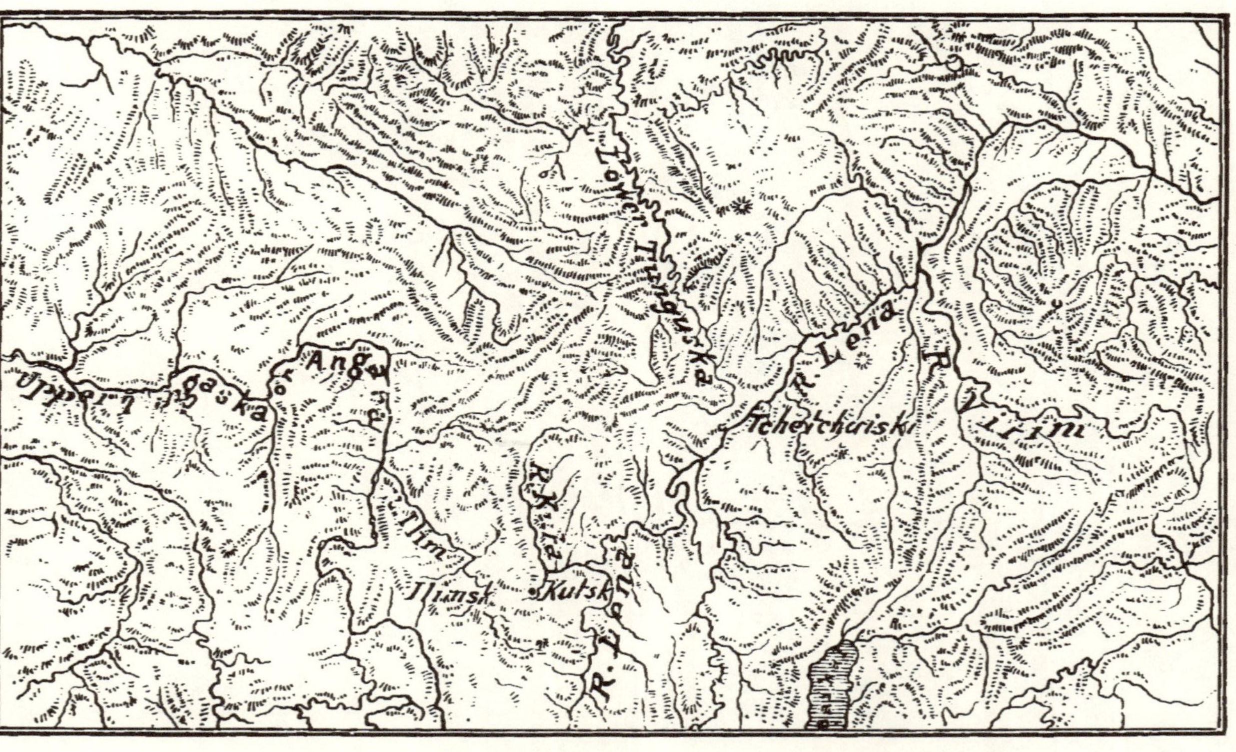

MAP SHOWING THE COMMUNICATIONS BETWEEN THE YENISSEI AND LENA RIVERS

the Stanovoi, which is considered by some as the prolongation of the Yablonoi, the mountains on the east of Lake Baikal, while by others it is considered as the continuation of the Khin-gan chain, which, starting in Manchuria, traverses the Amur river. The orography of the region, as we shall see later, is very little known.

While the north-western part of Siberia is a vast plain only slightly raised above the level of the sea, on the south and east the country gradually rises to a considerable elevation, and then falls abruptly to the Pacific. This difference in the two slopes is already noticeable in Trans-Baikalia, as we pass from the basin of the Selenga to that of the Amur; but it is much more marked in the north, where the plateau, formed by the plains rising eastward, reaches to a very short distance from the Sea of Okhotsk. The narrow slip of land hemmed in between the sea and the plateau is thus full of natural difficulties, intersected by rapid mountain torrents, which have seldom space to unite and expand into navigable rivers.

The Russians on the confines of Asia found themselves in a similar position to their ancestors when they were stopped by the Ural, on the eastern frontier of Europe. A gradual, almost imperceptible, ascent had led them to a mountain chain. But the steep slope on the other side led to a very different country. Beyond the Ural they had found vast plains intersected by a network of rivers, offering means of rapid extension; while beyond the Stanovoi a narrow strip of laud enabled the Cossacks to behold, for the first time in their lives, the boundless waters of the sea—a strange spectacle for men who had spent years in traversing an immense continent. The uninviting character of the narrow plain was enhanced by the difficulties of access; the small rapid rivers are unfit for navigation, and the mountain paths during a great part of the year are almost impassable.[1]

While the Cossacks were deterred for some time from settling on the shores of the sea of Okhotsk, they advanced boldly in the north-east to the shores of the Arctic Ocean. When the Russians explored the lower course of the Lena, they found it ill adapted for their usual methods of eastern expansion. The tributaries on the right are inconsiderable and lead to a mountain chain (the Verkhoyansk mountains), which, though not very high, is covered with snow the greater part of the year, owing to the rigour of the northern climate. The difficulties of the portages requiring reindeer sledges and the reluctance to quit their boats obliged the Cossacks to alter their methods. Instead of passing from the middle course of one river to that of another by adjoining tributaries, they boldly adopted the plan of exploring the still unknown rivers right from the mouth, though this method involved the necessity of steering their rough vessels among the ice-floes of the Arctic Ocean.

In 1636 the Cossack Elisei Buza was despatched from Yenisseisk with orders to explore the frozen stream. He started with only ten men, but after wintering at the *ostrog* of Olekminsk, on the Lena, forty trappers joined the expedition. They descended the Lena in two weeks, and, passing through the western branch of the delta, reached the sea, where, after a day's navigation, they discovered the mouth of the Olenek, a river to the west of the Lena. Here Buza started collecting tribute, and, after wintering, found a shorter land route to the Lena.

---

[1] From September to April, when the north-west winds are prevalent, the gusts blowing down the gullies are terrific. Men and beasts struggle vainly for days to climb up in the teeth of the wind, which often blows them down, hurling the pack-loads to the precipices below (see Zapiski in the *Siberian Section of Russian Geographical Society*, iii. 1857).

In 1638, with two vessels, Buza started from the mouth of the Olenek, and with a favourable wind in five days he reached the mouth of the Yana, a large river to the east of the Lena. For three weeks he ascended the new river, collecting tribute from the Yakute inhabitants, who had probably emigrated from the south. He returned to Yakutsk, but in the following year, 1639, he started again with instructions to explore another river further to the east, the Indighirka. The voyage was very successful; he collected tribute from a new people, the Yukaghires, built an *ostrog* (1640) on the Indighirka, and spent three years in his explorations, returning to Yakutsk in 1642.

Buza, during his long explorations, had greatly increased the knowledge about North-eastern Siberia, by the important discovery of three large rivers; but the reports he had heard from the natives were considered of still greater importance. He had been informed of the existence of another river, a week's distance by reindeer sledge from the Indighirka, where rich silver mines were to be found. This news caused great excitement among the Russians, as a new source of wealth was needed by the impatient adventurers whose reckless hunting and trapping had already greatly diminished the numbers of the fur animals.

The Cossacks flocked to the new region, but the search for the silver mines was unsuccessful, so they had to fall back on the old system of collecting tribute in furs. Their exactions caused revolts among the Yukaghires, who were also provided with some firearms which they had obtained from the Russians in defiance of the strict orders neither to give firearms nor teach their use to the savages. The insurrection was finally subdued in 1645.

The situation of the native races in the north at that

time was very distressing. They were precluded from
escape to the south, as it was occupied by more warlike
tribes, and as they gradually retreated eastward they
reached the north-eastern corner of Asia, where the continent narrows, constituting a perfect *cul de sac*, and where
they were hemmed in by the advancing Russians on one
side, and by the ocean on the other. Moreover, the cruelty
and lawlessness of the Cossacks, as we have already
noticed, increased the further they advanced from the
Ural. The power of the *voivodes* or military authorities
in Siberia was absolute and too often harshly used; to
obtain redress was almost impossible, as it took a year for
news to reach Moscow from Yakutsk. The Russian
proverb, 'God is too high and the Tsar too far,' had all
its terrible significance, at that time, in Eastern Siberia.
We learn incidentally what abuses were committed by a
curious report of Bugor, the Cossack who had defeated
the Buriats. He also started for the newly discovered
lands of the north-east, but carefully avoided passing
Yakutsk. He therefore felt obliged to write to the Tsar
explaining and justifying his irregular conduct. He and
his companions stated that they had not reported to their
military chief, the *voivode* of Yakutsk, on account of the
cruelties they had suffered from that commander. They
wrote, 'We endured from our former *voivode*—we
endured without cause—the "knout" and fire, and every
indignity, exposure and cold;' and then they give the
length and thickness of the rods and describe the savage
beatings. From the sufferings of the Cossacks we may
judge of the treatment of the natives.

In 1645 Michael Stadukhin discovered another large
river, the Kolyma, which (as he was given to exaggeration) he described as equal to the Lena. This completed
the series of Siberian rivers flowing into the Arctic Ocean.

Stadukhin built a *zimovie* and then an *ostrog* on the Kolyma, and was lucky in finding huge heaps of mammoth tusks which served to start a new profitable trade. The communications with the new region watered by the Yana, Indighirka, and Kolyma were maintained by the sea-route from the mouth of the Lena. The route was not very long, but it was very difficult for the Cossacks, who had to launch on the Arctic Ocean the rude river vessels with which they had traversed the greater part of the continent. Yet with these rough boats they began a series of daring maritime explorations.

We have an account of the dangerous navigation of Timothy Buldakoff, who seems to have been unlucky from the beginning of his voyage. He started from Yakutsk in 1649, but was obliged to winter on the Lena, and only on June 2 of the following year he reached the mouth of the river. Here winds blowing from the sea [1] detained him for a whole month ; a change of wind then enabled him to reach the neighbouring bay of Omoloeva on the east. But there he was caught by the ice, which drifted his battered boat, after eight days, on to an unknown island. Here he lost another week, until a fresh change in the wind brought him back to the bay of Omoloeva, but the same difficulties with the ice obliged him to return to the mouth of the Lena, where he found eight Russian vessels also bound for the east. Encouraged by this reinforcement, Buldakoff started again, and, after a continual struggle with the ice, reached Cape Sviatoi, beyond the mouth of the Yana, towards the end of August. He had employed nearly three months in

---

[1] Nordenskiöld notices the fact that, when the wind blows from the sea, ice accumulates on the shores and impedes navigation ; while, when the wind blows from the land, the ice is driven away and the sea becomes navigable.

traversing not much more than 200 miles in a straight line !

Worse hardships now awaited Buldakoff and his companions : the channel which they navigated, owing to the vicinity of ice-fields, began to freeze, a thin icy crust covering the whole surface of the water ; though with the assistance of their sails they were able to cut their way through, the broken ice hacked and splintered the sides of the boats. At last in one night the whole sea froze hard around the vessels, the ice became thick, and all hope of escape was lost. While they were preparing to reach the land in sledges, on St. Simon's day (September 1, Russian New Year at that time) the wind blew from the land, detaching the ice-fields, which drifted away with the ice-bound vessels. After five days the ice stopped and the whole sea froze. Men sent out on the ice to explore met the vessel of a Cossack, who informed them that the land lay to the south ; but, though two men proceeded in that direction from morning until late evening, no land was found. As it was impossible to remain in the vessels, these had to be abandoned, a portion being broken up and converted into sledges. In the midst of danger and hardships Buldakoff did not relax from that rigid sense of duty to the Emperor which animated all the Cossacks ; his first thoughts were directed to save the government stores. But he encountered much opposition, as his men, especially the traders and trappers attached to the party, refused to be encumbered with needless articles. They said : 'We do not know where to find the land or whether we shall live to reach it ; we cannot carry those things without sledges and dogs.' After much discussion the traders consented to carry one pound of government stores per man, the soldiers carried each three pounds, while Buldakoff himself carried twenty pounds. They procceded on their weary journey, weakened by scurvy, and were obliged to drag the sledges with ropes; after nine days, exhausted by cold and hunger, naked and barefooted, they reached land near the mouth of the Indighirka. Thence they continued their journey to a *zimovie* of tax collectors on one of the affluents of the Indighirka.

The sufferings of the refugees continued, and we learn another dark feature of Siberian life at that time: the inhuman speculation of the few provision dealers. Buldakoff was informed that a man who detained a stock of 500 poods of wheat and flour had secreted it to barter privately with the natives, while he refused to sell it on credit to the starving Cossacks, who were ready to bind themselves as serfs in security. The grasping dealer would only part with his goods at an exorbitant price, and only five soldiers obtained provisions. Buldakoff and the rest were obliged to live on larch-prickles, and on this food they had to travel a whole month until they reached the river Mazeya, almost perishing with hunger.

Similar trials were endured by the other Cossack navigators, who recklessly ventured on the ocean with their rude vessels, and who bitterly repeated the Russian proverb, 'Who has not been at sea has not seen trouble.'

Among the daring adventurers who chose the sea as a new route of discovery the most glorious figure is that of the Cossack Dejneff. The explorations of the Russians on the rivers Yana, Indighirka, and Kolyma brought them to the north-eastern prolongation of the Stanovoi chain of mountains, which had delayed their advance further south on the sea of Okhotsk. In the north the chain was still more barren, and the rigour of the climate rendered the passage less inviting. Vague reports of another river on the other side of the mountains were collected from the natives, and the Russians directed their attention to discover a route to the new region. Motora and Stadukhin (the boastful explorer of the Kolyma) were anxious to be the pioneers in the new land, but they were preceded by Simon Dejneff. The latter started from the mouth of the Kolyma on June 20,[1] 1648, and after being separated from his companions by storms, with a single vessel he was able to coast round the whole north-eastern corner of Asia. He passed through the straits of Behring eighty years before the Danish navigator who had given them his name, he reconnoitred the islands opposite the East Cape, and about October reached the mouth of the Anadyr.

Dejneff found a barren country without forests: his provisions were almost exhausted, and it was difficult to catch fish. Twelve men (the whole party consisted of twenty-five) were sent to explore up the river Anadyr; they advanced for twenty days without finding a road or even a path, and then returned. But when only three days' march from the camp they broke down under the depressing effects of cold, hunger, and fatigue. They commenced to scrape holes in the snow to sleep. A trapper, Permiak, dissuaded them from remaining, as their companions were not far, but only another trapper followed his advice to proceed without halting. The rest, weakened by hunger, could not move a step. The torpor brought on by the cold is illustrated by the request they sent to their chief: they wanted Dejneff to send them bedding and old deerskins and something to eat, that they might drag themselves to the camp. When Dejneff

---

[1] This and all the other dates are Russian, *i.e.* old style; it would correspond to June 30 of the current calendar—the difference then being ten days. As Nordenskiöld remarks, this slight difference is important in recording northern navigations, which are often stopped by the ice in consequence of a few days' delay.

heard from Permiak the sad plight of the Cossacks, he sent his last bedding and blanket, but the unfortunate men could not be found. They had been probably buried in a snow-drift during one of those *purgas* which are the terror of winter travellers in Siberia.

Dejneff managed to struggle through the winter in a *zimovie*, which afterwards became the Anadyrsk *ostrog*. He thus had the honour of founding the most distant Russian settlement, over ten thousand versts from Moscow. He was soon overtaken by his rivals: Motoro and then Stadukhin reaching the Anadyr by the land route. The newcomers, however, only added to the distress of the forlorn party; Stadukhin, who had descended to the level of a common brigand, forcibly deprived Dejneff of the tribute he had already collected, and struck him on the cheek in the presence of the natives. Later he surprised Dejneff's party and robbed them of the provisions they were conveying to a station of tribute collectors. He also tried to deprive Dejneff of the glory of his discoveries, boasting that he had been the first on the Anadyr, and had doubled the Great Cape, as the Cossacks called the eastern extremity of Asia. Dejneff had to take refuge further south, where for several years[1] he was lucratively engaged in morse-hunting.

While these explorations were taking place in the north-east, the Russians were slowly establishing themselves on the shores of the sea of Okhotsk. The difficulties of the country have been already noticed; the rivers, descending from the edge of the Asiatic plateau to the sea, are short and rapid. The boats of the Cossacks were therefore often damaged on the rocks, men being drowned and provisions lost. When the narrow coast-

---

[1] Until 1654, after which date all trace of him is lost.

line was reached it could not be traversed on land, as it was intersected by numerous water-courses of the same torrent-like nature. The only possible communication was by the sea, in boats ill adapted for such navigation.

An *ostrog* was established at Okhotsk about 1647 by Ivan Athanasieff, who, with fifty-four Cossacks, routed more than a thousand Tunguses; but the natives continued to resist, and made several desperate efforts to drive out the invaders. The Tunguses, hemmed in between the mountains and the sea, had no escape from the extortions of the Cossacks, and the latter, degraded by constant contact with inferior races, and too far to feel the control of Moscow, now lost their best qualities— the spirit of comradeship and the sense of discipline. Savage fights among the men, and insubordination to their chiefs, were of frequent occurrence. The struggle with the Tunguses now assumed a savage character; the Cossacks, infuriated by the sight of the mutilated and tortured corpses of their companions, who had been surprised by the enemy, retaliated in the same spirit.[1]

In 1654 the Tunguses succeeded in burning the *ostrog* at Okhotsk, and it was only rebuilt when fresh reinforcements came from Yakutsk. The scanty numbers of the Russians, and their distance, even from the nearest Russian settlement, Yakutsk, rendered their position very precarious. It was only by a long struggle and with heavy losses they were able to subdue the natives and secure peace for their settlements on the sea of Okhotsk.

But even worse disorders broke out among the Cossacks in a still more distant region across the sea—in the peninsula of Kamchatka.

---

[1] In blaming the cruelty of the Cossacks, account must be taken of the general ferocity of past centuries. Calvin, a cultured man, the founder of a religious sect, had Servetus burned slowly so as to prolong his agony, and it was only for a trifling difference of opinion.

The Asiatic continent, as it narrows on the north-east, throws out a mountainous peninsula to the south; its existence was long ignored by the Cossacks, as it lay out of the track of their routes, and was connected with the mainland in a region of cold and desolation. The rigorous climate and extensive wastes of the north-eastern corner of Asia presented such difficulties to the Russians that their advance was slow and conquest incomplete; the Tchukchis succeeded, after many defeats, in preserving their independence, which they have kept to the present day. The Cossacks were content with establishing an outpost—the Anadyrsk *ostrog*—and for some time renounced all further explorations. The magnitude of the difficulties encountered may be measured by the fact that, while it took less than seventy years for the Cossacks to advance from the Ural to Behring Straits, it required nearly fifty years to reach Kamchatka from the Anadyr.

The discovery and conquest of Kamchatka were due to Vladimir Atlasoff. His father, Vassil, a peasant, had been compelled by poverty to emigrate across the Ural, and Vladimir from his early years grew up under the wild influences of the rough life of Eastern Siberia. After wandering about the settlements on the river Lena he finally enrolled among the Cossacks of Yakutsk, and rose to the rank of a commander of fifty men.[1] He was appointed to collect tribute in the distant *ostrog* of Anadyrsk, and started with thirteen Cossacks from Yakutsk in the spring of 1695. The long wearisome journey through woods, swamps, and over mountains was accomplished on foot, on horseback, with reindeer, or by water, according to circumstances; only after fifteen

---

[1] The Cossacks' officers commanded detachments of ten, fifty, and a hundred men.

weeks Vladimir Atlasoff reached Anadyrsk, towards the end of summer.

The commander of the lonely *ostrog*, at such a distance from Yakutsk, was virtually exempt from all control, and absolute master of the whole surrounding country and its native inhabitants. The feeling of independence, the exemption from the necessity of submitting for approval all his measures, aroused the ambition of Atlasoff to discover some new land for the glory of the Tsar and his own profit. As early as 1654 a native woman had stated that one of the companions of Dejneff, separated from him by a storm, had strayed to Kamchatka, a land rich in sables and valuable furs, where he and his party had been subsequently massacred. These vague reports had not been forgotten in the Cossack camps of the north, and were confirmed by the information which Atlasoff diligently collected from the natives. He therefore sent, in 1696, Luke Morozko with a party of fifteen Cossacks to explore the country.

Morozko was very successful in his expedition; he advanced to within four days' march of the river Kamchatka, and collected tribute from a tribe of Koriaks. He returned with rich booty and the agreeable news of the existence of a rich land which could be easily conquered by a stronger expedition.

In the spring of 1697 Atlasoff started from Anadyrsk with a force of sixty Cossacks and sixty Yukaghires. He collected tribute from three Koriak villages without resistance, but was opposed by the Kamchadales, whom he defeated with the loss of five men. To celebrate his first victory he erected, on July 13, 1697, a big wooden cross with an inscription. As the country was intersected by mountain chains, Atlasoff divided his forces, proceeding with one half along the coast of the sea of Okhotsk, while Morozko with the other half advanced along the shores of the Pacific. Shortly after the separation Atlasoff was exposed to great danger; his Yukaghire allies treacherously mutinied and suddenly commenced cutting the throats of the Cossacks; they succeeded in killing three and wounding fifteen (including Atlasoff himself) before they were overpowered. Undismayed by their reduced numbers, the Russians continued to advance until they were joined by Morozko. Proceeding in one body, the Cossacks, collecting everywhere tribute, traversed the whole peninsula until they reached Cape Lopatka at its southern extremity. On the return route Atlasoff built an *ostrog* on the river Kamchatka, which he called Verkhne Kamchatsk (Upper Kamchatsk), and left a garrison of sixteen Cossacks to hold possession of the country. After the departure of Atlasoff, the small party, discouraged by their loneliness and the general hostility of the natives, imprudently abandoned the *ostrog* and attempted to return to Anadyrsk, but were all massacred on the way by the Koriaks.

Atlasoff now perceived the impossibility of holding the country without a large armed force, and, leaving twenty-eight men in Anadyrsk, he proceeded to Yakutsk, which he reached in July 1700. Here the conquest of Kamchatka and the reports of its wealth were considered of such importance that Atlasoff was sent, with the tribute he had collected, to Moscow to arouse the attention of the higher authorities. The arrival (in the year 1701) of the conqueror of Kamchatka caused some excitement in the capital; over fifty years had passed since the conquest of Siberia, boldly undertaken by Yermak and rapidly carried on by his successors, had ceased to reveal new regions to the Russians. While almost every decade of the first half of the seventeenth century had brought

the discovery of new lands further east, the second half of
the century had passed without any fresh acquisition.
The adventurous voyage of Dejneff seemed indeed to
preclude the possibility of new discoveries, as it reached
the sea-bound limits of Siberia. It was therefore an
agreeable surprise for the people of Moscow to learn that,
attached to the north-eastern extremity of Asia, there was
a new land which moreover was rich in valuable furs.
The Siberian bureau (a kind of colonial office) reported
favourably that the tribute from Kamchatka was of no
indifferent quantity. In fact, Atlasoff had brought a large
collection of the rarest furs. The arrival of Atlasoff at
Moscow was somewhat similar to that of Ivan Koltzo,
the lieutenant of Yermak, when he appeared more than a
century before at the capital. Both brought reports of
new lands, and the rich tribute was a visible proof of the
importance of their conquests. In both cases they overlooked the antecedents of the successful adventurers.
Atlasoff therefore received every encouragement for
the prosecution of his enterprise ; he was promoted,
a body of one hundred men was appointed to accom-
pany him, supplies of military stores and provisions were
provided.

After leaving Moscow Atlasoff proceeded to Tobolsk,
where he recruited a part of the force destined for Kamchatka, and continued his journey towards Yakutsk.
Unfortunately he forgot the new duties incumbent on his
'altered position, and yielded to the evil habits contracted
in youth and freely exercised in the wild districts of
North-eastern Siberia. On the river Tunguska he met
the merchant Loghin Dobrynin with a raftload of Chinese
goods. The temptation was too strong, and, inspired by
' his plucky spirit,' he robbed the man of all his valuable
merchandise. The plundered trader lodged a complaint

in Yakutsk, and Atlasoff with ten of his Cossacks was imprisoned.

In the meantime affairs were proceeding unfavourably with the Russians in Kamchatka. When Atlasoff reached Yakutsk in the year 1700, Kobeleff had been appointed to take his place in the peninsula; this new commander proceeded to rebuild the *ostrog* of Verkhne Kamchatsk and to establish another at Bolsherietzk on the western coast. In the year 1702 Kobeleff was followed by Zinovieff, who built the *ostrog* of Nijni (lower) Kamchatsk. In 1704 Kolesoff was appointed commander of the Cossacks, and he made an expedition in the Kurile islands. But, from the mutinies which happened later, it seems probable that none of these commanders were capable of holding in proper subjection such a body of desperadoes as the Cossacks had become on the distant shores of the Pacific. In 1706 a general revolt of the natives commenced, and the Russians were almost completely driven out of the country; *ostrogs* were burnt, and the hated intruders massacred wherever they could be surprised.

In the sudden emergency the authorities of Yakutsk recollected that they had in their prison the first conqueror of Kamchatka, the redoubtable Atlasoff, now sufficiently punished for his transgressions by five years' imprisonment. He was therefore released and appointed commander of the Cossacks in Kamchatka, with orders to conquer and pacify the insurgent natives; he was given authority to punish his men with the 'knout' and with rods, and to inflict capital punishment on the rebels when necessary. As he had a bad reputation for cruelty, he was strongly cautioned to use his powers with discretion. But either the evil inclinations of his character or the conduct of his men rendered this warning of no effect, for even on the route to Anadyrsk the Cossacks forwarded a complaint to Yakutsk against his inhuman severity; but again it must be considered that the most ruthless cruelty was the only means to secure discipline and prevent worse excesses.

Atlasoff, proceeding on his journey, reached Kamchatka in 1707, occupied the *ostrogs* of Verkhne and Nijni Kamchatsk, and a month after his arrival, in August, he sent a detachment which defeated the natives near the bay of Avacha (the bay where Petropavlofsk is now situated). This victory was soon followed by another, and Russian authority was being solidly established in the peninsula, when, towards the end of the year 1707, the Cossacks, unable to bear the ferocity of Atlasoff, mutinied. They seized their chief, confined him in prison, and confiscated all his goods, which, according to the list, consisted of 1,235 sables, 400 red foxes, 14 grey foxes, and 75 sea-otters. As these must have been collected during a few months, and formed only a small item in respect to the government tribute, it shows how abundant furs were then in Kamchatka, and how ruthlessly the Cossacks despoiled the natives.

A fresh complaint was sent to Yakutsk, in which it was alleged that Atlasoff did not provide his men with food, that he hacked a man with his sabre, and that he incited the natives against the Cossacks, stating that the latter would deprive them of their wives, children, and goods. From the last accusation it seems probable that Atlasoff had attempted to institute order in the country, and secure some elementary rights for the natives against the lawless desires of his men. The allegations of the insubordinate Cossacks must be read with caution, and judged according to their general conduct towards the natives.

The authorities of Yakutsk were much embarrassed by the complaint against Atlasoff, and the consequent revolt of the Cossacks. It was difficult to find men adapted to govern such a difficult country, and the distance was so great that a commander starting from Yakutsk never knew in what condition he would find his soldiers and his native subjects. A year generally elapsed between the outbreak of a disorder and the arrival of the intended remedy. The indecision and helplessness of the superior authority at Yakutsk are shown by the quick succession of commanders appointed to Kamchatka. In 1707 Tchirikoff is sent, in 1708 Panintin, in 1709 Lipin, in 1710 Sevastianoff, in 1711 Kolesoff. None of these could firmly assert their authority, as on their arrival they often found the Cossacks had already chosen a chief, and if it had not been done, it was sure to happen when the titular from Yakutsk attempted to enforce distasteful discipline.

The confusion reached such lengths that in 1710 there were three commanders in Kamchatka: Atlasoff, who had escaped from prison, governing in the *ostrog* of Nijni Kamchatsk; Tchirikoff, who had not yet given over charge; and Lipin, just arrived to assume command. The Cossacks, however, found ghastly means to solve the difficulty and dispense with the authority of the three unpopular commanders. Lipin was murdered in an ambuscade while on his way from Nijni to Verkne Kamchatsk; Tchirikoff, as he was returning to Yakutsk, was seized near the gulf of Penjina (northern extremity of the sea of Okhotsk), bound and thrown into the sea. It was more difficult to remove Atlasoff, for he was justly feared as a dangerous man. A treacherous plot was devised to achieve the object with little risk. Three bold men were sent to bear a letter, with orders to set upon him while he was perusing it; but the messengers surprised him sleeping in his hut, and cut his throat without resorting to the stratagem.

The mutinous Cossacks elected Antzyphor and Kozyrefski as their chiefs, and proceeded to levy tribute from the natives. Their oppression must have been horrible, for insurrections broke out everywhere. In 1711 the Russians were besieged by the Kamchadales, who were defeated only after a severe struggle. Another hard fight took place near the river Bolshaya. The slaughter was so great that the channel of the river was clogged with the corpses of the natives. All open resistance was now broken, but the hatred of the natives, kept alive by ever-increasing outrages, resorted to treachery, and compassed the destruction of the murderous Antzyphor. The particulars of his death show how terrible must have been the crimes which could inspire such a reckless thirst for vengeance.

In February, 1712, Antzyphor, with twenty-five Cossacks, arrived at Avacha to collect tribute. He was received with every mark of respect, and a large wooden building, specially constructed for the purpose, was assigned for the accommodation of the party. The Cossacks, as was their custom all over Siberia when dwelling among the natives, required hostages; the principal men of the village were delivered, and they retired with the Cossacks to rest. The natives had already planned to set fire to the building in the night, and to avoid the destruction of the hostages a secret portcullis had been contrived for their escape. But when they went to rescue them, they found that their countrymen had been chained up. The hostages, however, begged their friends not to desist from their purpose, as they were quite willing to be burned alive provided the Cossacks were destroyed.

Order was slowly established in Kamchatka only when communications were made easier. Already in 1708 an *ostrog* had been built on the river Penjina, and in 1714 another was established at Kintorsk; but these only served to improve the communications between Kamchatka and Anadyrsk. The long journey between the latter place and Yakutsk, across the desolate north-eastern region, still remained to be traversed.

In 1714 the first attempt was made to find a more direct route by traversing the sea of Okhotsk instead of the circuitous way by land, with the long needless détour up north to Anadyrsk. The expedition started from Yakutsk, and by the rivers Lena, Aldan, Maya, and Yudom reached the Stanovoi mountains; thence by portage they descended to the river Urak, which brought them to the *ostrog* of Okhotsk. Here boats were built, and the sea traversed to Kamchatka. The discovery of the short sea-route led to the rapid pacification of the country, and also brought about far more important results at a later period.

The conquest of Kamchatka was a detached episode of the Russian invasion of Siberia, just as the peninsula itself is an appendix of the great northern region. It happened fifty years after the rapid expansion had been stopped by the Arctic Ocean and the straits of Behring; even the Russians of the time recognised it as an independent fact, treating Atlasoff as the discoverer of a new land, and not as one of the many continuators of the great work of Yermak.

The conquest of Kamchatka has been described in detail because it marks the last stage of degeneration of the Cossacks, corrupted by the constant intercourse with inferior races during a century's march across the continent. Moreover, the dark deeds of the peninsula will

acquire greater importance when we describe later events,
when, by the effects of that perspective which comes
from the observation of long periods, we shall find in
them the latent cause producing results of such magnitude that they will only be attributed to other
causes appearing more conspicuously at a nearer date.
It will be seen that the early possession of Kamchatka led insensibly to the necessary absorption of the
course of the Amur. The northern peninsula also
deserves notice because it gave Russia her first port on
the Pacific, Petropavlofsk, and indeed her only one, if we
wish to be geographically pedantic, as both Vladivostok
and Port Arthur are situated on the shores of the closed
seas of Japan and China.[1]

The conquest of Siberia is chiefly remarkable for its
extraordinary rapidity, contrasting strongly with the
general slowness of Russian expansion. Yermak crossed
the Ural towards the end of 1581, and the Cossacks
reached the sea of Okhotsk in 1636. Dejneff, in his
remarkable voyage, doubled the East Cape, and discovered
the straits of Behring in 1648. The northern part of the
Asiatic continent was traversed in only sixty or seventy years.
To measure adequately these facts we must bear in mind
that it took the Americans nearly two centuries to reach
the Pacific, and nearly a century for the Australians to
cross their island. The possession of firearms by the

---

[1] The conquest of Kamchatka was followed at the beginning of this
century by a further advance in North America which does not concern the
subject of this book. The Russians not only occupied Alaska, but in their
usual rapid way pushed southwards along the coast, attempting in 1807 to
found a settlement at the mouth of the Columbia river, and in 1812 establishing a colony of trappers at Bodega not far from San Francisco, where
the fact is recorded by the name of Russian river. They actually reached
the Pacific coast before the Americans! Treaties with the United States in
1824, and with Great Britain in 1825, fixed the limits of the Russian
possessions in America which were afterwards sold to the United States in
1867.

Russians was an advantage also shared by the Americans and Australians. The rigorous climate of Siberia, on the other hand, had presented special difficulties, stopped all travelling at certain seasons, and rendered the transport of provisions a necessity. If the attractions and requirements of the fur trade may seem to explain the rapid advance, it must be also remembered that the Hudson's Bay Company, formed in 1670, almost lost its privileges in 1749 for 'non-use,' and the only facts it could adduce against the plea were the existence of four or five forts on the coast and a corps of 120 regular employés.

Another important reflection is that the conquest of Siberia was but the continuation of the gradual expansion of the Russian people, a prolongation of its eastward march. It is curious to notice how unswervingly the race has advanced in the same direction to the east, with a slight trend northwards, from the earliest times. Without taking into consideration the probable historical hypothesis that assigns the banks of the Danube as the original home of the Slavs, it will suffice to note that the mother of Russian towns, the capital of the present Little Russia, Kief, is situated about 50° N. lat., that the later towns of Vladimir and Moscow on the east are about 55° N. lat. In Siberia we find the same direction; Tobolsk and Yenisseisk are situated about 58° N. lat., while Yakutsk, to the east, reaches 62° N. lat. The Russians seem to have steered by the compass, keeping on the same course through centuries from the shores of the Dnieper to the straits of Behring.

CHAPTER III

THE STRUGGLE FOR THE AMUR

WE have now to go back to the narrative of events which have been left out of their chronological order because they had slight immediate importance, and retarded rather than furthered the general conquest of Siberia. They constituted a series of daring exploits, which produced no apparent practical results, because the political tendencies of Russia, and the weak conditions of the Siberian colonies, prevented their full development. It was only in the middle of the nineteenth century, under altered conditions, after a long period of inactivity of 160 years, that the Russian Government seconded the latent aspirations of its people, and carried out the old plans of the bold Cossack pioneers. The events of the seventeenth century on the Amur, therefore, have little connection with the contemporary expansion in the rest of Siberia ; they constitute the early prelude of the permanent establishment on the Pacific, which forms such an important chapter of the world's history in the present century.

When the Russians came in contact with the Buriats, and explored the upper tributaries of the Lena, from Lake Baikal to the mountains coasting the sea of Okhotsk, they heard vague reports of the existence of a large river to the south, traversing a warm fertile region. The name of the river varied according as the informers spoke of the main stream, or of its numerous large tributaries. On the

west, near Lake Baikal, the Cossacks heard that beyond
the Vitim there was a river Shilka; while in the north
they were informed about the existence of the river Dji
(the Zeya), which flowed into the Silkar, a tributary of
the Mamur river, which reached the sea. The confusion
of the reports is not surprising if we consider that even
at present opinions differ : the Russians consider the Amur
the main river, while the Manchus, and after them the
Chinese, give the preference to the Sungari. These differences of opinion arise from the fact that the Amur,
like most Siberian rivers,[1] is formed by two rivers, which,
at their junction, seem of equal importance. This pe-
culiarity extends almost to the head waters, as not only
is the Amur formed by the equal rivers, the Argun and
the Shilka, but the latter in its turn is also formed by the
Onon and the Ingoda.

All the information collected by the Cossacks agreed
in describing the new region as fertile, abounding with
cattle, and inhabited by a settled population which even
tilled the soil. Some statements asserted the existence
of silver, either extracted from mines or obtained through
barter for furs from other races further south. This was
corroborated by a Cossack, Maxim Nerphilieff, who had
noticed silver buttons and rings in the possession of some
Tunguses.

To ascertain the truth of these reports, an expedition
of thirty-six men was despatched up the Vitim, right
tributary of the Lena, in 1638, under the command of the
said Nerphilieff. From the Lena he slowly ascended the
Vitim by tracking, and, after wintering on its banks, re-

---

[1] The three great northern rivers of Siberia are formed respectively by
the junction of the Irtysh with the Ob, of the Yenissei with the Angara.
and of the Lena with the Vitim, and in each case it is difficult to decide
which is the main stream ; in fact, the tributary has generally the longer
course.

sumed his journey up the Tzipa, a small tributary on the left
of the Vitim. Here from the Tunguse natives he gathered
information about the Silkar—the present Shilka. The
inhabitants on its banks, the Daurians, had firearms as
well as bows and arrows ; they gave cattle, grain, and
silver to the Tunguses in exchange for furs, which they
bartered in their turn for the silk goods of another people
(probably the Chinese) ; they had two silver mines, one
situated among rocks, and the other near the river Ura.
If Nerphilieff, instead of going up the Tzipa, had continued
to ascend the Vitim, he would have come much nearer to
the basin of the Amur, but he probably was unable to
distinguish the main stream.[1]

The information brought back by Nerphilieff, especially
that about the silver mines, was considered of sufficient
importance to justify another larger expedition. The
command was confided to Vassil Poyarkoff, the secretary [2]
of the *voivode* of Yakutsk,[3] a choice probably dictated by
the desire of having a clear, intelligible account of the new
regions by a man who had the habit of writing. He was
instructed to inquire carefully about the existence of
silver, copper, and lead mines.

The party consisted of 132 men, of whom 112 were
soldiers, and, besides a sufficient supply of powder and
lead, a half-pounder gun with 100 charges was provided
for frightening hostile natives. The route chosen was to
the east of the Vitim, one adopted by Nerphilieff, as it
was intended to reach the Zeya in a direction almost due

---

[1] Anonymous *History of the Amur*. The river Ura is not marked in
the maps. Perhaps the river Urka is meant.

[2] For the official correspondence, each *voivode* had a man skilled in
writing, then a rare accomplishment among the rough settlers of Siberia.

[3] This *voivode*, Peter Golovin, had met Nerphilieff on the Angara, and
had been informed of his expedition. He first sent a party up the Vitim
under Bakhteyaroff, which returned without bringing additional information.

south of Yakutsk. But to obtain this object a circuitous course had to be followed, as the Cossacks, in their usual way, proceeded along the rivers.

Poyarkoff started at the most favourable season ; he left Yakutsk on June 15,[1] 1643, and descended the Lena for two days, when he reached the mouth of the Aldan. On this river he had laboriously to track his boats for four weeks, until he reached the mouth of the river Utchur, a right tributary of the Aldan. This river was more rapid, and though the Russians impressed in their service the Tunguse natives as trackers, they spent ten days in reaching the mouth of another stream, the Gonom, which joined the Utchur on the left. Now they had reached high ground, and the course of the Gonom was full of dangerous rapids : they had to pass forty-two of these, and one of the Cossack boats was smashed and its cargo of lead lost. Five weeks were spent in overcoming these difficulties, and winter was now very near. As this terrible season of Siberia requires timely preparation, the Cossacks, after six days employed in ascending another small stream, began to fell timber and construct winter quarters.

Poyarkoff was impatient to advance, especially as the fertile lands of the Shilka were reported to be at no great distance ; so, after two weeks employed in directing the construction of the winter quarters, he decided to divide his party. A portion were left in charge of the boats and stores, with instructions to follow him on the Zeya next spring ; the remainder, ninety men, were led by him southward towards the basin of the Amur.

It is difficult to give an exact description of the nature of the country he traversed, because, as I have already stated, the orography of this part of Asia is very little known, even at present, the best authorities disagreeing.

---

[1] The anonymous *History of the Amur* states July 15.

While Schwartz states he found the sources of the Ghilini (an affluent of the Zeya) and of the Gonom (the affluent of the Aldan ascended by Poyarkoff) surrounded by mountains 6,000 and 7,000 feet high, Kropotkine maintains that the head waters of the two rivers flow from marshes on the high plateau. The latter, who is a great authority on this region, asserts that the long chain, which joins in most maps the mountains to the east of Lake Baikal to the mountains along the sea of Okhotsk, does not exist. According to him, the chain along the sea of Okhotsk is a prolongation of the Khingan mountains, which extend northwards from Manchuria across the course of the Amur.[1]

After proceeding on the frozen stream Niuemka, the passage to the basin of the Amur was effected on snow-shoes, with hand-sledges for the baggage, through deep snow-drifts. After two weeks they reached the river Briand, a tributary on the right of the Zeya. Here they remained for the winter, building boats for the coming spring (1644), when the rivers would be freed from ice. Then Poyarkoff descended the Zeya, built a small *ostrog* on a creek, and awaited the arrival of the rest of the expedition, which he had left on the other side of the plateau the preceding winter. Here he first met the Daurians, of whom so many reports had reached Yakutsk, and inquired anxiously about mines and precious stones, but was informed that none existed in the country.

The natives received the Russians very cordially at first, providing them with food, but gradually grew tired of the incessant demands of the famished strangers, whose provisions had run short. Quarrels broke out ; a Russian

---

[1] It is curious to note how Stieler in his Atlas follows *both* authorities; in the map of Asia the mountains are arranged according to one system, and in the map of Siberia according to the other.

VIEW ON THE AMUR

detachment was attacked, and ten men killed. The situation of the isolated party in the desolate region amid hostile barbarians was most distressing : forty men died of hunger and disease before the arrival of their companions with provisions.

Poyarkoff, with his whole force, now descended the Zeya and reached the Amur, which he mistook for the Silkar.

On the majestic waters of this river, between beautiful wooded banks, amid innumerable islands, the Cossack boats glided swiftly down the rapid stream. The Russians, coming from the colder regions of the north, were delighted at the sight of fruit trees, and considered the new region a perfect Paradise. The course of the Amur is an imposing sight even at present to the ordinary tourist, and it must have been far more striking then, with its forests intact, to the daring adventurers in their voyage of discovery. The shores were inhabited by different races, subject to a powerful Manchurian prince, who, in his turn, was a dependent of the Khan of Kitai.[1] The natives were surprised at the tall stature, thick beards, and long hair of the Cossacks, and frightened by their firearms, so Poyarkoff was able to proceed without danger. He passed through the gorges of the Amur, where the Khingan chain, crossing the course of the river, confines the stream for many miles [2] within a narrow bed, meandering among the hills, and where the current acquires extraordinary rapidity and violence. After three weeks Poyarkoff reached the mouth of the Sungari, and, as he thought, the commencement of the Amur, which flowed on to the sea. Here a halt was made, and a de-

---

[1] The Russians still give China the name which was so common in mediæval Europe.

[2] Over 100 versts.

tachment of twenty-five men was sent to reconnoitre the river to its mouth. After three days' navigation, having ascertained from the natives that the river flowed to the sea, they returned, but on their way the whole party, except two, was massacred in the night by natives dwelling between the Sungari and the Ussuri. This happened at a day's distance from their chief.

Poyarkoff decided to explore the lower course of the river with his remaining men, and in a week he reached the Ussuri, which, like the Sungari, also joined the Amur on the right. Continuing his voyage, he arrived at the mouth of the river, and the Cossacks at once commenced the usual preparations for passing the winter, which was fast approaching. Again the Russians suffered terribly from want of food in the inhospitable region : during the winter they had to subsist on the scanty produce of the chase and by fishing, and in spring they lived on roots and grass. When the beginning of summer (1645) freed the river and sea from ice, Poyarkoff was able to prepare for the voyage to Yakutsk. It was impossible to return by the Amur, as that route was too long and difficult : it had taken two months from the Zeya to the sea, drifting with the stream, and it would take many months to ascend the river against the swift current, especially in the long gorges. The only other way was by the sea of Okhotsk, which had been discovered a few years before (1636) by the Cossacks from Yakutsk.

This plan was very risky. The Russians had only the flat-bottomed boats with which they had come down the Amur, or such craft as they had been able to build at its mouth during the winter; they had no nautical instruments or knowledge of navigation, and it is almost certain that none of them had ever sailed on the sea or even seen it before in their lives. But the Cossacks were unacquainted with fear, and they daringly launched their vessels on the boundless expanse of water, so strange to their continental experience. They kept close to the shore because, if they had lost sight of the land, they would not have been able to find it again. After three months' navigation, amid incredible hardships and dangers, their shattered boats were driven ashore, and they landed near the mouth of the small river Ulia. Here they found an old abandoned *zimovie*, which sheltered them for the winter.

The following spring, Poyarkoff, leaving twenty men to collect tribute from the local Tunguses, started with the scanty remainder of his expedition, crossed the mountains, and reached the upper waters of the river Maya. The Cossacks were now on familiar ground; they again built boats, drifted down the Maya and the Aldan, and thence ascended the Lena to Yakutsk, which they reached on July 12, 1646.

This remarkable voyage, one of the most daring performed by the Cossacks, lasted a little over three years, during which time more than 7,000 versts were covered. It cost the lives of eighty men, nearly two-thirds of the whole expedition, and the sufferings endured by the survivors were terrible. The pangs of starvation had compelled many to devour the dead bodies of the natives and of their companions who had perished through want of food. It was the most disastrous expedition undertaken in Siberia, and it produced no practical results, because at that time the Russians were not able to establish themselves on the Amur.

Poyarkoff brought back 480 sables, and reported that the conquest of the Amur was not very difficult. It would require 300 men and the construction of three *ostrogs*, each garrisoned by fifty men, the remaining 150 serving to collect tribute from the surrounding natives. But even this small force, which, as we shall see, would have been insufficient, could not be spared by the *voivode* of Yakutsk. The only useful results of the expedition were the written account of all that had been seen and heard, and the plans of the rivers that had been explored. According to Poyarkoff, the Shilka flowed into the Sungari, the Sungari into the Amur, and the latter into the sea.

The failure of Poyarkoff and the sufferings of his men did not deter others from attempting the same task, and a new expedition was quickly organised; but it was due to private enterprise and it chose a different, shorter route.

Erothei Pavlof Khabaroff, a peasant of Ustiug Veliki, in the province of Vologda,[1] emigrated with his brother and son to Siberia in the year 1636, and settled on the Yenissei,[2] where he busied himself with husbandry. He was an intelligent, energetic man, and his attention was soon directed to the reports about another river lately discovered (the Lena), where the sable trade was easy and remunerative. The Russians having reached the third Siberian river only a few years before—Yakutsk was founded in 1632—the slaughter of the fur-bearing animals had not yet diminished their numbers. Khabaroff, therefore, in 1638, proceeded to the river Lena. As he had already made some money, he was able to hire a body of twenty-seven trappers and start trading in furs. Sables were then abundant on the Lena and its tributaries, the Olekma and Vitim. They were collected by gangs of trappers, consisting generally of thirty men, who pro-

---

[1] A province in North-east Russia, south of Archangel province.

[2] In Chap. ii., 'Conquest of Siberia,' the fact was mentioned that in 1630 500 men, besides women, were forwarded for the colonisation of the country around the newly discovered river Yenissei. Khabaroff was probably incited to emigrate by the news of this exodus.

ceeded in decked boats, heavily laden with flour, salt, and other necessary provisions, to the spots frequented by the sables. Only bows and arrows, nets and traps were used, as the muskets of that period were too cumbersome to be carried about in the woods. At the approach of winter *zimovies* were built, and the hunters awaited the time when the snow on the ground and the ice on the rivers could bear sledges; then they dispersed in small parties, burying their provisions in the ground along the route for fear of being robbed by the natives. The hired trappers were of two kinds: some received all the articles they required from their master, and were obliged to give a third of the furs they collected, besides repaying all that had been given except their food; others delivered to their master half the animals they had trapped and provided for their own wants, receiving only five or six roubles for the winter.

Khabaroff engaged men of the first class, and spent two thousand roubles in providing over thirty tons of stores for their use. His trade flourished, and he began new speculations, acquiring land on the river Ilim, near the important portage between the Yenissei and the Lena. There he started another profitable business, employing his men as carters for transporting the large traffic between the two rivers. Constant success urged Khabaroff's active mind to find new sources of profit, and in 1640 he started a salt-boilery at the mouth of the river Kuta, which, however, was soon stopped by the authorities. Undiscouraged, Khabaroff, the following year, asked permission to cultivate fallow lands at the mouth of the Kirenga, on condition of receiving only one year's exemption from taxes.

Khabaroff gradually acquired great wealth, and employed a large number of men in his various speculations.

His position in Eastern Siberia was very similar to that of the Stroganoffs, the patrons of Yermak, in the preceding century, on the banks of the Kama near the Ural. He was also similarly situated—to the east beyond the mountains (the Yablonoi). There was an unknown region along the banks of the river Shilka, which vague rumour asserted was also very rich. His trappers, in their eager search for unfrequented spots where the hunted sables sought refuge, had probably reached the upper waters of the Olekma and brought back valuable information of what they had seen and heard.[1] Not content with the safe and rapid accumulation of wealth in the lands arduously discovered by his predecessors, Khabaroff, with the restless adventurous spirit of a Cossack, desired to explore new lands and subjugate unknown tribes.

In 1649 he sent a petition to the *voivode* of Yakutsk, declaring that he knew a short route, by the river Olekma, leading to the new region, and asking permission to enlist a body of about 150 men. He promised to provide them with money, food, boats, arms, and ammunition. Permission was granted, and Khabaroff was instructed to build a small *ostrog* on the Shilka, to keep a record of the tribute collected, to describe the people he met, and to draw plans. He was stringently cautioned not to use firearms except in extreme necessity, and to prevent his subordinates committing violence on the natives.

Khabaroff, with a small body of seventy men, started in the spring of 1649. From the Lena he went up the Olekma, where the rapid stream greatly retarded his pro-

---

[1] Gregory Vyjitzoff, at the sources of the Tughir, tributary of the Olekma, had heard of Prince Ladkai on the Shilkar. Ivan Kvashnin with three Tunguses had reached the Shilkar by the river Amazar, and, to avert danger, had announced the near arrival of a Russian army to conquer Ladkai.

gress. Worse difficulties were encountered when he found the usual rapids of Siberian rivers. Khabaroff was able to write—a rare accomplishment at that time in Siberia—so we have a forcible description of one of his misadventures : ' In the rapids the rigging was broken, the rudder smashed, the men were bruised ; but, by the help of God and the imperial good luck, all ended happily.' It took the whole summer to reach the mouth of the Tughir, an affluent of the Olekma, and on its banks they stopped for the winter. In January of the following year (1650) the Russians, with sledges and snow-shoes, crossed the portage with great difficulty, on account of the deep snow and stormy weather. In descending from the plateau they found the small river Urka, which led them directly to the Amur.

On their way down the Amur the Russians found five native towns, entirely deserted by their inhabitants ; the first, situated at the mouth of the river Urka, was the residence of Lafkai, a Daurian prince, well known to the Cossacks, as all the reports about the Amur mentioned his name. The Russians were agreeably surprised to find the houses built of stone, with large windows [1] covered with paper (an article probably purchased from the Chinese), and greatly astonished to find the inhabitants had fled. Their wonder increased as they proceeded to the next towns and also found them abandoned. At the third Khabaroff halted and succeeded in conversing, through an interpreter, with five native horsemen, who, however, kept at a distance and remained on horseback. Lafkai, who was among them, inquired who they were ; but when Khabaroff said they had come for trade, he

---

[1] The Cossacks in Northern Siberia had very small windows in the log-huts where they dwelt in winter ; the native hostages confined in the close suffocating air were often found dead, and they were treated, if not better, at least as well as the Cossacks.

answered that it was useless to try deceit as he knew their intentions. A Cossack (probably Ivan Kvashnin) [1] had threatened to come back with 500 men to kill the natives and take their goods, wives, and children. Khabaroff promised him the protection of the Tsar if he paid tribute, but Lafkai only answered : ' Well, we shall see what kind of people you are,' and galloped away with his men.

The Russians found in the fifth town an old woman—it is said she was the sister of Lafkai—from whom they extorted the information that Lafkai, with other princes, was waiting for the Russians at a town two weeks' march from the residence of the rich Prince Bogdoi. This chief had cannon to protect his town, which was a great centre of trade, where gold, silver, and precious stones were to be found in great abundance. These particulars were probably the embellishments of the interpreter, desirous to please his masters, or a trick of the frightened old woman to send away the unwelcome visitors.

The news of the warlike preparations to receive the Russians convinced Khabaroff of the imprudence of advancing further with only seventy men. He therefore retreated to the first city at the mouth of the river Urka, and, leaving his men to garrison the place, returned to Yakutsk in May 1650. Though not very important for the moment, some useful results had been obtained by the expedition. Khabaroff brought back information about a part of the Amur which had not yet been visited, as it was situated much higher than the mouth of the Zeya, whence Poyarkoff had commenced his exploration, and he had tested practically the advantages of his new

---

[1] The anonymous *History of the Amur* puts his name in the mouth of Lafkai, though probably the latter referred to him without mentioning the foreign name.

route—they were indeed evident, because he had travelled from Yakutsk to the Amur and back in about a year. He reported to the *voivode* that fish was abundant in the Amur, especially sturgeons, which were bigger than those of the Volga; indeed, all the fish were larger. The inhabitants were Daurians; some devoted to agriculture, others to cattle-grazing. Besides dense forests containing fur animals there were fields and meadows growing barley, millet, oats, buckwheat, peas, and hemp; stocks of grain had been found in the towns abandoned by the natives. These facts were important for the future plans of conquest on the Amur, as it became unnecessary to send supplies of grain from Yakutsk to revictual the expeditions. The time required to cover the distance was also inconsiderable, especially returning from the Amur, as it was only a hundred versts from Lafkai's town on the Urka to the *ostrog* built by Khabaroff on the Tughir, and thence, floating down the Olekma, in two weeks Yakutsk could be reached.

Khabaroff, however, took a quite different view from Poyarkoff about the military requirements of the question, and his estimate was certainly more correct. He said 6,000 men were required to conquer the whole land of the Daurians, by which he probably meant the basin of the Amur. It was quite impossible to raise this force, as even in 1662 the whole population of Siberia amounted to only 70,000 souls; and much later, in 1720, it was estimated [1] that the regular soldiers did not much exceed 2,000 men. Khabaroff therefore contented himself with enlisting about 150 volunteers, and the *voivode* of Yakutsk added a detachment of twenty

---

[1] Andrievitch, *History of Siberia*, part ii. (from 1660 to Empress Elizabeth).

Cossacks,[1] three guns, and a supply of powder and lead, besides promises of assistance in case of need.

With these reinforcements Khabaroff went back to the Amur in the autumn of the same year, 1650,[2] but this time he found no abandoned towns. The Daurians had decided to resist, and had given much trouble during his absence to the men left at the mouth of the Urka, who had sustained many sieges, though with little loss, as the natives had only bows and arrows. Khabaroff descended the Amur and met the Daurian army near the town of Albazin, where an obstinate battle was fought from mid-day to evening, and ended with the rout of the natives. This victory was obtained at the cost of only twenty wounded men, and it gave the Russians Albazin with its stores of grain. The town was conveniently situated, not far from the portage employed in passing from the Olekma to the Urka ; so Khabaroff had the fortifications improved, and established a garrison of fifty men. Albazin played a great part in the Russian colonisation on the Amur in the seventeenth century, and the heroic sieges it sustained rendered its strange Daurian name famous in the Cossack camps of Eastern Siberia.

From the information communicated by the prisoners Khabaroff began to have fairly accurate notions of the political state of the country. The banks of the Amur were inhabited by many races—they said nine—which were all tributary to the Shamska Khan (the governor of Manchuria was probably meant), who in his turn was tributary to another prince with a still stranger name.

---

[1] The anonymous *History of the Amur* gives only 117 volunteers with 21 *strielitz*.

[2] The same anonymous author states 1651 ; if Khabaroff returned after September 1, 1650, it would have been in the following year, *i.e.* 1651 of the old Russian calendar.

The tribes at the mouth of the river, however, did not pay tribute.

Khabaroff employed the winter in making an expedition on sledges, when he met and defeated a body of natives; and, in writing a report to the *voivode* of Yakutsk,[1] he pointed out the importance of the Amur which he said could become a second Siberia—the land of the Daurians alone could support 20,000 people. His ambition even went beyond the present frontiers of Russia, for he wished to conquer Manchuria. Again he came back to his favourite postulate—the necessity of a large army. It was difficult to bring the Shamsha Khan under the subjection of the Tsar, because he had large towns provided with cannon ; his country was only seven days' march from the Amur, and it abounded with silver mines, pearls, and precious stones.

News about Khabaroff had reached Moscow, and it was decided to assist his bold plans. Reinforcements were despatched, consisting of 132 soldiers, volunteers, and trappers, under the command of Trenka Tchet-cheghin, with a large supply of lead and gunpowder, besides a ream of writing-paper, which was a very rare article in Siberia, and was probably forwarded to encourage Khabaroff's literary activity, which furnished such valuable information about the new region. It was also decided to send an embassy with a letter from the *voivode* of Yakutsk to the Shamsha Khan, in which it was shown that the Daurians had been unable to withstand the terrible arms of the Russians, and that the Shamsha Khan himself had better give as much gold, silver, and precious stones as he could : ‘For our Lord Tsar Alexis Mikhailovitch is strong and great and terrible, but gracious and just, and

---

[1] He also built a town, by which it is generally understood that he repaired and fortified Albazin.

not bloodthirsty. And our Lord has in an empire of Siberia a great multitude of soldiers, trained to the business of war, and they fight desperately.' All these cunning suggestions and covert threats were wasted, however, because the embassy was massacred *en route* by the Daurians.

In the following year (1651), as soon as the river was free from ice, Khabaroff descended the Amur to continue his work of conquest. On his way he found a fortified town surrounded by a triple rampart and ditches, containing a large population, with numerous cattle, and he decided to besiege it. When they advanced, the Russians were astonished to behold some people in silk clothes—probably Chinese—who, instead of flying for shelter within the walls, retired to some distance, and with characteristic coolness watched the operations. Khabaroff through an interpreter summoned the besieged to submit and pay tribute. But the natives answered that they already paid tribute to the Bogdoi Khan (the Chinese Emperor) and could not pay it again to the Russians. The attack then commenced, and though the Daurians shot showers of arrows on the besiegers, the Russian cannon soon made a breach in the outer rampart, through which the Cossacks, protected by their armour, were able to penetrate and drive the besieged into the second enclosure. This, as well as the third, was breached and stormed, the natives slaughtered, and the town with a thousand head of cattle fell into the hands of Khabaroff, who had only four men killed and fifty wounded. The next day one of the men in silk clothes, who, the prisoners said, were tribute collectors, came to confer with Khabaroff, but none of the interpreters understood his language, so he was dismissed with presents. The Russians rested in the conquered town for a month and a half.

Khabaroff learned from his prisoners that he was only three days' distance [1] from the mouth of the Zeya, the river down which had floated the boats of the first Russian expedition under Poyarkoff. He proceeded in that direction, and, arriving unexpectedly in a town, seized some of the princes. Here again he was confronted by proofs of the Chinese suzerainty: he could only collect sixty sables, the natives offering as an excuse that they had just paid tribute to the Shamsha Khan and had had no time to trap more animals. Another difficulty also presented itself: though the princes were in his hands, the inhabitants all fled. Hitherto, all over Siberia, it had been sufficient to hold the chiefs as hostages to secure the submission of their tribes. But on the Amur it was different; the princes declared that their people acted independently, or, as they put it very forcibly, ' If we fall into your hands, it is better we alone should die than that all our race should perish.' All intimidation failed before this fact, and the Russians were forced to recognise that the Daurians cared more for themselves and their land than for their princes.

As it was impossible to establish winter quarters in a country deserted by its inhabitants, Khabaroff descended the Amur on September 7, passed through the gorges, and reached the mouth of the Sungari about September 14. All the way the Cossacks lived by plundering the natives—the Dutcheri—a quiet race unable to resist the fierce strangers. In his search for suitable winter quarters Khabaroff again proceeded down the Amur to the mouth of the Ussuri, where, in the present century, the town of Khabarofsk has been built to record his exploits. The position is favourable, at the confluence of two great rivers—the mighty Amur and the

[1] Six, according to the anonymous author.

picturesque Ussuri—and Khabaroff, with his keen military insight, selected a spot adapted for his necessities. The subsequent events fully justified his choice. A rocky eminence, jutting out with almost perpendicular sides into the river, was connected by a narrow neck with the high banks and formed a small sheltered cove, which could only be reached by the river.

Khabaroff anchored his boats in the cove, cut a path in the rocks, and commenced building a fort on the cliff. As he had arrived on September 24, it was necessary to collect provisions without delay for the approaching winter. Game was abundant in the mountains, and fish in the river, and a foraging expedition of 100 men was sent up the Ussuri to find the other provisions required. Several villages were plundered, but the alarm soon spread over the country, especially as the Manchurian authorities must have been already informed by their tribute collectors of the Russian attacks on the Amur. Khabaroff therefore, on his return, had to run the gauntlet of the Chinese troops cantoned on the banks of the Ussuri. As he approached a town, a fleet of boats put out, stretching across the river to intercept him. Khabaroff's generalship saved him from the imminent danger; he ordered his men to reserve their fire until they came to close quarters, and then to sweep the two nearest boats. The strong current and a stiff breeze were also in his favour, and in the confusion caused by the concentrated volley he was able to cut through the line and escape before the discomfited Chinese could alter their course.[1] This

---

[1] This episode on the Ussuri, as well as the description of Khabaroff's fort, is taken from Atkinson, who never gives his authorities ; but as he had been for many years in Siberia, and knew the Russians well, and moreover was on the Amur at an important historical moment (at the time of Muravioff's expeditions) when old stories would be revived, and traditions repeated, it is probable that he had reliable foundation for his account (pp. 465–470 of Atkinson's work).

perilous encounter taught the Cossacks prudence, and they passed the other towns on the Ussuri at night-time.

During the absence of their chief the Cossacks left in the fort were also exposed to danger. The neighbouring natives—of the Atchan [1] race—as soon as they discovered the departure of the large expedition up the Ussuri, plotted to massacre the garrison ; they had, however, a just dread of firearms, and they found difficulties in climbing the palisades of the fort. They resolved at last to collect a quantity of straw, and attempt to burn the enclosure. But seventy Cossacks made a sortie and vigorously attacked them, while others from the walls fired muskets ; then, as Khabaroff writes, 'the fear of God fell upon the heathen dogs, and they could not stand against the terror of the Tsar and our weapons, and they fled, and we ran at their backs, killing many and seizing prisoners, and the heathens threw themselves into their boats and paddled away on the great Amur.'

When the party returned from the Ussuri with provisions, the Cossacks settled down for the winter, strengthening their fortifications. In the meanwhile the Manchurian authorities had realised the danger that threatened their almost nominal suzerainty over the natives dwelling on the banks of the Amur, and had made great warlike preparations to drive out the unwelcome strangers, despatching bodies of troops to different points of the river. A force of 2,000 men with eight guns, thirty gingalls, and twelve earthen petards, intended for blowing up the walls,[2] suddenly appeared before the Russian fort at Atchansk, under the command of Prince

---

[1] Khabaroff's fort was built on the site of one of their villages called Atchansk.

[2] Khabaroff says they contained forty pounds of gunpowder.

Isinei, and commenced a vigorous artillery attack. Luckily for the Cossacks, the Chinese gunners were very bad marksmen and made more noise than execution. The siege lasted for some time, but, by a bold sortie of Khabaroff, it ended in the total defeat of the Chinese, who lost two guns, many muskets, eight flags, and 830 horses. Khabaroff, with his usual lively style, gives a picturesque description of the fight.

'On March 24, at daybreak, the Bogdoi (Chinese) army, horsemen and armoured men, came upon us Cossacks in the town of Atchansk, and our Cossack *esaul*,[1] Andrew Ivanoff, shouted in the town : "Brother Cossacks, arise quickly, and put on your strong breastplates !" and the Cossacks, in their shirts only, rushed to the town wall,[2] and stood to the guns and the muskets, and fired on the Bogdoi army. And we Cossacks fought with them, the Bogdoi people, from dawn to sunset ; and the Bogdoi army fired on the Cossack huts, so that we Cossacks could not go about in the town, and the Bogdoi people with their flags surrounded the town wall. The Bogdoi men broke down the wall of our town to the ground, and then the Bogdoi Prince Isinei and all the great Bogdoi army shouted : "Do not burn nor strike the Cossacks, but take them alive !" and our interpreters repeated these words of the Prince Isinei to me, Erothei, and hearing these words of the Prince Isinei, we Cossacks put on our armour, and I, Erothei, and the regular[3] and the volunteer Cossacks, praying the Saviour and our Blessed Virgin and Saint Nicholas, took farewell of each other. And I, Erothei, and Andrew Ivanoff, and all our Cossack army, said : "Let us die, brother Cossacks, for the Christian faith ;

---

[1] A kind of lieutenant.

[2] It must have been a wooden one.

[3] The regular Cossacks of Siberia were the descendants of the companions of Yermak on the river Irtysh (Sadovnikoff).

let us stand by the Saviour, the Virgin, and Saint Nicholas; let us serve the Emperor Alexis Mikhailovitch, Grand Duke of all Russia; and let us Cossacks all die to the last man against the Tsar's enemies, but never shall we fall alive in the hands of the Bogdoi men." And the Bogdoi people were talking near the fallen walls, and we Cossacks wheeled up to the breach a large brass gun, and we began to fire cannon and muskets, while from the walls they fired some iron guns upon the Bogdoi people. And, by the grace of God and the imperial good luck and our efforts, many of those dogs were killed. And as the Bogdoi men retreated from our cannon and the breach, at that moment 156 men, regular and volunteer Cossacks in armour, sallied forth upon the enemy, while fifty men remained in the town. As we sallied forth upon them, we captured two iron guns; and by the grace of God and the imperial good luck we fell upon the enemy, capturing the muskets of their best men. And a great fear came upon them, our force seeming innumerable, and the remaining Bogdoi men fled from the town and our arms. And we counted the dead around the town of Atchansk; of the Bogdoi men there were 676 killed, and of our Cossacks ten, but wounded in that battle there were seventy-eight men.' [1]

[1] Atkinson gives a rather different account of the sortie: he says Khabaroff was reduced to great straits and obliged to retire, but, before leaving, resolved to give the Chinese a parting remembrance. He proposed to burn the Chinese camp with only six men and asked for a forlorn hope; all the Cossacks volunteered, but on condition that their chief should not go and expose his valuable life. An officer, therefore, was selected who proceeded in a boat with his small party to a ravine at the back of the Chinese camp. Then, during the night, the Cossacks fired all their guns, and Khabaroff headed a sortie; while the Chinese were busy repelling the attack, the small party stealthily approached and set fire to the tents. The sight of the flames in their camp threw the Chinese into confusion, and they fled. Atkinson elsewhere mentions that the Cossacks of the Argun (a river marking a part of the frontier between Manchuria and Transbaikalia)

The first encounter of the Russians with the Manchus had resulted in a brilliant victory, but Khabaroff was too shrewd to overestimate its importance.   From the prisoners he learnt that the Shamsha Khan, the viceroy of the Emperor of China, had received complaints about the Russians from all the natives on the Amur, and was still making great warlike preparations.   Another larger army might advance at any moment, and at Atchansk Khabaroff was too far from his only base of supplies, the portage between the river Olekma and the small river Urka on the upper Amur.   He prudently decided to retreat up river, and in April 1652 he abandoned the spot which he had so sagaciously chosen and bravely defended.

The *voivode* of Yakutsk, having received no news from Khabaroff for a long time, sent a small reinforcement under the command of Trenka Tchetcheghin.   But when they reached the upper Amur they found that Khabaroff had gone down river the preceding year, and nothing had been heard since.   The junction with Khabaroff was necessary for the safety of both detachments, their united forces being barely sufficient to face the dangers that threatened them from the Chinese.   Tchetcheghin therefore despatched a small party under Ivan Naghiba to scour the Amur and discover Khabaroff.

The task was by no means easy.   The gigantic river, when not confined by the parallel ranges of the Khingan mountains, which cross its course, enjoys its liberty by spreading its waters for miles in the plains; numerous islands intersect the channel and hide the banks, which are sometimes difficult to distinguish in the confused mass

had many traditions about Khabaroff, and he may have heard these details from them. His particulars have an air of probability, as they would explain the victory of 156 men against 2,000 with the slaughter of 676, and as they are striking and interdependent they might have been handed down by oral tradition through two centuries.

of water and grassy meadows. The Cossack boats, moreover, lying low in the water, were not easily discernible at a distance. Naghiba steered through the intricate creeks, occasionally leaving marks and inscriptions on the islands to attract the notice of the strayed party. In his vain search for Khabaroff, Naghiba descended the whole course of the Amur and reached the sea, as Poyarkoff had done seven years before; but this second exploration was fraught with greater dangers. The party was smaller, while the natives had become more hostile, and were on their guard at the approach of the strangers. Several times Naghiba was completely surrounded—horsemen on the banks and a flotilla of big boats on the river precluding all possibility of escape—and in this dangerous situation had to halt, fearing by an untimely attack to risk a disastrous defeat. Near the mouth of the Amur the Ghiliaks thus kept him blockaded in the river for two weeks, until the want of provisions compelled the Cossacks to land with the courage of despair and plunder a village. When the sea was reached, Naghiba was faced by the same dilemma as confronted Poyarkoff—to return up river against the strong current amid hostile natives, or to choose the dangerous sea-route. The latter course was similarly selected, and Naghiba's party rowed out to sea until they were caught by the ice, which drifted them for ten days, and threw them on a desert coast. After endless privations they were able to cross the mountains and return to Yakutsk by the Lena and its tributaries.

Tchetcheghin also started in search of Khabaroff, but was more fortunate, as he met him in the gorges of the Amur, where he probably had halted in the certainty of not missing the boats in the narrow channel. Khabaroff had been obliged to proceed very cautiously in his retreat from Atchansk. At the mouth of the Sungari a Manchu army of 6,000 men with cannon and muskets was waiting for him, and he owed his escape to a strong breeze blowing up river, which enabled him to face the swift current and steer in the middle of the stream, crowding on all the sail his boats could carry. Alarming rumours were current among the natives : an army of 10,000 men—others said more—was ready ; the Shamsha Khan, bent on driving out the Russians, was collecting 40,000 men for that object. Worse misfortunes now came upon Khabaroff : the defection of his men and the persecution of his superiors.

On August 1, 1652, Khabaroff halted at the mouth of the Zeya, where he proposed to build a fort ; but some of his men, preferring a roving life of piracy, seized three boats, which contained the government stores—cannon, gunpowder, and armour—and fled down the Amur. The deserters numbered 136 men, and Khabaroff was left with only about 200 ; but the material loss was trifling in comparison with the moral consequences. With his forces intact, it would have been difficult, even for the daring resourceful mind of Khabaroff, to achieve success against the hostile natives and the Chinese armies, but the task became hopeless when the mutiny of his men added to his dangers. His attempts to conciliate the natives and induce them to submit failed ; he was held responsible for the incoherent violence of the men who had escaped his control. He proceeded on the Zeya for six weeks, summoning the inhabitants to submit, but they answered : ' You deceive us, for, behold, your men run away and plunder our lands.'

His power seems to have been entirely crippled by the desertion and consequent filibustering of his men, for he accomplished nothing remarkable after, and his last report to Yakutsk was written on August 5, 1652, in which he described his difficult position and asked for assistance.

Reports of the daring voyage of Poyarkoff and of the successful expeditions of Khabaroff had spread over Siberia; the stream of adventurers which had spread over the northern plains reaching the Lena about twenty years before had been lately struggling with the difficulties of the Arctic Ocean and of the inhospitable north-eastern region. The discovery of a fourth great river was hailed with delight, especially as it lay in the south, and was described as fertile. The scanty settlers on the Lena were eager to abandon their cold barren land for a warmer region, and began to emigrate with such frequency that orders were issued to stop them on the Olekma and prevent their passage. The welcome news had reached even Moscow, where it was resolved to despatch 3,000 *strielitz* on the Amur; this measure was probably suggested by the statement made in 1650 by Khabaroff, that 6,000 men were required to conquer the country. But even with half the number demanded, it is very probable that the daring and skill of Khabaroff might have firmly established the Russian domination on the Amur in the seventeenth century. The 3,000 *strielitz*, however, never arrived; they were either not sent or were absorbed *en route* by the military necessities of the districts through which they passed.[1] The small force which did arrive had a *voivode*, Zinovieff, appointed to govern the country, who foolishly abused his power. When he met Khabaroff at the mouth of the Zeya he scolded him, pulled his beard, accused him of concealing treasure, and sent him for trial to Moscow—some say even in chains.

[1] This often happened with convoys of provisions which never reached their distant destination, but were detained for the urgent needs of the nearer garrisons.

This shameful treatment of their beloved *ataman*, the attempt to enforce distasteful discipline, and to oblige them to cultivate the land, disgusted the Cossacks, who were not appeased even by the distribution of money sent from Moscow to reward their exploits.

In the winter of 1655 Khabaroff arrived at Moscow, where he was tried—it is not known for what crime—and acquitted. Rewards were now given to the old man who had been so harshly treated ; the title of ' son of a *boyar* ' was bestowed on him, and he was appointed chief of a district on the Lena ; but he never returned to the Amur, where he had been so ungratefully requited for the heroic exertions of four years. He died on the Lena not far from Kirensk, and it is said his descendants are still to be found in Siberia.

After Yermak, Khabaroff is the most conspicuous figure among the Cossack conquerors of Siberia ; he not only possessed the daring courage and unhesitating resolution to face difficulties and privations, which were common to all the Russian pioneers, but he had the intellectual qualities necessary for a commander. The best proof of the clearness of his intellect is shown by the statement he made in 1650, when he had returned from his first raid on the Amur after he had passed but a few months in the region, that 6,000 men were required for conquering the country. All the disasters that followed show the correctness of his first rough estimate. He discovered a short route to the Amur, which rendered possible the quick despatch of reinforcements and ammunition. He was the first to meet a large Manchu army, and inflicted a severe defeat, which raised the military reputation of the Russians and surrounded them with a prestige which compensated for their numerical weakness. His keen discernment of strategical positions is evinced by the fact that the two spots he preferred, the mouth of the Ussuri and the mouth of the Zeya, have been chosen as the site of the principal Russian towns now on the Amur—Khabarofsk and Blagovieshensk.

In the meanwhile events were taking place in another region which bore the most lasting consequences for the Russian aims on the Amur. It has been shown that, notwithstanding their preference to advance in the northeast, and their reluctance to engage the more warlike races of the south, the Russians had been compelled by special reasons to attack the Buriats dwelling around the Lake Baikal. Their first appearance on the eastern shores of that lake was in 1644, when Skorokhod with thirty-six men reached the river Barguzin, which flows into the Baikal nearly in the centre of its eastern side. In 1647 Kolesnikoff built the *ostrog* of Verkhne Angarsk on the upper Angara, a small river at the northern extremity of the lake, considered to be the upper course of the lower Angoras, which flows past Irkutsk. In 1648 an expedition of sixty men under Ivan Galkin crossed the Baikal and built an *ostrog* near the mouth of the river Barguzin, which afterwards became the town of the same name. The Barguzin *ostrog* was for a long time the base of operations for all the expeditions engaged in the conquest of the lands beyond the Baikal. In the following year, 1649, the Russians pushed on south and built the *ostrog* of Verkhne Udinsk at the confluence of the river Selenga with its tributary, the Uda. The establishment of the Russians in the extensive river basin of the Selenga[1]

---

[1] This should be considered the principal source of the Baikal, and the head of the Angara. It is not only much larger than any other river of the Baikal system (a course of over 700 miles), but the researches of Dibowsky and Godlewsky in 1876, proving the existence of a transverse chain of mountains under the surface where the depth is only 200 feet, while the rest of the lake has a depth never less than 800 and sometimes

led to the colonisation of the region now called Transbaikalia, the most picturesque and fertile province of Siberia. In 1653 Peter Beketoff started with an expedition which achieved the most important results : he ascended the Selenga and then its right tributary, the Khilok, and reached Lake Irghen, where he built the Irghensk *ostrog*. He had thus gradually mounted the plateau gently rising from the Baikal and was close to the Yablonoi crest, which parts the waters falling into the Baikal and thence into the Yenissei, from those belonging to the Amur river system. In the following year, 1654, he crossed the Yablonoi, which presented no great difficulties, especially on the western side, and by the rivers Ingoda and Shilka (formed by the junction of the Ingoda and the Onon) he reached the mouth of the tributary river Nertcha, where he built the Nertchinsk *ostrog*.

His eastern march had brought Beketoff on the upper waters of the Amur, thus discovering a third still more favourable route to reach the much-coveted new region. Poyarkoff's long disastrous voyage had shown the inconveniences of the route by the river Aldan, and it was abandoned as soon as Khabaroff discovered the shorter one by the river Olekma, which had, moreover, the advantage of leading to a point more than 500 miles higher up the Amur. But the second route was also long and laborious, requiring several months' tedious tracking up the Olekma ; and the expeditions on the Amur therefore received very slowly reinforcements and ammunition from their distant headquarters at Yakutsk. It was, however,

over 4,000 feet, establish the fact that the Baikal is really composed of two great depressions, and the so-called upper Angara has no connection with the lower Angara, which is really a prolongation of the Selenga.

the only practicable route as long as the Cossacks kept to the northern part of Siberia.

The advance of the Russians in Transbaikalia, in the land where the waters part to flow either eastward to the Pacific or westward to the Baikal and thence to the Arctic Ocean, rendered possible the adoption of the third still more advantageous route, which was, indeed, the course of the Amur itself almost from its sources. The settlements on the upper waters of the Amur, within easy distance of the Baikal, through the fine Selenga river and its affluents, the Uda and the Khilok, became the natural base of operations for the conquest of the middle and lower courses of the Amur. The fact must have been recognised at the time, because in 1656 Transbaikalia was detached from the authority of Yakutsk, and Athanasius Pashkoff was appointed as independent *voivode* in Nertchinsk.

After the departure of Khabaroff, the task of collecting tribute and subduing the natives was entrusted to Onuphrius Stepanoff, who, notwithstanding the presence of the Chinese armies, prosecuted the work with great spirit. In the summer of 1654 he went up the Sungari, where he met a large Chinese army, on shore and in boats ; the Cossacks made a vigorous attack and drove the Chinese out of their boats, forcing them on shore, where they took refuge in their entrenchments. Stepanoff attempted to carry the position by storm, but was repulsed, and the want of provisions obliged him to retreat up the Amur. He was joined by Beketoff, who, after discovering the third route to the Amur and building the Nertchinsk *ostrog*, had sailed down the Shilka.

Though reinforced, Stepanoff was aware of the dangers that threatened him, and made the most elaborate preparations to give the Chinese a warm reception. He concentrated his forces at Kumarska[1] and employed the autumn in erecting formidable fortifications, which showed considerable skill. The camp was square, and surrounded by a rampart of double palisades filled in with sand; cannon were mounted at the angles; the approaches were defended by a ditch seven feet deep and fourteen wide, and by caltrops strewn on the ground. In the centre of the fort an earthen elevation with sloping sides (a 'cavalier' of the old system of fortification) enabled the artillery to fire over the ramparts on the surrounding country. To extinguish fires, a well was dug and water kept running in gutters. To prevent surprises, fires were kept burning during the night. These works, especially the ditches, cost immense labour, because in the Amur region very little snow falls in winter, the ground is frozen to a great depth, and never thaws completely even during the high temperature of the short summers. The Cossacks had to light huge fires to thaw the ground before breaking it with their spades.

With the spring the expected enemy arrived. On March 13, 1655, the Manchu army, 10,000 strong, appeared before Kumarska; their siege appliances were as numerous and far stronger than the defences of the Russians. Besides fifteen guns they had boat-hooks, firewood, straw, wooden shields covered with felt or hides, mounted ladders with one end on wheels and the other provided with hooks to grapple on the walls, and long sacks (140 feet long, it is said) filled with gunpowder, probably intended as portable mines to blow up the rampart. After a great deal of useless cannonading and attempts to burn the camp with fire-arrows, the Chinese commenced the assault on March 24, but notwithstanding their abundance of appliances for scaling the walls

[1] At the mouth of the Kumara, a right tributary of the Amur.

it is probable they were not eager about using them in the face of 500 Cossacks at bay, desperately resolved to sell their lives dearly; it was found more congenial to resume the distant cannonade, which was kept up day and night until April 4, when, perceiving they had produced no effect, the Chinese retired.

The position of the Russians was not much improved by the repulse of the Chinese, as scarcity of provisions obliged them to abandon Kumarska. Stepanoff had not the high qualities of Khabaroff, and was unable to restrain the Cossacks, always inclined to disorder in distant regions. Their capricious violence and wasteful plunder exhausted the resources of the natives, who could easily have supported the Russians if the requisitions had been made with order and intelligence. The dearth on the Amur was also increased by order of the Chinese authorities, who, despairing of driving away the Cossacks by force of arms, hoped to succeed by starvation. The natives were forbidden to cultivate the lands on the shores of the river and enjoined to retire southwards with their families. Stepanoff, however, was equal to the emergency; when he found no more grain on the deserted Amur, he went up the Sungari and commenced his depredations on that river. His boldness was so great that he penetrated into the heart of Manchuria as far as the town of Ningut. Then he descended the Amur and wintered at its mouth, building the *ostrog* of Kosogorski on the Amgun.

His recklessness cost him his life and ruined the Russian power on the Amur. If the Cossacks had settled and cultivated the land after their success at Kumarska, they would probably have been left alone, as the Chinese had very little interest in the Amur, and were averse to wasting lives to drive out the formidable strangers. But they could not tolerate the filibustering raids in the province of Manchuria, the home of the dynasty which had lately ascended the dragon throne of China. They were now convinced that there was no limit to the rapacity of the Cossacks, and determined to exterminate them.[1]

Stepanoff continued his daring raids up the Sungari every spring, but the Chinese collected a large army at its mouth and concealed a fleet of forty-seven large boats among the islands. When the Cossack boats came down on June 30, 1658, the Chinese fleet suddenly appeared and surrounded them. The Russians, thus caught in a trap, lost heart and fled, and their chief, who had not the skill of Khabaroff to extricate himself, perished with about 270 of his men. Only about 200 succeeded in escaping. This disaster, the heaviest sustained by the Russians in Siberia, ruined their domination on the Amur; it destroyed their reputation for invincibility which hitherto had enabled their scanty forces to struggle against such overwhelming numbers.

In the same year Albazin, the *ostrog* founded by Khabaroff in 1651, and which had been besieged since 1657, was abandoned by the Cossacks on account of want of provisions, and burnt by the Chinese.[2] The Amur was thus entirely freed from the Cossacks—but it did not long remain so.

In 1638 Nikiphor Romanoff Tchernigofski, a Polish prisoner, had been deported to Siberia and sent to the Yenisseisk *ostrog*, and thence transferred to the Ilimsk *ostrog*. In 1650 he was put in charge of the Tchetchuiski portage, which, as we have seen, served for the com-

---

[1] Besides Stepanoff there was also a band of about 300 cut-throats under Sorokin, who, after robbing the Russian settlers and merchants on the Lena, spread desolation on the Amur.

[2] This siege is given on the authority of Atkinson, who must be correct, because from other sources it is known that Albazin was founded in 1651 and rebuilt in 1665.

munications between the Yenissei and the Lena, and in 1652 he was appointed overseer for a salt boilery at Ust-Kutskoe. In 1665 he formed part of a convoy which Obukhoff, the *voivode* of Ilimsk, led to the Kirensk fair, and, on the return voyage, he prevailed on the men to mutiny and murder the *voivode*.[1] To avoid punishment, Tchernigofski incited the accomplices of his crime to follow him and settle on the Amur : he reached Albazin with eighty-four men and built an *ostrog* on the site of the former one burnt by the Chinese in 1658. The origin of this second settlement at Albazin was therefore similar to that of the Zaporoghians on the Dnieper two centuries before—it was a refuge for outlaws. It is probable that, even after the defeat of Stepanoff, Russian trappers and traders continued to roam on the Amur; all these adventurers now congregated at Albazin, which became in a short time a considerable place. In 1674 it had already a government office, a guard-house, and barracks. Before this date, in 1669, Tchernigofski, perceiving the impossibility of holding his ground without assistance, had asked the protection of the *voivode* of Nertchinsk, and proffered his submission to the Tsar. The offer was graciously accepted, as, owing to the scarcity of population, the Russian authorities in Siberia at that time could not be particular about the quality of the settlers, and a commander was appointed in Albazin. In 1672 the sentence of death on Tchernigofski and his companions was remitted, and they received a reward of 2,000 roubles for their meritorious work on the Amur.

Tchernigofski decided to restore the work of Khabaroff and Stepanoff, and undertook the task with great energy.

---

[1] The anonymous author often quoted states that the *voivode* had taken a fancy to the wife of Tchernigofski, who in revenge committed the crime. This version explains the event and corresponds to the state of lawless violence then prevalent in the outlying districts of Siberia.

From his headquarters at Albazin he despatched successive expeditions to rebuild the ruined *ostrogs* and collect tribute from the natives. Manchuria itself was not spared by his raids. The reconquest of the region proceeded so quickly and thoroughly that in 1681 Tchernigofski had surpassed his predecessors, having extended the Russian power over the river Ussuri and part of the Sungari up to the mountains.[1] Again Russia had the chance of establishing her power on the Amur in the seventeenth century, but again she let the precious opportunity slip away. Instead of sending the requisite forces demanded by the daring adventurers on the Amur, as well as by the *voivode* of Yakutsk, the ministerial offices at Moscow responded with insignificant measures; they acted as they had done with Khabaroff more than twenty years before, and appointed a *voivode*—Alexis Tolbuzin. Though this hero, who afterwards acquired everlasting fame in his defence of Albazin, was a man far superior to Zinovieff, he could not accomplish his arduous task with insufficient forces. Yet there was no time for delay; Káng-hsi, the greatest of the emperors of the present Manchu dynasty, and one of the most remarkable that ever sat on the throne of China, incensed by the ravages of the Cossacks and their audacious invasions of Manchuria, had summoned Tolbuzin to evacuate Albazin and retire from the Amur.

As the summons of the Emperor received no answer, the Chinese, in 1684, commenced their warlike operations by destroying all the Russian posts on the lower Amur, reserving the attack on Albazin for the following year. In

---

[1] Ragosa says that, besides the fortress of Albazin, there were the *ostrogs* of Kumarska, Zeiska, Kosogorska, and Atchansk on the Amur; those of Ust-Oelinsk and Ust-Nimelensk on the Amgun (a tributary on the left of the Amur near its mouth); that of Tugursk on the river Tugur (a river flowing into the sea of Okhotsk). There were also villages along the Amur, where peasants cultivated the land.

the beginning [1] of June, 1685, a Chinese army of 15,000 men with 150 field and fifty siege guns appeared before Albazin and established batteries on an island opposite the town.

Tolbuzin had made the best preparations for defence; he had burned all the houses outside the fortifications and withdrawn the inhabitants within the walls, sending to Nertchinsk the non-combatants; and though he was able to collect only 450 men with three guns and 300 muskets, he peremptorily rejected the summons to surrender.[2] After the usual long preliminary cannonade, the Chinese commenced [3] a series of assaults, which were bravely repulsed by the small garrison. At last, however, want of ammunition compelled Tolbuzin to capitulate on honourable terms, the Cossacks being allowed to proceed to Nertchinsk with their arms. The Chinese, after burning Albazin, retired to Aigun, a town which they had lately built near the mouth of the Zeya, to counteract the influence of the Russian fortress.

Albazin, like the much-quoted phoenix, had the faculty of rising from its ashes. Tolbuzin was determined to make another attempt to hold the Amur, and as soon as he ascertained from his scouts that the Chinese had left, he returned with reinforcements, and on August 7, 1685,[4] began reconstructing the fort. The approach of winter gave him leisure to finish his fortifications before another attack was possible. Other posts were established and tribute collected from the natives as before.

[1] Atkinson gives the 4th, Ragosa June 10.

[2] This was written in Polish, probably by some Polish prisoner who had fallen into the hands of the Chinese and was used as an interpreter.

[3] On June 22, according to Atkinson.

[4] This date is given by Atkinson. Ragosa places the return in 1686, but this does not give sufficient time for the events following; so I think Atkinson must be right. Perhaps the difference is due to the Russian calendar of the time.

The Chinese, alarmed at the pertinacious reappearance of the Russians, despatched an army of 5,000 foot and 3,000 horse with forty guns to besiege Albazin. The Chinese advanced in June 1686,[1] and commenced the attack on July 2. Tolbuzin, profiting by his experience of the former siege, had collected a larger garrison, but still he had only about 800 men[2] with eight brass guns. The Cossacks made a gallant defence against the superior numbers of the Chinese, harassing them by continual sorties, but in one of these they had the misfortune to lose their heroic *voivode*, who was killed by a cannon-ball. The command then devolved on Athanasius Beiton,[3] who proved himself a worthy successor of Tolbuzin; he defended the place so vigorously that the Chinese were obliged to retire, and the approach of winter suspended all military operations.

In the following spring the Chinese renewed their attacks, but Beiton, with bulldog tenacity, continued to hold out, notwithstanding the dwindling numbers of the defenders. The long siege, the losses by the enemy, a fearful outbreak of scurvy, diminished the small garrison daily, sometimes hourly. The Cossacks were reduced to sixty-six men, and their provisions and ammunition were almost exhausted, but Beiton continued the desperate resistance until the Chinese retired. The peace negotiations between the Governments of Russia and China then put an end to the warlike operations.

[1] Ragosa gives a year later, 1687, as he gives a year later for the return of the Cossacks to Albazin; but Atkinson's date (1686) is also given by Andrievitch.

[2] Ragosa gives 736, Andrievitch 826.

[3] Atkinson says he was an Englishman—Beaton—but I do not know what authority he had for his statement. The anonymous author says he was a German, a term which then in Siberia might be loosely applied to any foreigner. His name, Athanasius, does not sound English. At all events, he was a man worth claiming by any nation. A Cossack station 38½ versts beneath Albazin now bears his name.

By the treaty of Nertchinsk, concluded in the following year (1689), Russia relinquished all claims to the Amur, and Albazin was again destroyed by the Chinese, who then confidently imagined it would never rise again. In fact, more than 150 years passed before the pertinacity of the Russians restored the town so heroically defended by their ancestors.

The events which took place on the Amur, so abruptly closed by the treaty of Nertchinsk, are interesting when considered as the prologue of the historical drama enacted in our times. They form also a brilliant though detached episode of Siberian history; nowhere else do we find such a rapid series of remarkable men. With the exception of Yermak, no man rises into prominence; the conquest of Siberia was the work of numerous nameless pioneers, all gifted with the common qualities of endurance and fearlessness, but deprived either of the opportunity or of the qualities to excel as leaders. Dejneff was only a daring and successful navigator. On the Amur we find, besides the striking figures of Khabaroff, Tolbuzin, and Beiton, also Poyarkoff, Stepanoff, and Tchernigofski, all conspicuous for their ability. Yet in the region where the Cossacks had the most brilliant chiefs they failed, were obliged to relinquish their conquests, and had to halt for nearly two centuries before resuming their advance.

This failure was mainly due to the power of China. In Northern Siberia the Cossacks met natives armed only with bows and spears, who could not withstand the few bold pioneers provided with firearms. In the south, on the other hand, they found the Chinese as well armed as themselves, and though the firearms were perhaps not handled so skilfully, this deficiency was compensated by overwhelming numbers. The Russians were also unfortunate in encountering the Chinese at a time when they were far more warlike than they have ever been since. The Manchus had lately conquered China, and the hardy virtues acquired in their native mountains had infused a short-lived vigour into the old empire. The liberal-minded favour shown to the Jesuits also gave the Emperors of the Manchu dynasty all the resources of the science of Western Europe. We shall see later what important assistance China received from her Jesuit *protégés* in her relations with Russia.

The Cossacks on the Amur were also very disadvantageously situated in their struggle against the Chinese; they were, to use a military expression, at a great distance from their base. Setting aside the long laborious route chosen by Poyarkoff, which was quickly abandoned, even the shorter one employed by Khabaroff on the Olekma was full of difficulties, especially proceeding from Yakutsk to the Amur, when the greater part of the journey had to be performed by tracking the boats against the stream. The Chinese, on the contrary, had Manchuria and a settled population reaching almost to the banks of the Amur, with two easy routes down the Sungari and the Ussuri. The discovery of the third and natural route along the course of the Amur itself, starting from the Baikal, did not profit the Russians much, because Transbaikalia, the proper base of operations, was a newly conquered region, containing a scanty reserve of soldiers and settlers from which no reinforcements could be drawn. This third route was also discovered late, when the Chinese had already been alarmed by the attacks of several expeditions. The Russians at that time were so few and so scattered all over Siberia that the real base for any considerable operation was at an enormous distance : it lay in European Russia.

Now while the Cossacks on the Amur were confronted

with a power formidable to their small numbers, they were unable to arouse the home authorities to provide the forces indispensable for success. In Moscow they continued the traditions of Ivan the Terrible; they were glad to receive valuable furs, and willing to send small parties of soldiers to collect tribute and *voivodes* to govern, but they were adverse to despatch large military expeditions. The indifference at Moscow rendered hopeless the task of struggling against China on the Amur.

As the struggle proceeded the action of the central authorities grew more mischievous; not content with neglecting the gallant adventurers bravely resisting at Albazin, they interfered, and by the treaty of Nertchinsk gave China all she demanded and recalled the heroic garrison which had victoriously sustained the long siege.

CHAPTER IV

THE HALT IN THE FAR EAST

It has been shown that while in the north of Siberia the conquest of the Cossacks followed its natural course and proceeded until it reached the ocean limits of the continent, it was abruptly and permanently stopped in the south, on the Amur, by the action of the Government. Before describing the negotiations which led to this result it will be necessary to cast a hasty glance at the history of Russia in the intervening period of over a century. It has been consistent with clearness to abandon the chronological order of narration, because the contemporaneous events in European Russia had slight influence on the eastern expansion in Siberia; but now that we have arrived at the time when, by the treaty of Nertchinsk, the Government of Moscow exercised direct and important influence on the destinies of Siberia, and by its action stopped for a long period the process of expansion, we have the opportunity for a retrospective survey of the history of the mother-country.

The brief sketch of Russian history was broken off when Yermak had already commenced the conquest of Siberia, at the death of Ivan the Terrible in 1584. The dreaded Tsar, who had ruled with an iron hand, might well have adopted the phrase attributed to Louis XIV., 'Après moi le déluge,' for the disasters which followed his death are unparalleled in Russian history. The country sank to the lowest point of degradation, and almost fell to pieces by the giving way of all social organisation.

As Ivan the Terrible had murdered his eldest son Ivan, the throne devolved on Theodore, who was young and feeble-minded. A kind of regency therefore became indispensable, and this led to trouble and intrigues among the rival nobles competing for the supreme influence in the government of the State. The principal families in Moscow were the Mstislav, the Shuiski, and the Romanoff. The latter had given a wife to Ivan the Terrible, the mother of Theodore. Boris Godunoff, the brother-in-law of Theodore, was also a candidate for the regency. Even the accession to the throne of the new Tsar was not effected without some trouble, caused by the partisans of a younger brother, Demetrius. They wished to secure an appanage to the young prince, but their object was defeated and Demetrius relegated with his mother and relations to the town of Uglitch. The unfortunate child is only famous on account of the impostors who assumed his name.

The first to undertake the direction of the State and the guidance of the weak Tsar was his uncle, Nikita Romanoff; but he died in 1586, and then Boris Godunoff took his place. He encountered strong opposition from the Shuiski family, but succeeded in thwarting their intrigues. He showed great administrative ability, and, besides favouring intercourse with Western nations, he effected several important changes: the institution of serfdom [1] and the creation of a Patriarch in lieu of the Metropolitan of Moscow. The latter measure gave the Russian equal rank with the other Eastern Churches.

[1] The peasants were permanently bound to the soil to prevent their leaving the service of poor landlords in favour of rich ones—a practice which, owing to the scanty population of the country, caused extensive regions to be left uncultivated.

Unfortunately a mysterious crime attributed to him by the suspicions of his contemporaries has obscured his fame in the eyes of posterity. In May 1591 the news spread over Russia that Demetrius, the young brother of the Tsar, had been assassinated by men sent by Godunoff. Commissioners, among whom was the head of the Shuiski family, were despatched to investigate the case, and they reported that the young prince had killed himself in a fit of epilepsy; but this explanation did not satisfy the people, who adhered to their suspicions. The murder had the most disastrous consequences for Russia, because the Tsar Theodore was childless, and when he died, in 1598, the long line of Ruric, which had ruled the nation for over seven centuries, came to an end.

The successor to the throne was chosen by the principal boyars and churchmen. But Godunoff had been practically the Tsar for twelve years; his enemies had been banished and his friends raised to high places; the Patriarch himself, the most important person in Russia after the Tsar, was his staunch supporter. Thus every measure had been taken betimes to secure the coming election. The vacant throne was therefore offered to Godunoff, who, after declining, was forced to accept. As titular Tsar Godunoff displayed the same qualities as when he exercised the supreme power in the name of his brother-in-law. He continued to cultivate relations with Western powers, and favoured foreigners residing in Russia; he paid great attention to the education of the nation, and sent young men abroad to study; in fact, he commenced the reforms which were carried out a century later by Peter the Great. But he lacked the essential quality for a man living in those troubled times who wished to found a dynasty—he had no military talents. Through indecision he neglected the opportunity of securing the Baltic coast lands for Russia when the war between Sweden and Poland freed him from the menace of these two formidable neighbours and rendered his alliance, or even his neutrality, of such value that he might have dictated his own terms. He was also addicted to petty suspicion, and on the throne could not forget the enmity of his rivals. A persecution of the principal noble families commenced, and all the Romanoffs were included in the list of proscription; the eldest, Theodore, son of Nikita Romanoff, was tonsured and confined in a monastery under the name of Philarete, his wife was obliged to become a nun, and all the brothers were exiled to different towns. These unpopular measures were followed by famine and pestilence, which increased the general discontent and converted the starving peasantry into bands of robbers, who even infested the neighbourhood of Moscow.

At this critical moment there appeared on the stage of history an extraordinary figure. George Otrepieff, the son of a soldier, to escape poverty had become a monk; being clever and able to write, he was chosen as copyist for the Patriarch; but his reckless words that he would be Tsar in Moscow were repeated to Godunoff, who ordered he should be transferred to a distant monastery. But Otrepieff fled to the Polish frontier, discarded his monk's frock, and, after frequenting a school at Gashtch and living among the Zaporoghian Cossacks, entered the service of a Polish nobleman. At a favourable moment he declared he was Demetrius, the son of Ivan the Terrible, who had escaped from his murderers. This extraordinary news rapidly spread among the neighbouring gentry, and was generally believed. One nobleman, Mnishek, especially patronised the false Demetrius, and promised him his daughter in marriage. As a preliminary step he was secretly admitted into the Catholic Church, and then, in 1604, Mnishek introduced the young prince to the Papal Nuncio, who presented him to the King of Poland. Sigismund was very desirous of aiding the young pretender and thus weakening Moscow by civil war, but he feared to break the truce concluded with Godunoff. He contrived to satisfy his political jealousy without a flagrant infraction of the law of nations by prompting his nobles to secretly support the Russian exile.

Mnishek furnished his future son-in-law, the young pretender to the throne of Moscow, with 1,600 adventurers gathered from the rabble of all Poland, and this small force was quickly reinforced. The experience of all countries in the dark ages has shown that the ignorant multitude has ever refused to believe in the violent extinction of dynasties which, from their long duration, seemed immortal as compared with the brief span of the individual life. The followers of Perkin Warbeck, and the lingering hope of the Portuguese that their last King Sebastian had not perished in Africa, are conspicuous instances. It was natural therefore that many Russians should hastily acknowledge the runaway monk as the descendant of the line of Ruric. Moreover, the borderland between the two great Slav States of Poland and Moscow was full of desperate adventurers and of Zaporoghian Cossacks, who were ready to embark in any enterprise which promised the plunder of the wealthy settled regions. The qualities of Godunoff were also injurious to him at such a moment. His attempts to spread order and civilisation over the country had displeased the wild roving inhabitants of the steppes, and the Don Cossacks declared for the false Demetrius. As Godunoff had no military capacity, he had to trust to his *voivodes*, and, though they won some victories, the impostor was able to repair his losses by the arrival of fresh adventurers. While struggling against these difficulties, Boris Godunoff died suddenly in a somewhat strange way on April 13, 1605.

The throne devolved to Theodore, the son of Godunoff, but he was soon abandoned even by the most strenuous supporters of his father. A revolt broke out in Moscow, and on June 20, 1605, the false Demetrius entered the capital with great pomp. The head of the Shuiski family made an attempt to persuade the people that Demetrius was an impostor, but he was discovered and punished. The Patriarch also was degraded for his opposition. Demetrius, to remove all doubts, had an interview with his alleged mother, and then was crowned with the usual solemnity. To gain favour, he appointed the head of the Romanoff family, Philarete, as Metropolitan of Rostof. His reign, however, was brief and ended tragically. Though he showed considerable ability, he was beset with insurmountable difficulties. The assistance received from the Poles bound him to a nation hated by the Russians, and his marriage with the daughter of Mnishek increased his unpopularity. The powerful Shuiski family was actively intriguing, and at last, on May 17, 1606, roused the people against the hateful heretic. Demetrius tried to escape, but was killed, and his corpse exposed on the famous Red Square outside the Kremlin.

The death of the impostor left the throne again vacant, and on May 19, two days after the revolt, the people of Moscow again assembled in the Red Square to elect a Tsar. The choice naturally fell on Vassil, the head of the Shuiski family, who had principally contributed to the fall of the false Demetrius.

The new Tsar soon became unpopular. The sudden elevation to the throne of a nobleman, however distinguished, naturally caused jealousy and discontent among his former peers; moreover, the election of the sovereign was found wanting in necessary completeness. It had been hurriedly effected by the people of Moscow without consulting the other towns and awaiting the arrival of their delegates for a representative election by the whole nation. Vassil had not even the qualities to captivate the multitude and make them forget the haste and irregularity of his election. He was old and avaricious, and soon disgusted his adherents in Moscow. He was endured because there was no other available candidate for the throne. But this immunity from competition was of short duration. The attachment of the people to the line of Ruric, which had ruled from time immemorial, and the success of the false Demetrius encouraged the appearance of fresh impostors. A pretended son of Theodore,[1] Peter, was supported by the Cossacks of the Terek. A follower of the false Demetrius, who had escaped from Moscow during the massacre, fled to the Lithuanian frontier and spread the report that he was Demetrius, who had falsely been reported killed at Moscow. In those times of confusion he readily found credence, and soon gathered followers among the turbulent border population.

The appearance of the second false Demetrius alarmed Vassil, who ordered the corpse of the true Demetrius to be conveyed to Moscow and buried with great pomp in the Archangel Cathedral, glorifying the innocent youth cruelly assassinated. But as Vassil Shuiski had been in the committee which had declared that Demetrius had killed himself in a fit of epilepsy, this public recantation

---

[1] Theodore had only a daughter who died before him, but it was alleged she had been substituted by Boris Godunoff in lieu of the boy Peter.

of his former assertion rendered him still more con-
temptible in the eyes of the people. Bands of adventurers
began to rove about the country, arousing the serfs against
their masters and threatening even Moscow. Though
they were defeated, the confusion they spread favoured
the cause of the second false Demetrius,[1] who was now
supported by the Zaporoghian and Don Cossacks. Approaching Moscow, he established himself at Tushina
(1608), and, though often defeated, he was able to repair
his losses and increase his power. To strengthen his
position he seized the person of Philarete, the head of the
Romanoff family, and wished to appoint him Patriarch.
For a time the whole country was divided into two
factions with their respective capitals at Moscow and
Tushina, with separate tsars, courts, and armies; unscrupulous adventurers passed from one party to the other
whenever it seemed suitable for their unlawful interests.

The horrors of civil war were heightened by foreign
intervention. Polish soldiers of fortune and desperadoes
having powerfully assisted the false Demetrius, this served
as a pretext for Vassil to secure the aid of an army from
Sweden, the jealous enemy of Poland. A body of 5,000
Swedes, led by Prince Skopin-Shuiski, nephew of the
Tsar Vassil, a young nobleman of eminent qualities, completely defeated the partisans of the false Demetrius in
Northern Russia. This assistance, furnished by Sweden
in exchange for an alliance, awakened the suspicions of
Sigismund, King of Poland, who hitherto had refrained
from overtly assisting the false Demetrius. He now
perceived the necessity of promptly intervening in the
affairs of Russia, to prevent the formation of the powerful
coalition of his northern and eastern neighbours. He

---

[1] There were many more obscure impostors who pretended to be sons
and grandsons of Ivan the Terrible.

hastily gathered a small army and advanced to Smolensk (September 21, 1609), which he vainly summoned to surrender. The advance of King Sigismund brought on a crisis in Russian affairs: the Poles at Tushina, who formed the backbone of the army of the false Demetrius, were obliged to abandon him and join their sovereign who was besieging Smolensk ; this desertion broke the power of the impostor, who was obliged to abandon Tushina. On the other hand Vassil became jealous of the glory and popularity of his nephew, Skopin-Shuiski, and as the youth died strangely after a short illness, the people suspected foul play and hated still more their imbecile Tsar. A defeat of the Russian army by King Sigismund completed the misfortunes of Vassil, who was forced to abdicate on July 17, 1610.

The vacant throne was claimed by two candidates: Ladislaus, the son of the King of Poland, and the second false Demetrius ; the majority of the Russian nobles and boyars would have preferred to elect one of their own class, either Prince Galytzyn or young Michael Romanoff, the son of the Metropolitan Philarete, but they had not the power to follow their own wishes against such formidable adversaries supported by the Polish army and the rabble enlisted by the impostor. Their greatest danger was from the false Demetrius, whose wild army of Cossacks and lawless adventurers threatened to destroy all order in the country ; and when they ascertained that the impostor was preparing to secretly enter Moscow, favoured by the lowest class of the people, Prince Mstislav, the foremost boyar, invited the Poles to occupy the capital.

The Poles, now in possession of Moscow, skilfully used their advantage ; some of the foremost Russians were gained over to their cause by promises of rank and power in the new reign ; influential men like the Metropolitan Philarete were sent under pretext of an embassy to the King of Poland and kept in honourable confinement, which was indefinitely prolonged owing to the complicated negotiations proceeding between the Russian nation and the proposed new sovereign. The position of the Poles at Moscow was difficult, as they were few and generally disliked by the people, who justly considered them as invaders; they tried to legitimise their position by urgently requesting their king to send his son Ladislaus to occupy the throne, but Sigismund did not care to risk the youthful prince in the capital of such a disordered country. He expressed the intention of pacifying the country first; but this was repugnant even to the Russians who favoured the candidature of his son Ladislaus; they feared the annexation of their country by Poland, unless the two thrones were separated at once. But the greatest difficulty was the theological difference of faith; all the Russians, as first condition, insisted on the conversion of Ladislaus to the orthodox faith, while Sigismund was equally inflexible in refusing the abjuration of his son. The Poles at Moscow artfully contrived to postpone the difficulty by delaying the communication of these irreconcilable decisions, but they were tacitly understood by both parties.

While these negotiations were proceeding, the difficulties of the Poles were increased by the death of the false Demetrius. The dangers threatened by that impostor and his lawless army had alone reconciled the respectable classes of Russia to the candidature of Ladislaus; but when death removed the cause of their fears, their invincible repugnance to the heretic and the foreigner appeared in full force. This general feeling of the population was excited by the Patriarch Hermogen, who strenuously insisted that Ladislaus should at once abjure his heresies and adopt the orthodox faith. To stop his seditious propaganda, the Poles put him in prison, where he eventually perished from neglect and want of food. A revolt broke out in Moscow; the Poles were driven into the Kremlin and obliged to set fire to the town to keep back the infuriated populace. Their situation was improved only for a short time by this severe measure; an army of 100,000 men, composed of Cossacks and contingents from the different towns, concentrated around the Kremlin and reduced the scanty Polish garrison to great straits for want of provisions. But Russia had fallen into such chaotic social disorganisation that all united action was impossible until the stern experience of fresh disasters should again show its necessity. The armed citizens and Cossacks had little mutual sympathy and were suspicious of each other; the Poles artfully availed themselves of this latent motive of discord. They forged a letter of the commander of the citizen force, containing secret instructions for the Russian towns to kill all the Cossacks they might lay their hands on. The letter was given to a Cossack prisoner released for the purpose, who delivered it to his chiefs. The infuriated Cossacks refused to believe the denials of the supposed traitor and hacked him to death with their sabres.

This hasty murder broke up the Russian army and relieved the Poles from the dangerous siege; the armed citizens, disorganised by the loss of their general, were either massacred or disbanded and retired to their towns, while the Cossacks spread about the country, pillaging the towns and villages. During this confusion the Swedes, exasperated that a prince of the hostile Polish nation had been invited to occupy the throne of Moscow, advanced in the north-west and seized Novgorod. Another false Demetrius also made his appearance. Though the

Cossacks continued to war with the Poles around Moscow, no hope of national salvation could be based on these lawless adventurers. In this, the most critical period of Russian history, the nation was saved by the action of the clergy and of a few heroic individuals.

The Patriarch had been imprisoned by the Poles, but the celebrated Troitski Monastery at Serghievo, which had served as a refuge for the poor and the homeless during the long troubles, now became the centre of the national aspiration to drive out the foreigner and re-establish the power of Moscow ; letters were sent all over the country inciting the people to defend their faith and their country. When this patriotic missive was read to the people in the cathedral of Nijni Novgorod, a butcher, Minin, addressed his fellow-townsmen, exhorting them to sell their houses and pledge their families to obtain money for the holy war. The proposal was readily accepted, and when the people urged the necessity of an experienced commander, Minin suggested Prince Pojarski, who had been wounded in the battles around Moscow. The veteran accepted the command, and chose the patriotic butcher as his treasurer to collect the funds for the campaign.

These two men, fit representatives of the nobility and the people in the unanimous national struggle, diligently set to work to accomplish their difficult task. The early part of the year 1612 was taken up in collecting recruits and destroying the roving bands of Cossacks which kept the country in disorder. In August Pojarski approached Moscow, where the Poles had received reinforcements. At first the Cossacks refused to co-operate, but they yielded to the entreaties of a monk of the Troitski Monastery, and the Poles were defeated by the united Russian forces. A portion then retired to Poland, while the remaining garrison in the Kremlin was reduced by famine and obliged to surrender (November 27), and release the captive Russians, among whom was young Michael Romanoff. King Sigismund made an attempt to reconquer Moscow, but his insufficient forces were unable to advance, and he was forced to relinquish his purpose.

The failure of the union of the two great Slav states of Poland and Russia was mainly due to religious causes, and they appear very clearly in the action of the Troitski Monastery and in the energetic words of Minin. The conversion to the Greek faith by the Byzantine missionaries bore its fruits after 600 years, creating an impassable barrier between the two nations. From a Panslavistic point of view and in the narrow field of European history, this failure was regrettable, but it probably furthered the Asiatic mission of Russia. A premature union with Poland would have permanently engaged Russia in European politics, and drained her strength in struggles against the more powerful civilised nations of the West; remaining free, she has quietly expanded eastwards, while only desultorily engaged in the affairs of Europe.

After the expulsion of the Poles from Moscow it was decided, by the prompt election of a Tsar, to prevent the recurrence of foreign invasion and internal disorders. To avoid the irregularity and unpopularity of the preceding hasty elections, representatives from the clergy, towns, and principal classes of the population were invited to Moscow. It was decided to exclude all foreign candidates, and though this at first roused innumerable private ambitions, and created factions, at last all the votes gathered around one name, which was also shouted by the people assembled in the famous Red Square at Moscow—the name of Romanoff. The violence of their ambition had deprived the other great families of their popularity and chances to the throne : Godunoff and Shuiski had failed, while Philarete, the head of the Romanoffs, had been gradually advanced in the Church to the rank of Metropolitan by his successful rivals. The Romanoffs now obtained the throne due to their rank, and which they had not inordinately coveted, and on February 21, 1613, Michael, the young son of Philarete, was elected Tsar.

To justly appreciate the debt Russia owes to the Romanoff family, it is necessary to compare her present prominent position in the world with her desolate condition less than three centuries ago when the dynasty ascended the throne. The Swedes were at Novgorod, the Poles at Smolensk, Moscow had been burnt and only just recovered from the enemy, Cossacks and marauders ravaged the country ; the father of the Tsar, the Metropolitan Philarete, was still at the court of King Sigismund, whither he had been sent to persuade the Polish monarch to bestow his son Ladislaus as Tsar to the Russian nation. When, on March 14, 1613, the envoys from Moscow proceeded to offer the crown to Michael Romanoff, they found him in a monastery at Kostroma living with his mother, who had been compelled to become a nun when her husband was tonsured. Michael, who was then only sixteen, declined the offer, and was supported by his mother,[1] who strongly exposed the weakness of the royal authority and the dangers attending such a young sovereign. The envoys overcame these objections only

[1] She said to the envoys : ' My son is not of age, and the people of the Muscovite empire were cravens to the former sovereigns—Tsar Boris (Godunoff), the false Demetrius, and Vassil Shuiski. They swore allegiance and afterwards became traitors ; besides the Muscovite empire is entirely ruined, the treasures of the former Tsars are gone, the domains lost, the soldiers reduced to poverty, and how can the future Tsar pay his army, maintain his court, and resist his enemies ? Moreover, the Metropolitan Philarete is a prisoner of the Polish king, who, when he hears of the election of the son, will wreak revenge on the father.'

by the reflection that their persistent refusal would make
the Romanoffs responsible to God for the final ruin of the
Muscovite empire.

The youthful Romanoff received the blessing of his
mother and accepted the throne.   The coronation took
place on July 11, 1613, without the usual largesses to the
people, as there was no money in the treasury even to pay
the soldiers.   The new Tsar was reduced to such straits
in the first years of his reign that in 1617 he borrowed
7,000 roubles from the Shah of Persia, Abbas the
Great.   The Cossacks continued to revolt and had to be
subdued ; the Poles did not relinquish their pretensions
to the throne of Moscow, and war continued until
December 1, 1618, when the truce of Deulina was concluded, and the Metropolitan Philarete returned to Russia.
From this moment the state of the country began to
improve.   Philarete was appointed Patriarch and associated in the government, all public acts running in the
names of both father and son.   Philarete, who was a
wise experienced man, removed the favourites who had
usurped the authority of his young weak-minded son,
and by cultivating friendly relations with Sweden,
England, and Holland, favoured commerce and increased
the political influence of Russia.

When the King of Poland concluded the truce of
Deulina, he did not officially renounce his pretensions to
the throne of Russia, and the question was prudently left
in abeyance by the negotiators.   This latent claim gave
rise to much petty annoyance and offence, as the Polish
frontier authorities not only refused to give Michael
Romanoff his proper imperial title, but even wrote his
name with contemptuous brevity, which roused the wrath
of the Muscovites, who then were very punctilious about
official etiquette.   When Sigismund, King of Poland, died,

the Russians, who had been watching for a favourable opportunity, commenced war in the confused interregnum which always preceded the election of a new Polish king. At first the Russians carried everything before them; but when, after eight months, Ladislaus succeeded in obtaining his father's throne, he quickly altered the fortunes of war. He marched to the relief of Smolensk, and, by intercepting the retreat of the Muscovite besiegers, compelled them to submit to an ignominious capitulation. The unsuccessful siege of Bieloi and the advance of a Turkish army towards their frontier disposed the Poles to peace. It was concluded at Polianofka (May 17, 1634); and though the Russians had to give up some towns they had secured by the truce of Deulina, and to pay 20,000 roubles, they obtained from Ladislaus a renunciation of his claims, and recognition of Michael Romanoff as Tsar of Moscow.

The Cossacks living on the banks of the great rivers of Southern Russia never relaxed their efforts to cripple the power of the Turks. Their frontier raids and piratical attacks on Turkish ships in the Black Sea often brought Poland and Russia into difficulties with the Sultan, the Zaporoghians on the Dnieper being considered subjects of Poland and the Don Cossacks of Moscow. In the summer of 1634 the Don Cossacks stormed the fortress of Azof, and, besides destroying all the Mahometans, killed the ambassador of the Sultan, then on his way to Moscow. This violation of the law of nations involved Russia in great trouble, her frontier being ravaged by the Khan of Crimea by order of the Sultan. The Turks made great efforts to retake Azof, sending an army of 200,000 men, in the year 1641; but the Cossacks resisted heroically, repelling twenty-four assaults and obliging the enemy to raise the siege. The Osmanlis, however, were too powerful at that time for Moscow, and Tsar Michael ordered

the Cossacks to abandon Azof. The definite conquest of
this important town was not achieved even by Peter the
Great, and was reserved for the second half of the following century.

Michael Romanoff died on July 12, 1645, and was
succeeded by his son Alexis, who, like his father, in spite
of frequent wars, strove continually to improve the internal
conditions of the country. The most important event of
his reign was the protracted insurrection of Little Russia.
Poland, as we have seen, by the union with Lithuania,
had incorporated many provinces originally Russian, and
among the rest the ancient home of the race—Little
Russia. Difference of religion rendered the Polish domination irksome, and at times even tyrannical; while, on
the other hand, the insubordinate nature and violent
habits of the Cossacks, who formed a large part of the
population, rendered them disposed to rise against the
infidel foreigner. In 1647, Khmelnitzki, a Cossack captain
grievously injured by a Polish noble, having failed to
obtain redress from Ladislaus,[1] fled to the Zaporoghians,
and then to Crimea. From these crowded haunts of
adventurers he collected a large army and returned to
Little Russia. The defeat of the two Polish commanders
roused the suppressed hatred of the Russian peasants, who
everywhere attacked their Polish masters and destroyed
their castles. The revolt spread all over the Ukraine, and
King Ladislaus dying about the same time, Poland was
reduced to great straits. During the usual confused interregnum that followed, Khmelnitzki advanced into Poland
itself, levying contributions from towns in Galicia. The
election of John Casimir, brother of Ladislaus, restored

---

[1] The answer of the Polish king shows his appreciation of the lawless
state of the Ukraine—the wild border country on the frontiers of Russia,
Poland, and Turkey : ' You are warriors and wear sabres—prevent any one
disturbing you.'

the authority of the monarchy, and Khmelnitzki was summoned to return into the Ukraine and await the arrival of peace envoys. But hostile operations soon re-commenced, and the King of Poland was surrounded by a joint force of Cossack and Crimean Tartars, and reduced to a desperate state. John Casimir succeeded in detaching the Khan of Crimea by a large bribe and the promise of a yearly tribute, and then Khmelnitzki was also obliged to come to terms. He was granted a semi-independent position, with a registered force of 40,000 Cossacks. The royal army was forbidden to enter Cossack territory, where also no Jews or Jesuits were allowed to reside.

These favourable terms, so humiliating to the proud Polish nobility, were still insufficient for the Cossacks, now accustomed to the freedom and plunder of a successful war. After much squabbling about mutual non-fulfilment of the conditions of the treaty, a second revolt broke out, and Khmelnitzki again advanced with the Khan of Crimea, who once more abandoned the Cossacks at the critical moment. This defection caused a disastrous rout, and led to a new treaty with the Poles, much less favour-able to the Cossacks, whose registered army was reduced to 20,000 men.

The harder terms imposed by the Poles rendered the Little Russians still more averse to the foreign yoke, while experience had now taught them twice that they were not strong enough to shake it off single-handed. They naturally looked for assistance eastwards, where men of their race had founded an orthodox state which had absorbed all Great Russia. In 1653 negotiations commenced, and in the beginning of 1654 the Little Russians transferred their allegiance to Moscow on con-dition of preserving all their ancient rights, of keeping an army of 60,000 men, and of being allowed to elect their

Hetman, who could even receive embassies from all foreign countries except Poland and Turkey.

To support the Little Russians operating on the south-west, Alexis advanced against Poland from the east, while Sweden, seizing the favourable opportunity, attacked on the north. All these three invasions were successful, and Poland seemed threatened with destruction, when she was saved by dissension among her enemies. Sweden having tried to forestall Russia in her conquests, and having even attempted to intrigue with the Little Russians, Alexis was obliged to stop the war with Poland, and commenced a war with Sweden in 1656, which lasted until 1658. Poland, freed from the joint invasions of her enemies, gradually succeeded in recovering almost all her lost territory, while in Little Russia jealousy and quarrels among the Cossack chiefs, especially after the death of Khmelnitzki, weakened the national cause. Russia recommenced the war with Poland, but not with the same success, and in 1667 a treaty of peace was concluded at Andrusof. Though Alexis was obliged to renounce his claims to that part of Little Russia which lies on the right bank of the Dnieper, he acquired all the part on the left, and, by this first successful step, showed his successors the way to gradually reconquer the old country on the west.

At this important epoch in Russian history, when the first serious attempt at expansion on the west commenced, it will be interesting to glance at the contemporaneous events in the Far East. Khabaroff started on his first expedition to the Amur in 1649, when the first revolt in the Ukraine was at its highest; his first report of 1650, asking for 6,000 men to accomplish the conquest of the Amur, must have reached Moscow some time before Russia decided to interfere in favour of the Little Russians and wage war with Poland. The destruction of Stepanoff and his force, which ended the first Russian occupation of the Amur, took place in 1658, when a truce had just been concluded with Sweden and the second war with Poland was raging.

Alexis employed the rest of his reign in settling internal religious questions. His death in 1676 left the throne to three young sons ; the eldest, Theodore, was very sickly and reigned only six years; his death in 1682, without children, left the succession to the two young princes, John and Peter. The former was also very sickly, and the people, discouraged by the prospect of a rapid succession of weak sovereigns, clamoured to have Peter elected as Tsar, and though the younger he was consecrated by the Patriarch. This election was displeasing to his step-sister, Sophia, an energetic woman, who intrigued in favour of her own brother, John, and by means of a mutiny of the *strielets* she achieved her purpose—the maternal relations and partisans of Peter being either murdered or exiled. Then the two princes were elected joint sovereigns, and the real authority entrusted to Sophia as regent. It was after this period of palace intrigues and crimes, after a disastrous expedition against the Crimean Tartars, that the Government of Moscow undertook to interfere directly in the affairs of furthest Siberia and settle the Amur question with the Emperor of China.

The Siberian frontier authorities had entered into diplomatic relations with China some time before. In 1667 a Tunguse chieftain, Gantimur, subject to China, had emigrated and settled with his followers on Russian territory. As the Chinese authorities made persistent demands to have the exile delivered into their hands, the *voivode* of Nertchinsk, Arshinski, had sent to Peking in 1670 a Cossack embassy. The instructions given to these rude envoys treated the ' Son of Heaven ' in a very cavalier fashion, for he was to be invited to submit under the lofty hand of his Majesty the Tsar. If this frank proposal could have been communicated to the conceited Mandarins, it would have startled their quiet assumption of universal superiority.

The trouble caused by Tchernigofski, when he rebuilt Albazin, urged the authorities of Moscow to send an embassy, and in 1675 Spaphari was instructed to proceed to Peking and, besides other matters, to obtain free trade between the two countries. The Chinese answer was limited to three points: the delivery of Gantimur, the despatch of another envoy to settle their demands, and the inquiry whether the frontier Russians would live peacefully. The embassy was very long on its journey, as it left Moscow on February 25, 1675, reached Peking on May 15, 1676, and only returned on January 5, 1678.

The attacks of the Chinese on the Russian posts on the Amur alarmed the Government in Moscow, and the Tsars, John and Peter, sent two messengers, Veniukoff and Tkavoroff, to announce in Peking the early arrival of a special ambassador, Golovin, with powers to settle all frontier questions. They reached Peking on October 31, 1686, and left on November 14, with two despatches from the Chinese Emperor stating his grievances: the free-booting expeditions from Albazin, and the non-delivery of Gantimur. The Emperor declared that all offensive operations of the Chinese armies would be stopped pending the result of the negotiations with the coming pleni-potentiary, Golovin.

The despatch of the two messengers had been decided in view of the urgent military requirements on the Amur, and in anticipation of the length of time required by a numerous mission to traverse the enormous distance between Moscow and Peking. The plenipotentiary,

Golovin, besides a becoming suite, was accompanied by a body of over 500 Moscow *strielitz*, which was to be reinforced by 1,400 soldiers drawn from different Siberian towns. This large force was intended to impress the Chinese with an idea of the military power of Russia and to guard against surprises, but, as we shall see, it was insufficient.

The slow advance of this mission through the waste plains of Siberia, separated by vast distances from its points of departure and arrival, with intermittent instructions from the home Government, and scanty information from the seat of the war which it was sent to terminate, is very curious and throws much light on the treaty which followed.

The embassy left Moscow on January 26, 1686, and by September 28 it had only reached the Rybenski *ostrog* near the mouth of the upper Tunguska or Angara, where a halt had to be made for the winter. Here couriers brought the news of the end of the siege of Albazin and the withdrawal of the garrison to Nertchinsk.[1] On May 15, 1687, the advance was resumed by boats on the Angara to the Bratski *ostrog*, which was reached in July, and where news was received of the repulse of the Chinese at Albazin with a loss of 1,500 men.[2] In September 1687 Golovin reached the *ostrog* of Verkhne-Udinsk in Transbaikalia, and received new instructions from Moscow ordering him to require:

1. The frontier between the two empires to be the river Amur, or, in an extreme case, the river Zeya.

2. If it proved impossible to obtain the above frontier, to require permission to carry on trade in those regions.

3. If consent were refused to the above, to insist that

---

[1] This must have been the first siege of 1685.

[2] This must have referred to the beginning of the second siege of 1686.

the settlement of the business should be deferred to another time.

On October 25 Golovin left Verkhne-Udinsk, and approached the Chinese frontier, stopping at Selenghinsk, where he despatched a messenger to Peking. In the first act of his mission he unfortunately committed a mistake, which, readily seized upon by the Chinese, became irreparable, and bore its consequences up to the end of the negotiations. Besides informing the Chinese of his arrival, he proposed to treat about the selection of a place for the conference of the plenipotentiaries. The messenger returned in June 1688 with a despatch, choosing Selenghinsk for the seat of the conference ; the negotiators were to be guarded by a force of 500 men.

In July 1688 an official arrived from Moscow with the following fresh instructions :

1. To proceed at once to Albazin with great haste.

2. On arrival at that place, to interview the Chinese envoys, and to treat about the frontier, as instructed before.

3. If, by the persistent demands about the frontier and the freedom to trade on the Amur, it were impossible to agree, to renounce the claim of the Russians to free trade on the Amur.

4. If the Chinese envoys had already left for China, to write about the above to China.

5. To ask Kutukhtu to mediate and stop the trouble with the Chinese in the Daurian land.

When Golovin received these instructions he had returned to Verkhne-Udinsk, where he was met by a Chinese colonel, Kuluphunzillu, with a despatch from the Chinese plenipotentiaries, informing him that they had been prevented from advancing through Mongolia on account of an outbreak of hostilities between Kalmucks and Mongols. They proposed, as autumn was already near, to postpone their meeting to next summer. It was now the opportunity as well as the duty of Golovin to appoint Albazin as the future seat of the conference, but he contented himself with again leaving to the Chinese the choice of the place, and frittered away precious time by employing his armed escort in petty border warfare with the nomads. It is impossible to justify his inactivity and flagrant disobedience of the categorical orders from Moscow to proceed to Albazin.

Golovin, in January 1689, sent a messenger to Peking with a draft of a proposed frontier, but he only received the answer that the Bogdoi Khan had chosen Nertchinsk for the seat of the conference of the plenipotentiaries, who were to be guarded by an escort of 1,000 men. Golovin now hastened towards Nertchinsk, but on the way received the disagreeable news that the Chinese envoys had already reached the town on July 21, and that, under pretext of conveying their provisions, a large army [1] had also arrived, and had encamped in close vicinity to the town. Golovin now tardily recognised his fatal mistake in leaving the choice of place to the Chinese, and neglecting to proceed to Albazin. Instead of meeting the Chinese at that out-post, under the walls of the fortress which had just repulsed their attacks, he allowed them, under pretence of negotiations, to advance without opposition into the heart of the Russian territory, and encamp within sight of the provincial capital at Nertchinsk. The result of the negotiations was now clearly foreshadowed, especially as the Chinese plenipotentiaries had been instructed by the Emperor K‘ang-hsi : ‘In case of necessity, to corroborate their demands with arms, and to skilfully avail themselves of a suitable opportunity.’

The Chinese possessed, besides their military, also a

---

[1] Ten thousand men, according to Ragosa.

diplomatic superiority. Golovin, a man of weak will and understanding, was ignorant of the country with which he was treating, while the Chinese were assisted by two Jesuits, who, by their education in Europe and by the information derived from Polish prisoners and deserters on the Amur, must have had a clear knowledge of the condition of Russia. Another advantage was also scored in the choice of the language for the negotiations— the Latin. Though Golovin knew that tongue, and one of his suite is stated to have been a fluent speaker, they were probably far inferior to the Jesuits.

In the first sitting Golovin proposed as frontier the river Amur—the left bank to belong to Muscovy, and the right to China. The Chinese plenipotentiaries, on the other hand, proposed Lake Baikal or, according to a Chinese author,[1] even the river Lena, which they stated had belonged to Genghiz Khan. In the following sitting the Chinese consented to extend the frontier as far as Nertchinsk ; but when they found Golovin bent on exacting fresh concessions, they remembered the instructions of their sovereign, and threatened a siege, commencing to surround the town with their troops. Golovin was also privately informed by the Jesuits that the Emperor K'anghsi would never consent to relinquish the Amur, as he drew a rich tribute of furs from that region. At the same time news arrived that a body of nearly 3,000 Buriats, lately tributary to Russia, had deserted to the Chinese. In this critical situation Golovin had no choice but to accept the terms of the Chinese, and on August 27, 1689, the treaty of Nertchinsk was signed, which fixed as the frontier of the two empires the river Gorbitza, the line of mountains bounding on the north the basin of the Amur up to the river Uda, and the river Argun. After the sig-

[1] Quoted by the anonymous author of the *History of the Amur River*.

nature of the treaty Golovin issued orders to Beiton and the heroic garrison of Albazin to evacuate the place and abandon the Amur.

The events that compelled Golovin to yield could not have happened if he had followed his instructions, and chosen Albazin as the seat of the conference. The threats of a siege could then have been treated in a derisory manner, for where Beiton with a few hundred men had resisted successfully, the Chinese could not have entertained hopes when the garrison had been reinforced by the 2,000 men escorting Golovin. Even the desertion of the Buriats was probably caused by the advance of the Chinese army to Nertchinsk, which appeared as a military success to the tribesmen ignorant of the diplomatic incompetence of Golovin.

The treaty was inglorious and disadvantageous for Russia, as she not only gave up her best seaboard on the Pacific and the course of the Amur, indispensable for the development of the lands around the Baikal, but she abruptly stopped the eastern expansion, which had been going on steadily for two hundred years since she threw off the Tartar yoke. Russia weakly renounced the historic mission which had led her race for centuries from the banks of the Danube to found successively Little Russia on the Dnieper, Great Russia on the upper waters of the Volga and Don, and lately the Cossack settlements on the great rivers of Siberia up to the shores of the Pacific.

The treaty of Nertchinsk is remarkable as being the first concluded by China with a Western Power, and it is also the most glorious. In her successive relations with other nations, China has been obliged constantly to submit to disadvantageous conditions and suffer loss. Nertchinsk and Shimonoseki are the extreme terms of the series marking the gradual decline of the empire in the last two centuries.

A little over two weeks after the signature of the treaty of Nertchinsk, on September 12, 1689, Peter the Great assumed the government of the State, and his sister, the self-constituted regent Sophia, was relegated to a monastery. The chief amusement of the young Tsar had been boating on Lake Pereyaslav, the only navigation he could enjoy in his dominions. By the loss of the Amur and the territory around its mouth, Russia was deprived of access to an ice-free sea. Though the empire at that time was relatively not much inferior to its present extension, it only faced the sea on the Arctic Ocean and the Northern Pacific. The huge continental area, similar to the dominions of Genghiz Khan before his successors conquered China, was entirely deprived of outlets on the sea. The boyish enthusiasm of Peter the Great for shipping and navigation expressed the unconscious want of the whole nation. The pastimes of the boy prepared the work of the man, and the whole reign was employed in obtaining access to the neighbouring seas. The first campaign, the conquest of Azof, secured an outlet on the Black Sea; and though this was lost at the end of the reign, in consequence of the unsuccessful war with Turkey, Peter the Great had in the meanwhile, by his persevering struggle against Charles XII. in the great northern war, secured permanent access to the Baltic. To bind irrevocably the nation to the new policy, and prevent any relapse, he undertook the bold plan of transferring the capital to the shores of the newly conquered sea, on the Finnish frontier of Sweden. He thus also secured the permanence of his social reforms: the transformation of the half-Oriental state of Muscovy into the fully recognised European empire of Russia. To use the picturesque expression of Algarotti: 'he opened a window into Europe.'[1] By directing the activity of the nation to the sea and to commerce, and by establishing the capital at St. Petersburg, he returned to the early times of the monarchy, to those of Ruric, when the political centre of Russia was in the north, at the great commercial emporium of Novgorod. A man of extraordinary genius like Peter the Great must be judged by his peers, and his work is placed in its true light by Napoleon: 'People have not rightly understood the true genius of Peter the Great. They have not seen that he won for himself what is wanting to the greatest man born on a throne: the glory of the self-made man, and the trials which that glory requires.'

The work of Peter the Great was continued by his successors, and under Catherine II. Russia obtained the coast on the Black Sea with the Crimea (1783), and, through the last partition of Poland (1795), an extension of the Baltic littoral. Thus, in little over a century after the accession of Peter the Great, Russia had recovered possession of the sea-coast on the west and south. The maritime programme of the great sovereign had been carried out in Europe, and the time had come to resume the natural eastward expansion of the empire. Tradition avers that Peter the Great, in his unquestionable thirst for the sea, had directed his attention also to the Pacific, and, besides recognising the necessity of securing the mouths of the Neva and Don, had intended to conquer the mouth of the Amur; but the great wars in Europe prevented the execution of this vast plan. In the last year of his life he is reported to have expressed the wish to go to Siberia, and then further and further to the land of the Tunguses,

---

[1] 'Pétersbourg est la fenêtre par laquelle la Russie regarde en Europe.' Algarotti quoted by Pushkin.

and to the Great Wall of China.[1]   Catherine II., who had
carried out his views in Europe, also took up his plans in
the Far East, and sagaciously remarked : ' If the Amur
were useful only as a convenient way to supply our possessions in Kamchatka and on the sea of Okhotsk, its possession would be important.'[2]   But these plans received
no execution, and the action of the Russian Government
was confined to the conclusion of a series of conventions
regulating frontier questions and the overland trade through
Kiakhta.[3]

The French Revolution and the general war it produced in Europe diverted Russia from her true purpose.
Instead of profiting by the dissensions in the West to
prosecute her natural expansion in the East, she chose to
engage in the general crusade against France.   The
transfer of the seat of government to St. Petersburg, the
long wars with Western neighbours, had permanently
fixed the attention of Russian statesmen on Europe, and
they had forgotten the old traditional policy of Moscow.
Napoleon, with the keen insight of genius, had seen that
the true mission of Russia lay in the East.   He vainly
attempted to convince the Russians of the wrong course
they were pursuing.   For a moment he hoped to succeed
by securing the friendship of the Emperor Paul, a man in
advance of his times, who had even studied the question
of the emancipation of the serfs ; but the prejudices contracted during a century of interference in Western
politics, the blind adherence to views that had ·become
obsolete when the plans of Peter the Great had been
carried out, proved too powerful to be controlled, and the
Tsar was assassinated.

[1] Quoted from Ragosa.
[2] Also from Ragosa.
[3] Treaties of Buria and Kiakhta, 1727, 1728 ; supplementary articles in
1768 and International Act of 1792.

The new Tsar Alexander also for a time fell under the fascination of Napoleon; but he was young and vain-glorious, and preferred to parade his handsome person over the Continent as the saviour of Europe, and to earn the barren glory of destroying the greatest man of the century. He thus neglected the most favourable opportunity for the permanent aggrandisement of his country. By favouring the realisation of Napoleon's dream of the reconstruction of the empire of Charlemagne, he might not only have secured then the present Asiatic expansion of Russia, but also the heritage of the Byzantines, and have extended his empire to the shores of the Bosphorus. The Crimean War, the indifference of Prussia, and the covert hostility of Austria revealed half a century later the fatal mistake.[1]

Besides neglecting her true interests, Russia, by engaging deeply in European politics, remained subject to the influence of Western diplomacy: she bound herself to the principle of *statu quo* so dear to Metternich and his school, but unnatural and harmful to a young race irresistibly impelled to expansion. This pernicious doctrine corrupted the atmosphere of the Foreign Office, and became a plausible pretext for senseless inactivity and obstructiveness. While in this torpid state Russia was not disposed to take much interest in her distant possessions in Siberia, but a series of events gradually arose which recalled her unwilling attention.

In consequence of a conspiracy at the accession of Nicholas I. in 1825, many prominent members of the Russian aristocracy were exiled to Siberia, and remained there with their families until the death of the Tsar in 1855. The long residence of these intelligent, cultivated

---

[1] It is strange that Napoleon was destroyed by England and Russia, the two great colonising powers, whose interests, lying outside Europe, ought to have induced them to allow him a free hand on the Continent.

persons contributed to the development of the country by attracting the attention of the higher classes, while some of the exiles and their children were of great service later in the colonisation of the Amur. The gradually increasing importance of the Russian settlements in Kamchatka, the fur trade of the Russian-American Company in Alaska, the frequent appearance of whalers in the seas of Okhotsk and Behring, showed the necessity of finding a short convenient line of communications with the eastern extremity of the empire. Great labour had been spent in inproving the only route to Kamchatka—that by land from Yakutsk—but very little had been effected. The great natural difficulties presented by the steep transverse valleys leading down to the sea of Okhotsk had prevented the construction of anything better than paths, only accessible to pack-animals during a short period of the year. Even these rude paths it had been impossible to extend along the shore to Kamchatka, owing to the mountains and extensive wastes and *tundras*. The road being thus incomplete, the journey had to be prosecuted by sea, and this gave a momentary importance to the little town of Okhotsk, which was much frequented by shipping, though inconveniently situated near the mouths of shallow, difficult rivers.

The deplorable consequences of the treaty of Nertchinsk, which had reduced the Pacific coast of Siberia to the narrow strip of land confined between the Stanovoi chain and the sea of Okhotsk, now began to be felt, when the important settlements of Kamchatka were almost completely cut off from the rest of the empire. After a long interval of more than 150 years, the cession of the Amur was clearly recognised as an irreparable loss for Siberia, and Nicholas I. resumed the idea of its recovery laid aside by Peter the Great and Catherine II. The question was fraught with many difficulties. The geography of the coast was little known, even after the explorations of La Pérouse, Broughton, and Krusenstern. The island of Saghalien was supposed to be joined to the continent, precluding all access to the Amur from the south, while the river itself was stated to be unfit for navigation at the mouth. The Russian Foreign Minister at the time, Count Nesselrode, a humble and zealous follower of Metternich, either through indolence or ignorance, was averse to all expansion in the Far East, considering Siberia as a land only useful for the banishment of criminals, and fearing China as a formidable enemy. He employed all his obstructive resources to dissuade the Tsar from his purpose, but in vain. An expedition was fitted out in 1846 to explore the mouth of the Amur. Lieutenant Gavriloff was sent in command of the brig 'Grand Duke Constantine' with instructions to proceed in the strictest incognito as a foreigner, because it was reported that numbers of escaped convicts had settled around the mouth of the Amur. Gavriloff reached the estuary, and in a boat proceeded twelve miles up the river; but, through want of time and means, he soon returned, bringing back fragmentary and erroneous information. Count Nesselrode, in his report to the Emperor about Gavriloff's expedition, complacently wrote : 'The mouth of the river Amur has been found inaccessible to sea-going vessels, as its depth varies from one and a half to three feet, while Saghalien is a peninsula : therefore the Amur has no importance for Russia.'

With these words the Minister for Foreign Affairs confidently expected to bury the Amur question and to comfortably enjoy his routine work undisturbed by difficulties in distant unknown lands. But Tsar Nicholas was gifted with an iron will which seldom relaxed its hold from the plans it had once taken up. The superficial, perfunctory nature of Gavriloff's explorations was so apparent that it was insufficient for hastily deciding such an important question : the report required to be supplemented and confirmed by fresh information. At the same time, events in the Far East drew the attention of the Russian Government in that quarter. For over a century and a half, Russia was the only European nation which had concluded international engagements with China : she had secured later even the official permission to trade overland. Though the profits were not extraordinary and were purchased at the cost of some humiliation, the treaties constituted a monopoly which the imagination, aided by distance, supposed might lead to great future benefits. This privileged position of Russia came to an end when, by the first China war, Great Britain obtained the opening of five ports and the legal right for her merchants to trade. The activity of England in the Pacific stimulated the Russian Government to advance in the north, especially as exaggerated suspicions circulated about probable British conquests in the Far East. The Russians had always coveted the Amur, and by a natural aberration of judgment they supposed that others were equally eager to acquire possession of the region ; they were now in constant dread of being forestalled by England, whose occupation of the mouth of the Amur would destroy for ever the prospects of Siberia and permanently arrest the eastern expansion on the Pacific.

A series of circumstances were thus working together about the middle of the present century to push Russia towards the Amur. A superior man was only wanted to grasp the complicated factors of the situation and skilfully direct them to the accomplishment of the work of Yermak, of that eastern expansion which had been suspended for 160 years. Tsar Nicholas took care to find the right man at the proper moment.

CHAPTER V

THE ANNEXATION OF THE AMUR REGION

On September 6, 1847, Tsar Nicholas passed through Tula in the night, and ordered the Governor, General Muravioff, to meet him at the neighbouring station of Sergiefska. In the interview, which took place at seven o'clock in the morning, the Emperor informed the young Governor that he had been appointed Governor-General of Eastern Siberia. He must proceed quickly to St. Petersburg to study the principal Siberian questions: the development of the production of gold, the correction of abuses, the Kiakhta trade relations with China and the Amur region. Nicholas added that the last question would be discussed more fully later.

The nomination of Muravioff, which had been known a few days before, caused great sensation in Russian official circles. The new Governor-General was only thirty-eight years of age, and had been raised to the governorship of Tula the preceding year; his distinguished services in the Turkish war and in the Caucasus were forgotten by his detractors. The choice had been made by the Emperor himself, who appreciated the administrative abilities of Muravioff, and wanted as Governor-General of Eastern Siberia a firm, energetic man. Muravioff, as we shall see, fully justified the Emperor's expectations. Siberia never had a better official; his untiring energy and rapidity in the despatch of business never slackened amid the torpid influences by which he was surrounded. During his tenure of office the principal questions affecting the region received their solution, and his far-seeing intellect foresaw future difficulties, and indicated the measures required for their removal.

By the end of September Muravioff was already in St. Petersburg, and with his usual alertness began studying the questions relating to his new office. He at once recognised that to secure the use of the water-way of the Amur, indispensable for the future development of Eastern Siberia, it was necessary to hold not only the sources of the river, but also the territory adjacent to its mouth. This object could only be effected by the co-operation of the navy; his own task being confined to strengthening the position on the upper course of the river.

At the capital he became acquainted with Captain Nevelskoy, who, at the end of 1847, had been appointed commander of the brig 'Baikal,' destined for service on the coasts of Kamchatka and in the Okhotsk sea, and was awaiting the launch of his vessel then in construction at Helsingfors. Muravioff expressed his opinion about the necessity of a more thorough exploration of the mouth of the Amur, and converted the enterprising naval officer to his views. Nevelskoy became his zealous cooperator, and contributed most effectively to the execution of his plans.

The territory to be governed by Muravioff stretched from the Yenissei to Behring Straits. This enormous tract of the continent had been deprived by the treaty of Nertchinsk of the only easy means of communications between its south-eastern and north-eastern extremities— Transbaikalia and Kamchatka. Therefore, when Muravioff was granted a farewell audience on January 8, 1848, Tsar Nicholas remarked that probably he would be unable to visit Kamchatka owing to the difficulties of the voyage and the loss of time it entailed. To point out the distance he added: 'Thus, if they take Kamchatka, you will only know it half a year later.' The young Governor-General modestly answered that he would try to visit the peninsula. The promise was kept, and had important results for Russia.

Muravioff left for his provincial capital, Irkutsk, at the beginning of 1848; Nevelskoy sailed from Cronstadt on August 21, 1848; their next meeting was at the other end of the continent in the following year. Important work was done by both during that interval.

Shortly after his arrival at Irkutsk, Muravioff was asked by the Naval Ministry to give his opinion about a new port which it was intended to establish in the bay of Tugur at the southern extremity of the sea of Okhotsk. This projected port, Constantinofsk, was to take the place of Okhotsk, found to be unserviceable both on account of being ice-bound the greater part of the year, and surrounded by dangerous sand-banks. It was also proposed to connect this new port by a land route with Transbaikalia. Muravioff showed the impracticability of the land route, and suggested that Nevelskoy should explore the coast from Tugur bay to the mouth of the Amur in search of a more suitable port. On January 20, 1849, the Tsar appointed a special committee to study the Amur question, and on February 8 he confirmed its proposal to send a maritime expedition to explore the mouth of the river. Nevelskoy, who would reach Kamchatka in a few months, was appointed to command the expedition, and Muravioff was ordered to communicate to him these instructions. As the winter post from Okhotsk to Petropavlofsk, the port of Kamchatka, had already left (there was only one in the season), Muravioff sent Staff-Captain Korsakoff to Okhotsk to wait for the opening of that port, and bear the instructions to Nevelskoy at Petropavlofsk. Korsakoff, however, was detained by the ice in Okhotsk until June, when, knowing that Nevelskoy must have already left Petropavlofsk, he sailed for the north coast of Saghalien, and cruised about in the hopes of intercepting Nevelskoy and his transport 'Baikal.' The search was fruitless, and Korsakoff was obliged to return to Ayan with the instructions undelivered.

Muravioff, in over a year's residence at Irkutsk, had acquired clearer views of the growing importance of the Pacific Ocean, due to the naval activity of England. Though at such a distance inland, by the decline of the overland trade through Kiakhta, he was able to measure the effects of the opening of China to maritime commerce. He therefore hastened to fulfil his promise to the Tsar to visit Kamchatka and its port, Petropavlofsk, the only possible Russian naval base on the Eastern Ocean. No governor-general had ever visited the distant peninsula, as the voyage was long, difficult, and supposed to lead to no useful results. Muravioff thought otherwise; the frequent visits of whalers on the coast had given the place a certain commercial importance, and he foresaw that, in the event of war, Russia must have a safe port on the Pacific.

Muravioff left Irkutsk on May 15, 1849, and reached Okhotsk on June 25, whence he sailed on July 4, arriving at Petropavlosk on July 25, after two months and ten days. He was charmed at the sight of the bay of Avacha, where Petropavlofsk is situated. This beautiful bay, which is said [1] to surpass in beauty and grandeur the celebrated harbours of Rio Janeiro and Sydney, with its numerous inlets protected on the north, west, and south

[1] **Dr. Guillemard.**

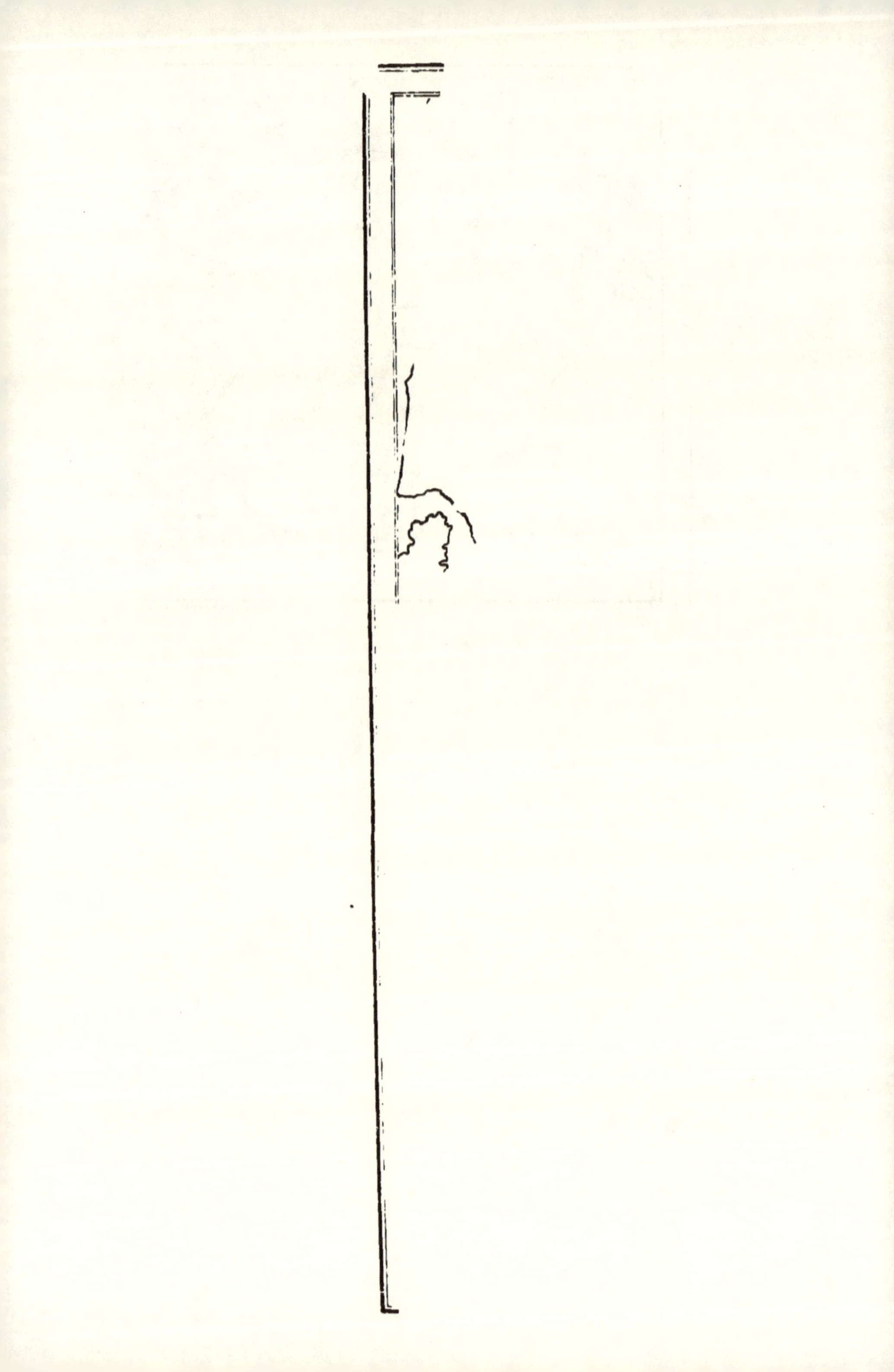

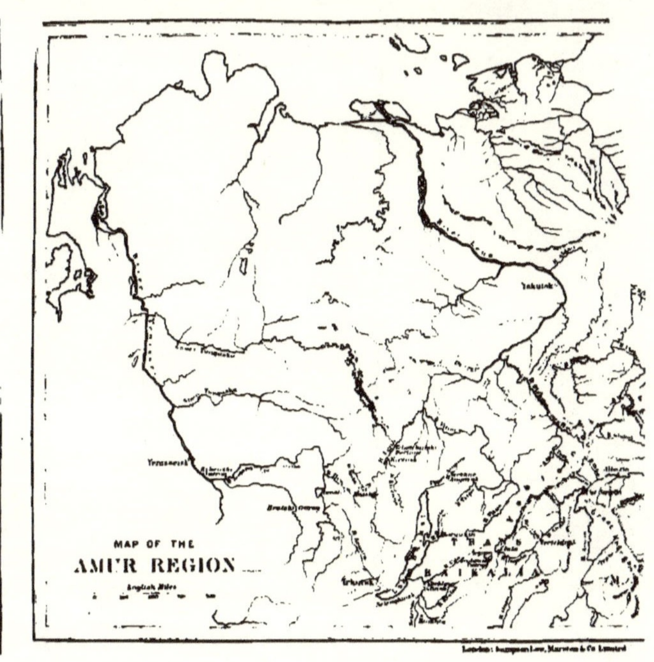

MAP OF THE
AMUR REGION
English Miles
London: Sampson Low, Marston & Co. Limited

by high volcanic mountains, with depth of water sufficient to allow vessels to unload on the quays, offered such advantages that Muravioff decided to transfer from Okhotsk the seat of the Russian naval forces on the Pacific. His enthusiasm is shown in his letters, where he declares that among the many ports he had seen in Europe and Russia none was comparable to the bay of Avacha.

He was there in the most favourable season, during that short summer when, if the weather be fine, the Siberian ports look so beautiful with their smiling sea, that one readily overlooks the long winter months and the frozen coast. Muravioff only a few weeks before had personally verified the irreparable defects of Okhotsk, and expressed his views by the forcible remark that he wondered the place had not ceased to exist a century before. At Petropavlofsk he fancied he had found the suitable place for establishing Russian naval power in the Pacific, and he resolved it should be the principal military port.

With his usual activity he projected a grand plan of fortifications, defended by 300 heavy guns to render the place impregnable to any attack from the sea. His practical mind was not led away by the visions of the future to overlook the modest possibilities of the present. He personally inspected the defences of the place, and found them to be of the most insignificant character; ten guns of small calibre, 200 Cossacks, and 500 sailors was the whole force ready to repel any sudden attack from the sea. Muravioff at once indicated to the commander of the garrison the best sites for the batteries, which could be erected in a short time, and pictured to himself so vividly the possible attacks of the enemy and the contingencies of the defence that, on choosing the site for battery No. 6 (called the lake battery),[1] he said: 'In case the enemy lands, when he comes round Mount Nicholski you can welcome him with grape-shot from this place.'

In his visit Muravioff received false impressions and committed the mistake, perhaps the only noticeable one in his life, of choosing Petropavlofsk as the future great military port of Russia on the Pacific. Time and the opportunity to choose on the coast south of the Amur showed the justness of the view of Nevelskoy, who wished for a port in a lower latitude. But his diligent observation and keen foresight saved Russia from a naval disaster, and perhaps worse, during the military operations on the Pacific in 1854.

Muravioff left Petropavlofsk on August 2, but instead of returning to Okhotsk he proceeded to the north of the island of Saghalien, hoping to find there Nevelskoy, who had sailed from Petropavlofsk in that direction since May 30. After a fruitless cruise he proceeded to the island of Shantar, and thence to Ayan on August 22, as he wished to inspect that port and the road connecting it with the interior. No news was heard about Nevelskoy in Ayan, and Karsakoff reported his unsuccessful attempt to deliver the instructions. Serious apprehensions were now entertained about the safety of the 'Baikal,' and it was feared she had been lost either on the way from Petropavlofsk or on the sand-banks reported to exist in the estuary of the Amur. At last, on the morning of September 3, the 'Baikal' appeared in the bay of Ayan. Muravioff could not restrain his impatience, and went to meet the vessel in a boat; he was hailed by Nevelskoy through a speaking-trumpet with the follow-

[1] It played, as we shall see, an important part five years later, during the attack of 1854.

ing words : 'God has assisted us . . . the main question is happily solved. . . . Saghalien is an island, and sea-going ships can penetrate into the estuary of the Amur both from north and south. An ancient error is completely dissipated. I now report to you that the truth has been discovered.'

Nevelskoy had left Cronstadt on August 21, 1848, and after a navigation of eight months and twenty-three days he reached Petropavlofsk on May 12, 1849, three days before Muravioff's departure from Irkutsk for Kamchatka. He found no instructions, but only a letter from Muravioff explaining the probable explorations to be undertaken around the mouth of the Amur, and stating that official instructions would follow quickly. Nevelskoy boldly decided not to lose precious time, and to proceed on his own responsibility. Having discharged all his stores by May 30, he sailed for the north of Saghalien and thence towards the Amur. After difficult navigation through shoals and sand-banks, being often obliged to anchor and send boats to sound for a navigable channel, he reached the gulf of the Amur on June 28. Here the 'Baikal' anchored, and boats were sent to explore the coasts of Saghalien and of the continent; the mouth of the Amur was discovered, and the river navigated for some distance. Then Nevelskoy decided to steer south, and continue his explorations between the continent and Saghalien.

This island extends for nearly ten degrees of latitude almost in a straight line along the meridian, forming with the curve of the continent two gulfs connected by narrow straits, where the Asiatic coast protrudes towards the island. This channel is only about four miles broad, and so difficult to discern by navigators coming from the broader waters of the bell-mouthed gulfs on the north and south, that all the maritime explorers who visited the coast at the end of the last and beginning of the present century—La Pérouse, Broughton, Krusenstern—imagined at this point a narrow isthmus separating the two gulfs and connecting Saghalien with the continent. Nevelskoy, steering south from the Amur, found instead of this isthmus a channel with thirty-five feet of water, and proceeding further south reached the parallel where Broughton in the last century had terminated his explorations, stopped by the imaginary isthmus. Having thus connected the results of his explorations with those of his predecessors, Nevelskoy recognised the insular position of Saghalien and returned north with his boat to the 'Baikal,' which had remained at anchor during the thirty days employed in making this important discovery. He then proceeded, as we have seen, to Ayan to meet Muravioff.

The geographical discoveries of Nevelskoy also brought practical results. As long as Saghalien was considered a peninsula, the Amur was accessible to sea-going vessels only from the north through the sea of Okhotsk, where the inclement winter keeps the coasts ice-bound for many months; the mouth of the Amur was therefore almost in the same conditions as the other ports of that sea, Okhotsk and Ayan. Now it was known that vessels drawing fifteen feet of water could proceed from the gulf of Tartary, where the sea is never frozen.

While Muravioff and Nevelskoy were undertaking long laborious voyages and collecting valuable information under the bureaucratic influence of Nesselrode and his school, a fantastic expedition was being organised at St. Petersburg. Some years before, in 1844–45, the academician Middendorf had made a scientific voyage on the Amur, and had seen in the country around the river Uda four posts, which he imagined had been erected by the Chinese to mark the frontier. These posts were the subject of much discussion, as it was alleged they did not correspond to the frontier fixed by the treaties. On this vague information it was decided in St. Petersburg, towards the end of 1848, to send an expedition by land to explore the whole frontier from the river Gorbitza to the sea of Okhotsk, and to especially verify the frontier posts between the river Uda and the sea. The matter was kept secret from Muravioff, and in February 1849 the authorisation of the Tsar was obtained for the despatch of this expedition. It was commanded by Lieutenant-Colonel Akhte, who was stringently ordered to avoid all collision with the Chinese and keep away from the Amur.

When, therefore, Muravioff returned to Irkutsk on November 20, 1849, he found Lieutenant-Colonel Akhte preparing for his expedition. He tried to persuade him to extend his explorations to the Amur and its estuary, but Akhte declined to depart from his instructions. The clear practical mind of Muravioff could not perceive the object of seeking for a frontier where it had never been marked by the treaties. This expedition was only the commencement of a long series of difficulties put forward by Nesselrode, and served as a pretext for a foolish despatch to the Chinese Government, which almost ruined the able plans of Muravioff. As we shall see later, on every occasion the occupation of the Amur was the result of a struggle between Muravioff and Nesselrode, rather than of negotiations between Russia and China. The worst enemies of Muravioff were not at Peking but at St. Petersburg.

The active Governor-General of Eastern Siberia was indefatigable in combating the opposition of his enemies and in arousing the attention of the Russian Government to the importance of the Far East. He had also influential friends in St. Petersburg—the Grand Duke Constantine and Perofski, the Home Minister—and in his correspondence with them he constantly pointed out the questions of the future. From Irkutsk, almost in the centre of Asia, his thoughts were directed down the Amur to the Pacific Ocean, which he perceived was destined to play a great part in the coming history of the world. Besides the immediate questions affecting Siberia, the growth of English influence in China, and the consequent development of maritime trade to the detriment of the overland trade of Kiakhta, he considered the whole colonial expansion of Russia. He referred to the early Russian settlements on the Californian coast, and their abandonment without any compensation.

By his perseverance he obtained the imperial approval for two measures—the transfer of the military port from Okhotsk to Petropavlofsk, with the creation of a Siberian flotilla, and the establishment of winter quarters at a place indicated by Nevelskoy in the gulf of Shtchastia to the north of the Amur.

In obedience to the latter orders, Nevelskoy sailed with the 'Baikal' to the bay of Shtchastia and founded the winter station of Petrofskoe[1] on June 29, 1850. This was the first Russian settlement near the mouth of the Amur, and it was established with the goodwill and satisfaction of the native Ghiliacks.[2] The place was, however, unfit for harbouring ships, because, like Okhotsk, Ayan, and other ports of the sea of Okhotsk, it was ice-

---

[1] This place was afterwards abandoned, and no traces of its existence are now visible (Ragosa).

[2] These poor savages received much bureaucratic attention at St. Petersburg, a special Ghiliack committee being created in their honour. Some years before, the academician, Middendorf, who was supposed to know their language, was almost sent to them on a *diplomatic* mission.

bound until June. Nevelskoy therefore decided on a bolder step than he had taken the preceding year, when he had acted in advance of his instructions, exploring the mouth of the Amur and the Saghalien coast. He now acted without instructions, and on his own responsibility. With a sloop, six armed sailors, and a one-pounder, he proceeded up the forbidden Amur itself, and at twenty-five versts from the mouth established a post, which, in honour of the Emperor, he called Nikolaiefsk. Here, on August 6, in presence of the Ghiliack natives, the Russian military flag was hoisted, and saluted by the one-pounder and rifles of the small party. It was the beginning of the occupation of the Amur, and Nevelskoy, leaving five men to guard the first Russian post on the long-coveted river, hastened to report personally to Muravioff.

On his arrival at Irkutsk, Nevelskoy met Korsakoff, who had just returned from Kamchatka, where he had superintended the transfer of the military post from Okhotsk. Both officers found instructions to follow Muravioff, who had left for St. Petersburg.

Muravioff always preferred to meet his adversaries, as he found their opposition most formidable when he was 4,000 miles away in the heart of Siberia. His arrival at St. Petersburg in November 1850 was most opportune. The creation of the post of Nikolaiefsk at the mouth of the Amur was severely criticised by Nesselrode and his party, who insisted that Nevelskoy should be severely punished for his arbitrary conduct. The question of the occupation of the mouth of the Amur was referred to the Ghiliack committee. This had been carefully formed with a strong majority of Nesselrode's partisans, who, it was hoped, would overpower all the efforts of Muravioff. also appointed on the committee. Nesselrode, who was the president, strongly opposed the occupation of the

mouth of the Amur, and expressed the opinion that the bay
of Shtchastia was sufficient as long as the river itself was
free. He decided that all settlements among the Ghiliacks
were dangerous and premature, and that the solemn foundation of Nikolaiefsk was sure to attract the attention of
the Chinese, and lead them to send a strong force. The
consequent destruction of the post, and insult to the
national flag, would diminish the prestige of Russia in the
eyes of the Ghiliacks. He advised an immediate withdrawal, without awaiting the complaints of the Chinese,
thus avoiding 'extreme danger.' Muravioff strongly
opposed these views, but found little support among the
members of the committee, one of whom, Tchernysheff,
the Minister of War, went so far as to reproach him
with ' the desire of building for himself a monument.' [1]

In the course of a few days the minutes of the discussion held by the committee were sent round for the
signature of the members present. The messenger had
instructions from Nesselrode to tell Muravioff to sign the
minutes and return them at once. Muravioff's vigilance
rarely slumbered, and on carefully perusing the minutes
he found, at the end of Nesselrode's speech advocating the
retreat from the mouth of the Amur, and showing the
dangers of collision with the Manchus, the following
words : 'Governor-General Muravioff, present at the
meeting, agreed with these views.' Muravioff offered the
messenger a tumbler [2] of tea, and, while he was drinking,
wrote a few short but energetic phrases, expressing his
decided disagreement with the contents of the minutes.

The action of Muravioff caused much discontent, and
Tchernysheff expressed his displeasure to him ; but the

---

[1] These words had a prophetic meaning which escaped the narrow-
minded Minister (*Life of Muravioff*).

[2] In Russia tea is generally taken in tumblers, and very hot.

minutes with the important additions had to be presented to the Emperor Nicholas. Nesselrode had hoped, with his diplomatic ruse, to outwit Muravioff, whom he probably considered an impetuous, hot-headed soldier ; but the mean trick, having been coolly detected and trenchantly exposed, produced an opposite effect. Nesselrode was removed from the presidency, which was given to the Tsesarievitch (afterwards Emperor Alexander II.), who, after an interview with Muravioff, convoked again, on January 19, 1851, the Ghiliack committee. Notwithstanding the renewed opposition of Nesselrode and his party, the Emperor Nicholas, after reading the discussion, ordered that the post of Nikolaiefsk should be maintained, and even guarded by a vessel during the summer months.

It was, however, to be considered as belonging to the Russian-American Company. On this occasion the Tsar pronounced the memorable words : ' Where the Russian flag has once been hoisted it must not be lowered,' which are remembered and often quoted by the Russians on the Pacific to this day.

The Chinese Government was to be informed at the same time that a post on the Amur had been established by the Russian-American Company, and that a cruiser was attached to prevent any encroachments of foreign powers and warn their men-of-war that all such proceedings must be authorised by Russia and China.

Muravioff had won his first battle, and secured the first footing on his beloved Amur. With his usual perseverance he determined to push his success further, and obtain the approval of another measure indispensable for the execution of the plans he prepared for the future. Being always possessed by the thought of the future occupation of the Amur, whenever favourable opportunities put an end to the wavering uncertainty of the Russian

Government, he perceived, like Khabaroff 200 years before, that the enterprise could not be carried out without a large military force. When he arrived in Siberia in 1848 he was struck by the insufficiency of the forces at his disposal. Over the immense territory of Eastern Siberia there were only four battalions of the line, without any field artillery. He now proposed a considerable increase of the military forces in his province. He met, as he had expected, the most determined opposition. Nesselrode brought forth his usual bugbear of China, and represented that any increase in the frontier army would alarm the Chinese. There were also more serious objections, on account of the state of Russian finances, which then did not allow any heavy charges for such an object. The resourceful mind of Muravioff succeeded in overcoming all these difficulties. He showed that the Chinese were accustomed to the sight of Russian officers and soldiers, and paid no attention to their numbers; that if Russia became stronger in the East she might even act as the protector of China,[1] and he suggested an adroit plan by which his forces would be greatly increased without drawing soldiers from Europe.

His plan consisted in converting the peasants registered at Nertchinsk into Cossacks. Those unfortunate peasants were subject to a kind of *corvée* for the working of the mines at Nertchinsk. The work was very hard; they were insufficiently remunerated, especially as they had to provide their own carts, wood, and coal; moreover, they had no means to free either themselves or their children from this endless bondage. In this last respect they were in far worse conditions than the convicts, whose maximum period of work at the mines was for twenty-

---

[1] Muravioff may therefore be considered as the originator of the recent Russian policy in the Far East.

five years, after which term they and their descendants were no longer liable to be called. This unjust treatment of the Nertchinsk peasants, which had no parallel in the whole empire, Muravioff was determined to abolish, though at the same time he intended that the reform should further the accomplishment of the plans he secretly cherished.

His scheme for the reorganisation of his army divided it into the following divisions :—

1. All the frontier Cossacks.

2. The Cossack regiment of the Transbaikalian towns.

3. All the native regiments—Tunguses and Buriats.

4. All the village Cossacks of Transbaikalia.

5. All the peasants of the mines in the Nertchinsk district.

The first four divisions, which already existed, were to form the cavalry of his force; the fifth, which constituted the projected increase, was to form the infantry. Out of a population of 29,000 males he intended to form twelve battalions (each 1,000 strong) of Cossack infantry.

The plan was so logical, removing a great injustice while increasing the frontier forces, that on April 27, 1851, Emperor Nicholas approved the conversion of the peasants into Cossacks. Later, on June 27, orders to that effect were issued, and the infantry battalions of the Transbaikalian army were created.

After nearly eight months' residence in St. Petersburg, spent in assiduous work at the different Ministries to obtain the full adoption of his measures, Muravioff returned to Irkutsk on August 12, 1851. Shortly afterwards, impelled by his constant desire of personal inspection, he proceeded to Transbaikalia to watch the arrangements for the conversion into Cossacks of the peasants registered at Nertchinsk. He had thus the pleasure of verifying the beneficent effects of his reform, and of witnessing the joy of the peasants at last freed from their ancient bondage.

Nevelskoy, who had so narrowly escaped degradation for his patriotic boldness, had returned to the Far East before Muravioff, with instructions to organise another expedition on the Amur. As soon as navigation was opened, he started from Okhotsk with his now renowned 'Baikal,' and the Russian-American Company's vessel, 'Shelekhof.' The latter leaked, and was only saved by running on a sand-bank in sight of Petrofskoe, while the 'Baikal' itself ran aground at the entrance of the bay. These slight disasters entailed a considerable loss of time, owing to the scanty crews at his disposal. Nevelskoy, even when reinforced by the people on shore (there were only three huts), and by the crew of the broken-down transport, 'Okhotsk,' had only fifty men under his command to unload the leaking vessel.

On August 5, 1851, Nevelskoy started with Lieutenant Boshniack and twenty-five men, in boats, for the mouth of the Amur. On August 9 he reached the post he had established the preceding year, and proceeded to choose the definite site for the town of Nikolaiefsk. He appointed Lieutenant Boshniack in command, and gave him twenty-five men, including the original small garrison. The Russians had much difficulty in obtaining provisions, being obliged to apply to the neighbouring Ghiliacks. They, however, lost no time in preparing for the long severe winter, and built the national bath-house, which is such an indispensable part of the Russian village.

The appearance of the Russians at the mouth of the Amur, and their activity during the last two years, had not roused the suspicion of either the Chinese or the natives, and the nice distinction drawn between the

Russian-American Company and the Government by the committee at St. Petersburg when it authorised the establishment of Nikolaiefsk had entirely escaped their notice. Friendly relations with the Chinese rather increased during the period.

The rigorous winter in the desolate, sparsely inhabited region did not prevent the Russians from continuing their explorations, and emulating the exploits of their ancestors on the Arctic Ocean two centuries before. In February 1852 Nevelskoy despatched by sledge Lieutenant Boshniack with a Ghiliack guide to explore Saghalien, ordering him to cross the island, as reports affirmed the existence of a good haven on the eastern coast of the sea of Okhotsk. Boshniack proceeded to Cape Lazareff,[1] and crossed the gulf of Tartary at its narrowest point.[2] Despite the exhaustion of his dogs and the scarcity of provisions, he traversed the island, meeting the river Tymi, which he explored down to its mouth. Suffering from ulcers in the legs, cold, and frost-bitten, with the dogs unable to run through want of food, the return voyage was most trying. Some fish, purchased from a Ghiliack, enabled him to reach Nikolaiefsk on April 3, 1852. Shortly after his return, on April 18, 1852, Nevelskoy sent an expedition up the Amur, which explored the river for some months.

From the information obtained by these expeditions on the coasts of the gulf of Tartary, and on the Amur, Nevelskoy reported the necessity of occupying the bay of De Castries, and of establishing a post on Lake Kizi. The Amur, in its great sweep to the north, when it

---

[1] When Nevelskoy discovered the insular character of Saghalien, he named the opposite capes, at the narrowest point, Lazareff and Muravioff.

[2] As we have seen here, the sea is only seven versts, or a little over four miles, broad, so that the channel long remained undetected, and was considered a bay limited by an isthmus.

passes the 51st parallel, begins to approach the shores of the gulf of Tartary, which also curve inwards about the same point. The proximity to the sea, maintained for the remainder of its course up to its mouth, is increased about 51° 30′ N. lat. by the fact that an eastern branch of the river forms a spacious lake (Lake Kizi), which extends almost to the shores of the gulf of Tartary. A narrow mountain-chain alone separates the waters of the lake from those of the gulf.[1]   At this point the gulf of Tartary forms the bay of De Castries, five miles broad, with an area of over twenty square miles. Its peculiar situation, close to the Lake Kizi, which communicates with the Amur, and forms part of that river system, gives the bay great importance; in fact, it may be considered as constituting strategically a second mouth of the Amur. Nevelskoy at once recognised, when these facts had been reported by the different expeditions, that an enemy in possession of the bay of De Castries could command the whole lower course of the Amur. To forestall this danger he proposed that this important point should be immediately occupied by Russia.

Nevelskoy feared his proposal would meet with opposition and procrastination at St. Petersburg, and as he had acted successfully on his own responsibility already on two occasions, he determined to follow the same course. In the summer of 1852 he therefore intrusted Lieutenant Boshniack to build winter quarters at De Castries. This was promptly done, and Boshniack, having wintered in the important bay, on March 4 of the following year, 1853, established there the post of Alexandrofsk. On the same day an employé of the Russian-American Company founded the post of Mariinsk, near Lake Kizi, thus

---

[1] It has even been proposed, by cutting the mountains or piercing a tunnel, to give the river a nearer access to the sea.

completing the occupation of the important natural line of communications between the Amur and the gulf of Tartary.

Boshniack continued his explorations of the coast, and, starting on May 2 with only three men in a Ghiliack boat, steered southwards until on May 23, in 49° N. lat., he discovered a fine bay, which he named Emperor Nicholas I. bay, in honour of the Tsar, and which now is more briefly designated as Imperatorski bay. Recognising the importance of this fine harbour, situated on the south route to the Corean frontier, he explored all the inlets and gave them names. From the natives he collected information about another large bay, twelve days to the south, with sheltered harbours at the entrance, and another bay still further south ; they also added that a large river in the vicinity led up to the watershed of the Ussuri. All this probably referred to the gulf of Peter the Great near Vladivostok, but Boshniack could not verify the reports of the natives, being obliged, from scarcity of provisions, to return to De Castries, whence he reported all his discoveries to Nevelskoy.

Shortly after the return of this expedition, on July 12, 1853, the 'Baikal' from Ayan arrived at Petrofskoe, bringing despatches from Muravioff, informing Nevelskoy that the Emperor had sanctioned the occupation of De Castries, Kizi, and the island of Saghalien. The first part of these instructions had already been carried out; it was therefore only necessary to attend to Saghalien.

The annexation of this island was necessary for the defence of the mouth of the Amur, as its possession by a European nation would have exposed to attack the passages both from the north through the sea of Okhotsk, and from the south through the gulf of Tartary. The Russian-American Company was appointed to effect the occupation, receiving for the purpose an adequate sum from the Government. Nevelskoy was ordered to survey the coast, and choose convenient places for occupation.

Nevelskoy, from Petrofskoe, sailed for the northern extremity of Saghalien, coasted the whole eastern side of the island, and then, having reached its southern extremity, passed through the straits of La Pérouse. He again sailed northwards into the gulf of Tartary, along the western coast of Saghalien, and found a suitable place at the mouth of the river Kusunai, where the island shrinks to its narrowest point. Here, on July 21, he established the post of Ilinsk with a garrison of six men. Crossing over to the opposite shores of the gulf of Tartary, he visited the places on the mainland lately occupied by Boshniack. At Imperatorski bay he founded the post of Constantinofsk, and hoisted the Russian military flag on August 1. Sailing northwards, he reached De Castries on August 5, founded the post of Alexandrofsk, and also hoisted the military flag. The same formal occupation was carried out at Mariinsk on August 7.

These occupations were a consequence of the explorations which had revealed to the Russians the importance of the coast south of the mouth of the Amur. We have already seen that the lower course of this river, when it turns northwards, runs almost parallel to the sea. This peculiar configuration of the country, bounded on the west by the river and on the east by the sea, is continued southwards by the course of the Ussuri. This important affluent of the Amur flows almost due north, also parallel to the sea, cutting off a broad band of territory, which is also bounded on the west by Lake Khanka and the river Sui-phun further south. This territory, which now forms part of the maritime province, was thus early recognised as indispensable for securing the free navigation of the Amur, the simple possession of the left bank being justly considered insufficient for the purpose.

Muravioff, with his usual vigilance, carefully followed all these movements, and provided for future contingencies. When Nevelskoy returned to Petrofskoe, after having again passed through the straits of La Pérouse and circumnavigated Saghalien, there awaited him orders to proceed in the 'Baikal' to Ayan and thence to Petropavlofsk to load provisions for De Castries, as in the spring of the following year, 1854, a body of 250 men would be sent down the Amur to guard the places occupied on the coast. The transport 'Irtysh' also took cargo at Ayan for the bay of Aniva at the southern extremity of Saghalien. Major Busse, specially sent by Muravioff, after loading provisions at Petropavlofsk and Ayan in the Russian-American Company's ship 'Nikolai,' proceeded also to the bay of Aniva, landed with eighty men, and built the post of Muravioffsk.

The winter sorely tried the scattered Russian vessels and expeditions. The transports 'Nikolai' and 'Irtysh' were obliged to seek refuge at the newly founded post of Constantinofsk in Imperatorski bay. Sub-lieutenant Orloff, who had been left with eight men at the Ilinsk post, after a month spent in exploring the neighbouring country, was obliged to start in search of the other Russian parties. He crossed over the narrow part of the island, bought a native boat, and sailed south towards the bay of Aniva, which is formed by the crescent-shaped southern extremity of Saghalien. Instead of doubling Cape Aniva, he dragged his boat overland from the bay of Mordvinova across one of the horns of the crescent, and reached the post of Muravioffsk on September 30. The 'Irtysh' took him over to Imperatorski bay, whence by dog-sledges he was able to proceed to Mariinsk on Lake Kizi.

After nearly two centuries the Russians now recommenced the occupation of the Amur, choosing, however, for this purpose again a different route. Their ancestors, in the seventeenth century, had already tried three different routes. Poyarkoff first discovered the one by the river Aldan, which was discarded when Khabaroff showed the advantages of the route by the Olekma; the latter was also superseded by the natural one chosen by Beketoff, who started from the head-waters in Transbaikalia, and followed the course of the river. The fourth route, now adopted, was in the opposite direction to the last, ascending the river from its mouth. The sea-route, only possible after Peter the Great had created the Russian navy, had the advantage of presenting at first few political difficulties, the mouth of the Amur and adjacent sea-coast being entirely neglected by the Chinese, who were only interested in the middle course of the river, which lies in a lower latitude.

Brilliant results had been achieved in a few years by a handful of men cast on the wild wastes of the eastern shores of Northern Asia at an immense distance from the civilised world. In 1850 permission had been granted grudgingly to erect a *zimovie* at Petrofskoe; in 1853 the most important harbours in the gulf of Tartary had been occupied, posts had been established in Saghalien, Nikolaiefsk had been founded at the mouth of the Amur, and the river navigated for 300 versts.

This had been accomplished amid all the difficulties of the inclement climate, and with scanty resources. Nevelskoy started from Cronstadt in 1848 on the ' Baikal ' with only thirty men and six officers, and he had received only slight reinforcements. It is amusing to note the first garrisons of the early settlements. Mariinsk was held by eight men ; Boshniack founded Alexandrofsk (at De Castries bay) with three Cossacks, afterwards reinforced to seven ; Nevelskoy left eight men at Constantinofsk in Imperatorski bay ; Orloff at Ilinsk had at first only six men, afterwards increased to eight.

The material at their disposal was equally scanty. In the spring of 1852 the expedition had only five boats, native and foreign, most of them small, so that in April Nevelskoy was obliged to commence building at Petrofskoe a decked boat 28 feet long and 7 broad. The boldness and endurance of fatigue and hardship exhibited by the small expedition of Nevelskoy recall to mind the exploits of Poyarkoff and Khabaroff, but it is gratifying to observe the difference in their conduct to the natives. While the unscrupulous Cossack adventurers plundered and often ill-treated the aborigines, the distinguished officers of the Russian navy showed them the utmost kindness ; indeed they were the victims of the greedy impositions of the Ghiliacks, who unconsciously retaliated for the losses of their ancestors. Nevelskoy remarked that after the Russians had been two years on the Amur the price of articles had increased tenfold.

Besides local hardships, Nevelskoy and his companions had to endure the dangerous secret hostility of a powerful party at St. Petersburg. Vice-Admiral Putiatin,[1] prompted by Nesselrode, declared his strong opposition to any occupation of the Amur or of the continent, and expressed his fears that the occupation of Saghalien[2] would create difficulties with Japan.

Muravioff, while Nevelskoy was occupying strategical

---

[1] Then appointed to negotiate with Japan.

[2] At that time Japan claimed rights over Saghalien, which she ceded to Russia later, in exchange for the Kurile islands.

points in the gulf of Tartary, had been busy at St. Petersburg engaging his enemies at close quarters. Since his return in 1851 he had devoted his activity to carrying out the measures already approved by the Government, and to the preparation of further plans which he hoped would be sanctioned. In the summer of 1852 he had again visited Transbaikalia to inspect the formation of the new Cossack army at Nertchinsk, and had been surprised at the progress achieved. He found twelve battalions of infantry well drilled and able to manœuvre with ease, and instead of the 300 cavalry which he expected, a brigade of 2,000 horse was already organised. The preparations for the future navigation of the Amur, an undertaking of which he was constantly urging the necessity at St. Petersburg, and anxiously awaiting the sanction, were progressing satisfactorily. After careful soundings on the Shilka had shown the possibility of steam navigation, a small steamer, the 'Argun,' had been laid on the stocks and the work was proceeding rapidly.

The results achieved by Muravioff at St. Petersburg had not been so rapid. He had not succeeded in obtaining the imperial sanction for the occupation of Kizi and De Castries, and he justly suspected that Nesselrode was the cause of the delay. The retirement of his zealous friend, Perofski, had alarmed Muravioff, who wrote a strong appeal for support to Grand Duke Constantine, who had expressed his readiness to further any scheme for the welfare of Siberia. Fortunately about this time Colonel Akhte, who, as we have seen, had been sent, without reference to Muravioff, to explore the left bank of the Amur down to its mouth, reported that the lower parts of the river, as well as the neighbouring sea-coast, were not occupied by the Chinese. This statement was important, as independent confirmation of the views repeatedly expressed by Muravioff. But it conveyed no fresh information, because Muravioff had already known three years before, from the reports of Nevelskoy, that the mouth of the Amur did not belong to China. Moreover, the presence and movements of Russian vessels had attracted no notice, friendly intercourse being kept up with Chinese and Manchurians. Muravioff, indeed, might have claimed far more ancient proofs of his statement, as Khabaroff, two centuries before, had been informed that the natives at the mouth of the Amur were independent.

At the beginning of 1853 the political situation of Europe was full of difficulties, which threatened to engage Russia in a war with the Western Powers. Muravioff therefore proceeded to St. Petersburg in March, in order to arrange measures for the defence of Eastern Siberia in case of hostilities. He presented a report to the Emperor, and in his usual comprehensive way examined exhaustively all the questions affecting Eastern Asia. He showed the increasing power of England in the Pacific, and the weakness of China requiring the protection of Russia. Distance alone had prevented the latter from exercising that influence which was due to her early expansion in the East. He deplored the lethargy which had come over Russia since 1812 in all matters concerning the further parts of Asia, and urged that all diplomatic communications with China should pass through the Governor-General of Eastern Siberia, the man most capable, by his position, of giving the necessary advice to the Foreign Office. By this plan a great deal of time would be saved, as the despatches from Peking could be at once examined at Irkutsk and commented on according to the necessities of the frontier provinces. Turning to the Pacific Ocean, he forcibly pointed out the important questions arising in the future in consequence of the eastern expansion of

England.   He denounced the sloth and ignorance of the Foreign Office, which twenty-five years before had ridiculed the prevision of the Russian-American Company when the latter urged the necessity of occupying California at once, as otherwise it would soon be annexed by the United States.   The Foreign Office then imagined that such an unlikely event could not happen for a hundred years, but Muravioff now pointed out that these previsions had been already realised.   He added sagaciously that the occupation of California would have been only a temporary measure, as the United States were destined to rule all North America, and that even Alaska [1] must in time be ceded by Russia ; but these concessions would serve to enhance the value of Russia's friendship with the United States.   Russia's legitimate ambition was to rule the Pacific shores of Eastern Asia.

The immediate result of Muravioff's report was the imperial order of April 11 for the occupation of Saghalien by the Russian-American Company.   This first success was soon followed by another.   On April 22 a conference was held in presence of Tsar Nicholas ; all the maps compiled by Colonel Akhte and the Staff of Eastern Siberia were exhibited, and Muravioff produced an able report on the necessity of the occupation of De Castries bay and the neighbouring Lake Kizi.   Emperor Nicholas, after carefully examining the maps and comparing them with the text of the treaty of Nertchinsk, pointed to that part of the Amur region which lies between the river Bureya and the sea, and exclaimed, 'So this should be ours !'   Then, turning to the War Minister, he added, 'We must arrange about this with the Chinese.' [2]   He

---

[1] It was, indeed, ceded to the United States in 1867, according to Muravioff's previsions.

[2] The treaty of Nertchinsk only determined the frontier of Eastern Siberia around the rivers Gorbitza and Argun ; the frontier in the regions

then examined Muravioff's general map of the Amur and said to him :

' All this is very fine, but consider that I must defend it from Cronstadt.'

Muravioff promptly rejoined, ' It is not necessary to go so far, sire ; it can be defended much nearer.'

And with his hand following up the course of the Amur, he pointed to Transbaikalia.

Tsar Nicholas, putting his hand on Muravioff's head, said :

' O Muravioff, really some day you will lose your wits with the Amur.'

Muravioff exclaimed : ' Sire ! events point out this route.'   But the Emperor, slapping him on the shoulder, concluded :

' Well, let us wait until events lead us thither.'

Within less than a year events led to the adoption of the course advocated by Muravioff.

Two important results were obtained by the conference : the issue of orders for the occupation of De Castries and Kizi, which, as we have seen, were duly received after they had been carried out by Nevelskoy ; and the decision of the Emperor to treat with the Chinese about the region between the river Bureya and the sea. The latter measure, which Muravioff justly considered as an important step for the acquisition of the left bank of the Amur, was perversely distorted by the Asiatic Department of the Foreign Office, and converted into a dangerous stumbling-block for Muravioff's future plans. The despatch to Peking on the subject was purposely delayed until Muravioff had left Russia for Marienbad, where he was obliged to go to

near the sea was left undetermined because neither the plenipotentiaries of the two nations, nor anybody else at the time, knew the exact geographical features of the country.

recuperate his health, much impaired by the many years he had passed in the rigorous climate of Siberia and by hard work. Then the Asiatic Department forwarded a note to Peking, conceived in terms so injurious to the interests of Russia on the Amur, that a Chinese mandarin might have proudly claimed its authorship.

When Muravioff returned to Russia in October of the same year (1853), he hastened to inquire of the chief of the Asiatic Department whether it were necessary to return soon to Siberia on account of the diplomatic negotiations with China. On receiving the answer that there were no special communications with China, he gladly delayed his departure, as there were still many important questions he wished to settle personally at St. Petersburg. He was greatly surprised when, towards the end of December, a courier from Irkutsk arrived with the information that Chinese plenipotentiaries were coming shortly to Kiakhta to discuss the Amur question in answer to a note of the Russian Government. Muravioff immediately demanded explanations from the Director of the Asiatic Department, who was then compelled to acknowledge not only the note, but to admit that the answer from Peking had already arrived. The note, which could no longer be concealed from Muravioff, was intended to convince the Chinese of the necessity for establishing frontier pillars[1] on the left bank of the Amur. This foolish document sacrificed the whole question at issue, as it had been Muravioff's persistent purpose to slowly induce the Chinese to acknowledge that the left bank of the river belonged to Russia.

The Chinese Government readily availed itself of the opportunity afforded by this note of June 16, 1853, and

---

[1] Since the supposed discovery of Middendorf, frontier pillars exercised a mesmerising influence on the Foreign Office.

declared its willingness to send officials to establish frontier pillars on the Gorbitza river, the only part of the left bank which had been clearly defined by the treaty of Nertchinsk. But after the purposeless demand of the Russian Government, as the question was supposed to refer to the whole left bank, the Gorbitza could be easily converted into a barrier shutting off the Russians from the Amur. Difficulties increased in consequence of the inconsiderate action of one of Muravioff's subordinates. When, in November 1853, the Chinese commission arrived at Urga, Rebinder, the town governor at Kiakhta, probably flattered at the prospect of acting a diplomatic part, took up the question, gathered all the documents and plans on the frontier question, and even went so far as to issue orders to the chief of the staff at Irkutsk and to communicate directly with Nesselrode.

Muravioff promptly reprimanded his subordinate for his rash zeal, reminding him that frontier questions could not be settled without imperial orders.

The end of the year 1853 left Muravioff in great difficulties; the decision of the Emperor to treat with the Chinese about the left bank of the lower course of the Amur, which he had joyfully considered as the first step towards the recovery of the long-lost river, had become a fresh obstacle through the foolish or criminal action of the Asiatic Department. The question, unless treated with great tact and firmness, threatened to destroy all hopes of realising his plans. Fortunately, at the same time, Muravioff received statements from Irkutsk showing that the yearly output of gold had exceeded the estimates by nearly a ton.[1] This new proof of his administrative ability and activity came opportunely to silence the opposition of his enemies.

[1] 55 poods 27 pounds, or 11 *zolotniks*.

The political events of 1854, which threatened to divert all attention from Siberia, were turned to the final accomplishment of his plans by Muravioff. Russia had become engaged in a war with Turkey which involved her also in a destructive war with England, France, and Sardinia. During two centuries Russia had neglected the Far East in order to concentrate her forces against her Western enemies. A continuation of this policy would have appeared necessary to most statesmen, to face the formidable coalition formed in Europe. But Muravioff, with singular boldness, saw the opportunity for achieving his plans, for satisfying his secret aspirations to acquire the whole of Siberia; and, thanks to his genius, the war which crushed the power of Russia in Europe secured her a lasting triumph on the Pacific.

His duties as commander of the military forces in Eastern Siberia had compelled Muravioff to prepare plans for the defence of the Pacific coast in the probable event of an attack by the allied fleets. In a lucid confidential report [1] to Grand Duke Constantine, Admiral-in-Chief, he set forth the requirements of the military situation.

After enumerating the forces at his disposal—16,000 infantry and 5,000 cavalry, out of which a total of 13,000, with twenty guns, could be sent across the borders—he showed the vast frontier, from Kamchatka to Kharazaya (10,000 versts by sea and land), which had to be defended. While in Europe the Western Powers could not inflict any serious loss on Russia, they might easily deprive her of Kamchatka and of the mouth of the Amur in the Far East. The empire of China, now insignificant on account of its military weakness, might become dangerous under the influence and guidance of England and France —Siberia might even cease to be Russian. The loss of

---

[1] November 29, 1853.

this vast region, capable of absorbing the excess of the rural population of European Russia for a whole century, could not be compensated by any victories or conquests in the West.[1] It was therefore necessary to guard Kamchatka, Saghalien, and the mouth of the Amur, thus also acquiring enduring influence on China. This was possible with the means now disposable in Eastern Siberia, prepared during the last five years, provided full powers were given to the Governor-General to settle all questions without the loss of time entailed by reference to St. Petersburg.

Rapid communications must also be provided, as the enemy's fleet could be informed by sea of the declaration of war and commence hostilities before the news could be forwarded overland through the vast plains of Siberia. The fleet of Admiral Putiatin should be recalled from its dangerous station in Japan and sheltered in the new port occupied by Nevelskoy; the steamer 'Vostok,' belonging to the fleet, could then be used for keeping up communications with Petropavlofsk in Kamchatka. At the same time troops, provisions, and artillery must be sent down the Amur; the steamer 'Argun,' now completed, serving to maintain communications between Nertchinsk and the mouth of the river. By this means there would be almost uninterrupted steam communications between Nertchinsk in Transbaikalia and Petropavlofsk in Kamchatka. It would not be necessary to send a large force down the Amur, as the English in their war with China had never been able to land more than 3,000 men. Besides, the coasts of Kamchatka, being little known, would present great difficulties for a descent. The navigation on the

---

[1] Muravioff here clearly pointed out the true policy of Russia. He was far ahead of his contemporaries, nobody then on the continent of Europe understanding those ideas of colonial expansion which have lately become fashionable in most countries.

Amur would not meet with much opposition from the Chinese, as three years' experience at the mouth of the river had shown they cared little about the question. Moreover, it was easy to explain that the measure was necessary for the defence not only of the sea-coast but of Manchuria itself, which would be exposed to great danger by the neighbouring conquests of the Western Powers. It was also necessary to bear in mind that the Chinese Government was fully occupied by its domestic troubles, half the empire being in the hands of the rebels.

The views of Muravioff were so sound, and the new conditions produced by the gigantic struggle in which Russia was engaged were so urgent, that the whole question was referred to a special committee under the presidency of the Heir-Apparent. Its opinion was favourable, and on January 11, 1854, the Emperor ordered that all questions relating to the frontier in the Far East should be settled directly by Muravioff with the Peking Foreign Office. The Chinese were informed of the change by a despatch of February 6, and a diplomatic secretary and interpreters in the Chinese and Manchu languages were attached to Muravioff. After long discussions it was also decided to start navigation on the Amur, even if the consent of the Chinese were not obtained, and to send reinforcements to Kamchatka by that river.

At last the hour had come for which Russia had waited over 150 years. In the opinion of Muravioff's biographer[1] it is doubtful whether all the efforts of his activity and energy would have achieved this object without the outbreak of the war in Europe. Thus the only enduring result of the Crimean war, unperceived at the time, was the opening of the Pacific to Russia.

Muravioff had achieved even more brilliant success in

---

[1] Barsukoff.

his second visit to the capital than in his first, and he hastened his return to Siberia to carry out the plans which had been sanctioned by the Tsar. He left St. Petersburg on February 10, and before the middle of March reached Irkutsk, where he at once commenced issuing orders for the approaching navigation on the Amur. He was not alarmed by the prospects of war on the Pacific coast, because, besides the enemy's ignorance of the country, he reckoned to be stronger than the allies, especially as by the new route of fluvial navigation he was now nearer to the ports exposed to attack.

While relying principally on the Amur to maintain his communications with the coast and Kamchatka, Muravioff also paid attention to the older routes. On his return from Kamchatka in 1849 he had passed through Ayan to inspect the road leading thence to Yakutsk; finding that regular communications were interrupted during several months, he obtained authorisation from St. Petersburg to establish settlers along the line in order to insure communications in winter. In 1851, 102 families had been transferred from Transbaikalia and the Irkutsk province, but the settlers complained of their condition in a country unfit for cultivation. As these accounts were not confirmed by official reports, Muravioff decided to have the matter verified by a reliable person. For this purpose he chose the son of Prince Volkonski, one of the Decembrists, or political exiles relegated to Siberia since 1825 by Tsar Nicholas. The young nobleman, like most of the persons selected by Muravioff, showed himself on every occasion fit for the duties he had to fulfil. Volkonski found the settlers in great distress; typhus and scurvy had prevailed, their cattle had mostly perished through scarcity of fodder, and they had been able to subsist only through loans of Government money; he also reported that the road required considerable improvements. To show the absolute necessity of the Amur route, it will suffice to mention that it took Volkonski, travelling alone, almost two months to accomplish the voyage [1] by the old route, amid incredible difficulties, travelling by boat, on horseback, and, at last, on foot over the mountains.

Muravioff, in the meanwhile, had commenced his first memorable expedition. When the news of the intended navigation of the Amur spread through Siberia, it was received with general enthusiasm. The daring exploits of the Cossacks on that river in the seventeenth century were still fresh in the memory of the people of Transbaikalia, who had never abandoned the hope of recovering the lost region and of rebuilding Albazin, endeared by its heroic sieges. The Amur was the direct route to the ocean, necessary for the future prosperity of Siberia, and the merchants of Irkutsk expressed their desire to subscribe funds for the expenses of the expedition. A banquet was offered to Muravioff by the same merchants before his departure from Irkutsk, and along the whole route he was received with wild joy amid feasts and recitals of verses.

A despatch had been sent to Peking stating that, on account of war with other Powers, the Governor-General had been ordered to forward officials and troops down the Amur for the defence of the Russian possessions on the littoral; the Chinese Government was also requested to appoint time and place for a conference of plenipotentiaries to settle frontier questions. Muravioff left Irkutsk on April 19, and reached Kiakhta on the 24th by the road around Lake Baikal; here, after obtaining information from Urga that Colonel Zaborinski [2] had not been allowed to proceed to Peking, he decided not to wait for

---

[1] He left Irkutsk at the end of April and reached Ayan on June 22.

[2] He was bearer of the despatch to Peking.

the answer from Peking, as the habitual procrastination of the Chinese would waste precious time. On May 7 Muravioff was on the Shilka, at a point seventy versts above the frontier, where the preparations for the navigation of the Amur had been actively proceeding under the direction of the Captain of the Navy, Kasakievitch, one of the ablest assistants of the Governor-General.

The Shilka then presented a very lively appearance, unusual in the quiet rivers of Siberia. Cossacks and soldiers of the line were hurrying along on the banks, while the stream was crowded with boats, barges, and rafts loaded with military stores and provisions. In the middle of the river was anchored the 'Argun,' the pioneer steamer on the Amur, built by orders of Muravioff with the generous gift of 100,000 roubles offered by Kuznetzoff, a rich merchant engaged in gold-washing. Great enthusiasm animated all classes at the arrival of the Governor-General, in whose honour a solemn fête was organised on May 9, his name-day. He was entertained at a banquet where appropriate verses were recited, and he was proclaimed the accomplisher of the ideas of Peter the Great. There was a display of fireworks and illuminations with transparent inscriptions recording the results of Muravioff's activity during the last four years ; the reforms in Transbaikalia ; the organisation of the Cossack army in the same province ; the increase in the production of gold ; the construction of a flotilla for the navigation of the Amur.

Muravioff neglected no opportunity to increase the popular appreciation of the historical importance of the event ; an old image of the Blessed Virgin, which tradition asserted had been brought from Albazin when the fortress was evacuated by the Russians, accompanied the expedition and served to impart a solemn blessing. Religion, which had contributed to establish the power of Moscow and had saved Russia from the Tartars and the Poles, now lent its powerful influence in the distant expedition towards the shores of the Pacific. Muravioff addressed the troops with a few impressive words: 'Children,'[1] the time has come to advance; let us pray to the Lord and ask His blessing on our journey.' 'We will do our best!' was the unanimous shout of the soldiers.

The expedition started on May 14, 1854, amid firing of guns and hurrahs. It consisted of a line battalion about 800 strong, a *sotnia* of Cossacks, and a division of mountain artillery; besides the s.s. 'Argun' there were seventy-five barges and rafts, the whole flotilla extending for two versts down the river. The boats were all heavily laden with provisions, some up to 1,500 poods,[2] destined either for the use of the expedition or for transhipment to Kamchatka. In the evening of May 17 the flotilla had reached Ust-Strielka, where the junction of the Argun with the Shilka forms the Amur. The night was passed at anchor, and on the following day, May 18, there was the solemn entrance in the forbidden river, closed to Russia since the treaty of Nertchinsk. The Governor's band played 'God save the Tsar,' the soldiers crossed themselves, waved their caps, and hurrahed, while Muravioff, filling a tumbler with the water of the Amur, drank to the success of the expedition.

On May 20 the flotilla passed the site of the old fortress of Albazin; the soldiers stood up and took off their caps while the band played hymns. Muravioff, with many others, landed to inspect the ruins,[3] and knelt reve-

---

[1] The common term used by Russian commanders addressing their men.

[2] Nearly 25 tons.

[3] Albazin is now a Cossack settlement on the Amur, but traces of the old rampart can be still discerned.

rently in prayer on the ground which contained the dust of their heroic ancestors.

The expedition having reached, on May 28, the mouth of the Zeya, at only twenty versts' distance from the Chinese fortified town, Aigun, Muravioff sent officers to inquire whether its Governor had received instructions from Peking. No answer had come to Muravioff's despatch about the navigation of the Amur, and the Governor of the isolated town was greatly embarrassed to find a solution to the unprecedented question suddenly forced upon him. He attempted to maintain the impossibility of allowing such navigation, but he was so scared by the sight of the numerous flotilla, and especially of the steamer, a kind of vessel entirely new to him, that he preferred to get rid of his unwelcome guests and hurry them away from his town.

The remainder of the journey was uneventful; the Sungari was reached on June 2, the Ussuri on June 5. At the confluence with the latter river Muravioff, admiring the beautiful situation, exclaimed, 'Here there shall be a town.'[1] At that time there were no charts of the Amur river, and distances were reckoned on the general map of Asia; therefore, when on June 9 a point had been reached 200 versts below the Ussuri, it was supposed that Lake Kizi must be in the neighbourhood. The mistake was not discovered until the evening of June 10, when a boat commanded by a Russian officer was seen sailing up the river. As it approached the banks Muravioff shouted out:

'How far is it to Mariinsk ?'

'Five hundred versts,' was the unexpected answer.

On discovering the distance which still remained to

---

[1] At present there is the town of Khabarofsk, the residence of the Governor-General of the Amur and Maritime Provinces, and of Trans-Baikalia.

be covered, Muravioff decided to proceed alone in the 'Argun,' and reached Mariinsk on June 12; the rest of the expedition, with the assistance of native pilots engaged by Nevelskoy, arrived on June 14, a month after its departure. The greater part of the navigation had been accomplished with great difficulties, as the course of the river was almost totally unknown. The lower part of the Amur presented a pleasant contrast, as the natives were very friendly, and offered every assistance. Muravioff, astonished at the order which prevailed, remarked that the region seemed to have always belonged to Russia. He was glad to verify the correctness of his inductions, that the lower course of the Amur had never been occupied by the Chinese, and that the independent natives were willing to accept the sovereignty of the Tsar.

Nevelskoy, who was at De Castries bay, came at once to Mariinsk to meet Muravioff and to behold the realisation of the plans they had discussed in St. Petersburg seven years before, and for which they had strenuously worked during all the intervening time.

Muravioff, with his usual activity, commenced his tour of personal inspection; he proceeded on foot, through a cutting in the forest, to De Castries, and thence on board the schooner 'Vostok' to Imperatorski bay to meet Admiral Putiatin. With the same vessel, he then sailed northwards through the straits of the gulf of Tartary to Petrofskoe, where he sent forward a part of his staff to Ayan by the 'Vostok,' and proceeded himself by land to Nikolaiefsk. At this post he found the answer of the Chinese Foreign Office, which had been forwarded after him down river; it stated that the Chinese were ready to appoint officials to inspect the places on the frontier. On the return of the 'Vostok' to Nikolaiefsk, Muravioff proceeded to Ayan on August 9, leaving that port on the 20th for Irkutsk.

During nearly two months spent in the region along the coast, Muravioff had been chiefly occupied in military preparations. He found, as was to be expected, the defences of the few scattered posts in wretched conditions; at Petrofskoe there were only twenty-five men with flint muskets; at Nikolaiefsk thirty men with the same weapons and two guns, of which only one could be fired; at Mariinsk eight men; at Alexandrofsk (in De Castries bay) ten men with one gun; at Imperatorski bay ten men; all these soldiers were armed with the same old-fashioned muskets. There were only sixty pounds of gunpowder and twenty-five charges for each of the three guns. The naval forces were equally insignificant; at De Castries there were the transports 'Irtysh,' 'Dvina,' 'Baikal,' and the schooner 'Vostok;' at Imperatorski bay the frigate 'Pallada' and the vessels of the Russian-American Company 'Nikolai' and 'Prince Menshtchikoff.' The frigate 'Pallada' and schooner 'Vostok' had formed part of the squadron of Vice-Admiral Putiatin, sent to Japan to conclude a treaty of commerce, but these vessels had been hastily recalled from Nagasaki when war appeared imminent. The corvette 'Olivutza,' also forming part of that squadron, had been sent to assist in the defence of Petropavlofsk. The Russian detachments stationed in the island of Saghalien had been withdrawn by order of Admiral Putiatin and concentrated in Imperatorski bay. This measure had been strongly opposed by Nevelskoy, who, instead of concentrating the Russian forces, proposed dispersing them along the whole coast, thereby inducing the enemy to declare a blockade, thus implicitly recognising Russia's occupation of the region. He argued that political considerations were of higher importance than the purely military requirements of the situation.

The much-needed reinforcements brought down the Amur by Muravioff were distributed as follows:—

The *sotnia* of Cossacks with four mountain guns was stationed at Mariinsk.

Two hundred men were destined for the defence of Nikolaiefsk.

Another force of 200 men was stationed on Lake Kizi with orders to cut a road through the forest to De Castries, as it was highly important to insure easy communications between that bay and the post of Mariinsk.

The remaining 400 men were sent on the transport 'Dvina' to Petropavlofsk.

The vessels of Admiral Putiatin, the frigate 'Pallada' and schooner 'Vostok,' were to winter at Nikolaiefsk, while the forces withdrawn from Saghalien were despatched to Alaska.

The detachment on Lake Kizi suffered great hardships, which it will be useful to describe in detail to show the endurance displayed by the Russian soldiers in the desolate, sparsely peopled region. The work of cutting a road through the virgin forest was attended with great difficulties; besides felling the huge trees, the soldiers had often to pave the way with fascines and to build bridges across the numerous streams which intersected the country. The mosquitoes and small flies [1] which infest the Siberian forests allowed the men no rest, tormenting them day and night, especially in the damp foggy weather. The food, principally consisting of salt meat, was spoilt and had to be thrown away, compelling

---

[1] The sting of these insects is such an unbearable torment, that all the gold-seekers and other frequenters of the 'taigas' or Siberian forests are obliged to wear veils to protect their necks and faces.

the soldiers to subsist on gruel and sugar. These provisions also soon came to an end, while still ten versts of the road remained unfinished. As the work could not be abandoned, the commander Glen sent back a portion of his men to Mariinsk to fetch provisions, but these did not arrive for many days, and the unfortunate men confined in the dismal forest were reduced to subsisting on roots and game. Sickness broke out, and perhaps the whole detachment might have perished if it had not been accidentally discovered by some officers of the Russian frigate 'Diana,' lately arrived at De Castries, who were hunting in the forest. Provisions and a doctor were sent from the ship, and the soldiers, recovering their strength, were able to finish the road.

On the return of the detachment to Mariinsk it received orders to proceed to Nikolaiefsk; but even here no rest was granted, for it was ordered on to Petrofskoe. Embarking on the old boats on which they had descended the Amur, with an escort of thirty sailors from the 'Pallada,' the soldiers sailed down the Amur; but on entering the sea of Okhotsk they were caught by a storm which smashed the flotilla on a sandy beach. The shipwrecked detachment had to proceed along the roadless coast to Petrofskoe, where, after a week, the transport 'Irtysh' conveyed them to Ayan. Here they were embarked, with four guns, on board the transport 'Kamchatka,' of the Russian-American Company, and sent on a cruise to capture English whalers; the search proving fruitless, after a few days they returned to Ayan. They remained encamped for four weeks, during which time they constructed two batteries for the defence of the port. At last, in the middle of September, Glen and his men were embarked again on the 'Kamchatka' and sent to Alaska. In about three months the detachment had built a road through a virgin forest, had sailed down the Amur, had been shipwrecked, had cruised about the sea of Okhotsk, and had built two batteries !

The other detachment which had been sent to Kamchatka was more fortunate : it had the honour of contributing to the most brilliant success achieved by the Russian arms during the war. When Muravioff visited Petropavlofsk in 1849, he was charmed by the beauty of Avacha bay, and projected a vast plan of defences ; but foreseeing that it could not be speedily carried out, he had given some useful advice for improving the fortifications of the place he had chosen for the principal naval station on the Pacific.

On receiving news of the war in Europe, the defences of the port were hurriedly strengthened ; and when the reinforcements sent from the Amur arrived, the men were employed in constructing batteries. These fears of naval attack were not exaggerated ; England and France had formed a powerful squadron in the Pacific with the intention of dealing a crushing blow at the principal Russian military port, thus freeing their merchant vessels from all danger of the Russian fleet. The allies, however, as Muravioff had justly foreseen, were handicapped by their scanty knowledge of the coast on which they had to land, and by the indecision which such ignorance invariably engenders. This will appear clearly in what follows.

Avacha bay is a large, almost circular, expanse of water with a narrow entrance, forming along its contour a series of minor bays or harbours. Petropavlofsk lies in one of these, formed by a narrow hilly peninsula running from north to south almost parallel to the coast of the mainland, enclosing an oblong sheet of water which is almost divided in equal portions by a long sandy spit jutting out from the mainland nearly right across to the peninsula. The northern part of the harbour is thus completely sheltered, being only accessible through a narrow entrance between the side of the hilly peninsula and the point of the sandy spit. The peninsula is formed by a long narrow hill, the Signal hill ; to the north of which there is a similar mountain, Nikolski hill ; still further to the north there is a lake. On the other side of the bay—on the mainland—there is another long hill parallel to the two former, called Krasny Yar (red cliff). The town of Petropavlofsk lies at the northern extremity of the bay, between Nikolski hill and Krasny Yar.

The defences of the harbour against a naval attack or descent were as follows :—

Battery No. 1, situated at the extremity of Signal hill (Shakoff point), defended the entrance of the harbour on the left (west) side. It mounted five guns.

Battery No. 2 was situated on the sandy spit which intersected the harbour, and defended the entrance on the right (east) side. This was the strongest battery and mounted ten guns.

Battery No. 3 was situated on the isthmus between Signal and Nikolski hills, and defended the town and harbour in its rear (to the east). It mounted five guns,[1] and was very much exposed.

Battery No. 4 was situated on the slope of Krasny Yar at its southern extremity, where the harbour of Petropavlofsk merges into the larger Avacha bay. It mounted three guns.

Battery No. 6 was situated on the shore of the lake, and could only fire when the enemy's landing parties turned round Nikolski hill. It mounted four guns taken from the 'Dvina,' and six almost useless old guns of small calibre.

[1] These guns had been landed from the frigate 'Aurora.'

Battery No. 7 was situated at the foot of the northern extremity of Nikolski hill. It mounted six guns.[1]

Petropavlofsk was therefore defended only by a total of thirty-nine guns ; moreover, owing to the peculiar situation of the town and the necessity for defending it on several sides, either against an attempt to force the entrance, or against a descent on the peninsula and Nikolski hill, the batteries were scattered about and their fire could not be concentrated ; there were only thirty-seven rounds for each gun. To increase the defences of the entrance, the 44-gun frigate, ' Aurora,' and the transport ' Dvina,' presenting a broadside of twenty-one guns, were anchored near it, behind the sandy spit which protected their hulls, leaving the guns free to fire as over a parapet. The total force under arms consisted of about 1,000 men,[2] including the reinforcements sent by Muravioff, a few natives, and some volunteers recruited amongst the officials and merchants of the town. In the event of the enemy landing he was to be repulsed by small detachments provided with a 3-pounder field-piece.

The Anglo-French squadron destined for the attack was composed of the following vessels : the English 52-gun frigate, ' President,' 44-gun corvette, ' Pique,' 24-gun corvette, ' Amphitrite,'[3] and steamer, ' Virago,' of six guns, 300 horse-power ; the French 60-gun frigate, ' La Forte,' 32-gun corvette, ' Eurydice,' and 18-gun brig, ' Obligado.' The allied fleet had a total of 236 guns.

A few months before, the frigates ' President ' and ' La Forte,' flying the flags of Admirals Price and Febvrier-Despointes, were anchored at the other extremity of the

---

[1] These guns had been landed from the frigate ' Aurora.'

[2] Barsukoff gives a total of 42 officers and 870 men ; Ragoza, 1,016 officers and men.

[3] This vessel is not mentioned by Du Hailly as taking part in the attack.

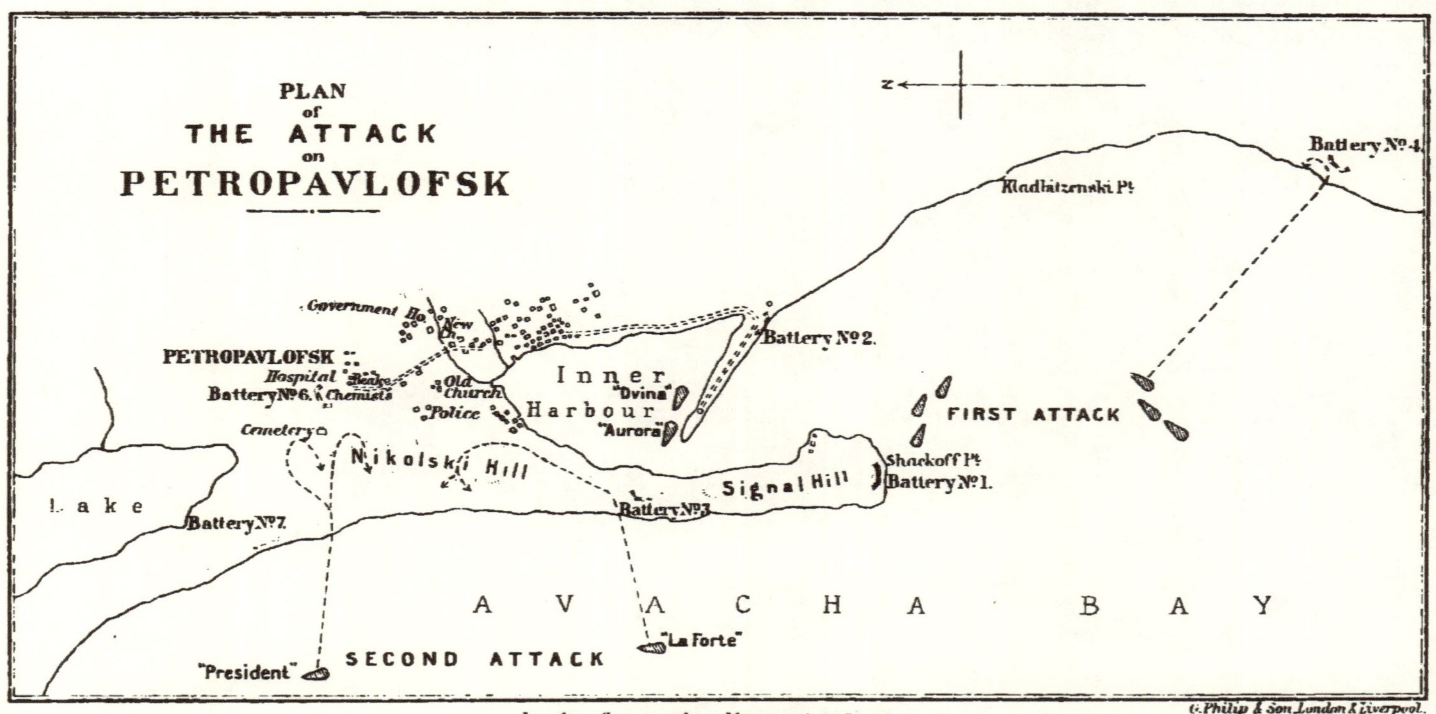

PLAN
of
THE ATTACK
on
PETROPAVLOFSK
N
Battery Nº 4.
Kladhitzenski Pt
Government Ho.
New
PETROPAVLOFSK ::
Hospital Bake
Battery Nº 6. Chemists
Old Church
Police
Cemetery
Battery Nº 2.
Inner
"Dvina"
Harbour
"Aurora"
FIRST ATTACK
Shackoff Pt
Signal Hill
Battery Nº 1.
Lake
Nikolski Hill
Battery Nº 7.
Battery Nº 3
A V A C H A   B A Y
"La Forte"
"President"
SECOND ATTACK
London : Sampson Low, Marston & Co. Limited
G. Philip & Son London & Liverpool.

Pacific, in the Peruvian port of Callao, and on April 26, 1854, they had saluted the departure of the Russian frigate 'Amora,' which had come all the way from Cronstadt. Though war had been declared in Europe, the news had not yet reached the South American Pacific coast, and the three frigates had to postpone warlike operations until their next meeting in Kamchatka.

The first news of the war was brought by the s.s. 'Virago' on May 7, and Admiral Price, as senior, took command of the allied squadron in the Pacific. He had a very difficult task to accomplish. The French and English vessels were scattered about the immense ocean, and there were no ready means—steamers or telegraphs— to recall them; there was no precise information about the number and position of the Russian vessels, nor exact knowledge of the Siberian coast. The number of British vessels trading in the Pacific justified the fear that the Russians might imitate Captain David Porter[1] and start destroying merchant shipping.

Admiral Price felt keenly the responsibility suddenly thrust upon him, and his anxiety to provide against all possible emergencies caused much delay. He left Callao only on May 17, stopped at the Marquesas until July 3, reached the Sandwich Islands on July 17, and, having at last brought together all his vessels, started for Kamchatka on July 25. At the Sandwich Islands he heard that the Russian frigate 'Dvina' had left at the end of June, bearing the news of the outbreak of war; she had therefore a clear month's start over him, and the consciousness that his procrastination had lost much precious time preyed upon his mind. On July 30, five days after

---

[1] This bold American seaman, during the war of 1812–14, cruised about the Pacific committing such depredations on commerce that British vessels crowded the ports, not daring to venture to sea.

the departure from the Sandwich Islands, two vessels were ordered to San Francisco for the protection of merchant shipping.[1] As the squadron approached Kamchatka it met thick fogs and drizzling rain, which made it very difficult to keep the vessels together. It was not till the evening of August 25 that land was dimly seen.

On the morning of August 17[2] (29), 1854, the lighthouse at the entrance of Avacha bay signalled that a squadron of men-of-war was in sight. Shortly after, a three-masted steamer flying the American flag entered the bay, and approached to within three miles of the Signal hill at the entrance of the harbour of Petropavlofsk, and appeared to be taking soundings. But when a boat put off from the shore, the steamer, finding that a ruse had been suspected, retired, joining the rest of the squadron outside the larger bay of Avacha. Admiral Price himself had reconnoitred the position, acquiring a sufficient knowledge of the defences. In the afternoon of August 18 (30) the allied squadron entered the bay, and, after exchanging a few harmless shots with the batteries of Petropavlofsk, anchored out of range. In the evening a council of war was held on board the ' President,' when it was decided to attack the following morning: the two flagships were to destroy the battery at Sharkoff point (battery No. 1), and the ' Pique ' was to destroy battery No. 4 on the opposite side.

Everything was ready for commencing the attack on

[1] Such anxiety was felt on this account that in the following year, 1855, the frigate ' Pique,' at San Francisco, alarmed at the presence of two small vessels of the Russian-American Company in that neutral harbour, sent her boats to watch them every night. The Russians, who were quite unable to attempt privateering, amused at these exaggerated precautions, humorously retaliated by also sending their boats to watch the frigate at night.

[2] Du Hailly gives August 28, and the same difference of a day occurs in all his dates; probably in his notebook he still kept the time of the American Pacific coast, and had not taken into account the change in longitude.

the morning of August 19 (31), when the news that Admiral Price had shot himself spread through the squadron. The exaggerated sense of responsibility which had been preying upon his mind for months, at last drove him to commit suicide in what must have been a fit of temporary insanity, as his religious sentiments and his usually calm character would have rendered impossible such an act while in a sound state of mind. He considered himself in fault for the delay in reaching Petropavlofsk, and his rapid but clear reconnaissance of the natural strength of the enemy's position probably rendered him doubtful of the success of the approaching engagement. He must have had a foresight of the disaster awaiting the allies, and he shot himself just before the attack he had prepared and ordered was to take place. This extraordinary event caused great confusion in the allied squadron ; the tact and uniform courtesy of Admiral Price were invaluable qualities for the commander of a mixed force. His death caused great changes. The supreme command of the squadron passed to the French admiral, while the English vessels were under the orders of the captain of the ' Pique ; ' and divergencies of opinion soon arose between these two officials.

On the morning of August 20 (September 1), a clear sunny day—a rare event in Kamchatka—the activity displayed in the squadron indicated the approaching attack of the allies. The steamer advanced, slowly towing the three largest vessels of the squadron, and placed them in a position to attack batteries Nos. 1 and 4. While the four men-of-war were slowly forming in a line, battery No. 4 on Krasny Yar, probably foreseeing it would not be able to resist long, boldly opened fire, which was promptly answered. A sharp engagement took place between the eight guns of the batteries and the eighty broadside guns of the ships, which ended naturally in the former being silenced after an obstinate resistance. Battery No. 1 was much damaged, because it was uncovered and backed by the rocky sides of the Signal hill, which, struck by shot, fell down in showers of splinters on the platform, wounding the men and hampering the working of the guns. When battery No. 4 was silenced the French landed a party and hoisted their flag; but Midshipman Popoff, who, after nailing the three guns, had retired with his twenty-eight gunners, promptly returned with reinforcements and attacked them with great bravery. The French, notwithstanding their numerical superiority, were thrown into disorder and retreated to their boats.[1]

After this successful attack on the cast, in the afternoon the larger vessels of the squadron advanced a little, taking up a position where they were sheltered by the Signal hill from the fire of the Russian vessels 'Aurora' and 'Dvina,' and commenced the attack on the battery No. 2. Though they had only ten guns against eighty, Prince Maxutoff, the commander of the battery, coolly directed his men not to waste powder, and to make up for their inferiority by the accuracy of their aim. The allies were much struck by the fearless indifference of a Russian sentinel, who continued on his measured beat throughout the whole cannonade. The engagement lasted almost until evening, but without decisive results. The allies at the same time made an attempt to land on the side of the Signal hill facing Avacha bay, near battery No. 3, at the isthmus of the peninsula; but as it failed, they retired to their anchorage after nine hours' fighting. 'La Forte' alone fired 869 rounds.

---

[1] Du Hailly says that the allies spiked the guns and then retreated; but this is not probable, as a descent to spike the guns of a silenced battery seems useless.

The whole night was spent by the Russians in repairing their batteries, with such activity, that on the following morning, with the exception of a few guns rendered unserviceable, the defences were almost in the same condition as on the preceding day. The loss of the Russians was six killed and thirteen wounded.

The night was spent by the allies in a stormy council of war, in which it was proposed to retreat; but this pusillanimous proposal was abandoned the next day. The men who had been sent ashore to bury Admiral Price had found two Americans, who furnished information about the land approaches of Petropavlofsk. They reported the existence of a good road to the north of Nikolski hill leading straight from the sea to the town. On this information Sir Frederick Nicholson, the captain of the 'Pique,' proposed to land near Nikolski hill, after destroying the shore batteries, and to march straight for the assault on the town. This plan had the defect of not utilising the chief strength of the allies—the guns of their ships—and of exposing the sailors to a disadvantageous land engagement with regular infantry; but it was adopted with enthusiasm by the officers and men, eager to fight and confident of victory. An attempt to force the entrance of the harbour, only protected by a battery and the two Russian vessels at anchor, though deemed risky by the captain of the 'Pique,' would certainly have had less fatal results than the course adopted.

In the early morning of August 24 (September 5) the allies commenced their preparations for the second attack. This was not directed, as the former one, against the defences of the entrance to the harbour, but against the batteries on the peninsula and Nikolski hill, which protected the harbour and the town on the west from a fleet operating in the broad waters of Avacha bay. The destruction of these batteries and a successful landing would enable the allies to occupy the hills, deliver a plunging fire on the Russian vessels anchored below in the harbour, and march towards the town. The Signal and Nikolski hills which shelter Petropavlofsk on the side towards Avacha bay are covered with low brushwood, and descend almost perpendicularly to the sea. They form a natural rampart covering the town and harbour, and only through the gap between them can the houses and ships be seen from the bay. Nikolski hill slopes less abruptly towards the town and has some steep paths towards the lake, while at the foot of its northern extremity there is a fairly good road—the one mentioned by the Americans—situated between the lake and the hill, leading straight towards the town through battery No. 6, an earthen fort well palisaded and protected by a ditch.

The weather was foggy when at 7.30 A.M. the steamer slowly advanced, towing the frigates 'President' and 'La Forte,' which took up a position in front of battery No. 3, at the isthmus of the peninsula, where a gap exists between the two hills. The Russians at once opened fire, which was answered by a broadside from the English frigate while she was still in tow ; at the same time the French frigate anchored close inshore, and the engagement became so hot that in less than half an hour the battery was completely destroyed. The English frigate then was towed in front of battery No. 7, which, after an hour's fierce cannonade, was also destroyed. The Russians fought their guns with skill and bravery, inflicting some damage on the ships, and only retired when the commanders of both batteries were wounded.

The first part of the attack—the destruction of the batteries—having been accomplished successfully, it was possible to undertake the second part—the landing of a force for the capture of the town. In about half an hour twenty-five boats landed nearly a thousand men [1] commanded by the French admiral. A portion of the advanced guard formed on the beach, and marching round the northern extremity of Nikolski hill advanced on the road near the lake towards battery No. 6. Here they were received with grape-shot, according to the instructions given by Muravioff five years before, when he chose the site for this battery in 1849, and were obliged to retreat in disorder. A second attack was also unsuccessful. This first repulse compelled the allies to climb the hill, whence they commenced firing down on the soldiers in the battery No. 6, and on the crews of the 'Aurora' and 'Dvina,' anchored below in the bay. Another landing was also effected at the isthmus lying between Nikolski and Signal hills.

Admiral Zavoiko, the Governor of Kamchatka, perceiving that battery No. 6 was in no danger, gathered all the men he had at hand, a little over three hundred,[2] and sent them forward to Nikolski hill with orders to drive the enemy into the sea at the point of the bayonet. When the Russians advanced they found the allies already in possession of the crest of Nikolski hill and commencing to descend the slope towards the town. Hiding behind the bushes, and in the ditch of the battery, the Russians opened an effective fire on the sailors, while the small field-piece swept them with grape-shot; then suddenly rushing forwards they charged with the bayonet. After a desperate hand-to-hand engagement the allies retreated

---

[1] Barsukoff estimates their number at 700, while Ragoza gives more than 1,000 ; these figures may be reconciled if we suppose the former estimates only the number landed in the first descent. Ragoza does not mention the second descent on the isthmus. Du Hailly, who must have known the exact numbers, gives 700.

[2] Barsukoff gives 312, Ragoza states *not* over 300.

in disorder up the hill, where a dreadful fate awaited them. The steep side of the hill towards the sea almost precluded retreat, and the sailors were either bayonetted down into the sea, or dashed to pieces on the rocks in attempting to jump down. The party which had landed near the isthmus now also retreated and joined the detachment which had been driven from the northern extremity of the hill ; crowding on the beach they embarked in confusion, under an incessant fire from the Russians on the hill. Many were killed in the water or in the boats, and others drowned. The total loss of the allies was estimated by the Russians at over 300 [1] men ; thirty-eight dead bodies were found on shore, besides which four officers, a flag, seven officers' swords, fifty-six rifles, and four prisoners were captured. The Russians lost thirty-one killed and sixty-five wounded, among whom were two officers.

The allies, after landing to bury the dead on the following day, the 25th, sailed away on the evening of August 27.

The gallant defence of Petropavlofsk, a detached little-known episode of the Crimean war, was an event of great importance in the Far East. It occurred at the most opportune moment and under the most favourable circumstances to further the far-reaching plans of Muravioff : it happened immediately after the first navigation on the Amur, and victory was won through the reinforcements sent down that river ; the unlooked-for success in a remote region contrasted forcibly with the uniform misfortunes attending the Russian arms in the other military operations at home.

---

[1] Barsukoff states 350, Ragoza 300 ; these figures must be near the truth, as Du Hailly confesses the allies lost a third of the landing party— 700 men.

The news of the victory spread rapidly through Siberia, arousing the greatest enthusiasm. The cause of the success was so plain that it appeared evident to all. Bishop Innocent, writing to congratulate Muravioff, said that without the men and provisions sent *viâ* the Amur 'now Petropavlofsk would be in ashes. Therefore it is doubtful whether you have more cause for joy on account of the timely opening of the Amur or on account of the saving of Kamchatka, which has so clearly shown the utility of the opening of that river.'

It had always been very difficult for Muravioff to arouse public interest in the Amur, as all were indifferent to that remote region. When he was in St. Petersburg, out of regard for his earnest patriotism they good-naturedly consented to listen to his plans, but as soon as he left for Irkutsk the subject was generally forgotten. The events of the war now directed the attention of public-spirited persons to the Far East. When Major Korsakoff, sent by Muravioff to report the first successful navigation of the Amur, arrived at the railway station of St. Petersburg, he was ordered at once, without being allowed to change his travelling uniform, to the War Office, and thence to the Tsesarie-vitch,[1] and to Grand Duke Constantine. The minutest inquiries were made about the expedition. The Tsesarie-vitch read Muravioff's report, in which he declared that Russia had gained 'firm footing on the Amur,' and modestly added that success was entirely 'due to Nevel-skoy, Kasakievitch, and Korsakoff.' 'Muravioff forgets to mention himself,' remarked the Prince. On the follow-ing day Korsakoff was presented to the Tsar Nicholas, who embraced him, and announced the promotion of all the officers of the expedition.

[1] The proper Russian name of the Heir-apparent—not Tsarwitch, as is usually written in the newspapers of Western Europe.

The news of the victory of Petropavlofsk coming shortly afterwards increased the general interest in the Far East, and convinced the most sceptical that Muravioff was not a visionary, and that his plans to defend Kamchatka *viâ* the Amur were of practical utility. His foresight and activity had spared Russia a disaster in the Pacific at the time she was suffering misfortunes in the Black Sea.

We have seen that Muravioff left Ayan on August 20, 1854—the same day the allies made their first attack on Petropavlofsk—*en route* for Irkutsk, which he reached on September 20; here he met Volkonski, who had been charged with the inspection of the settlements along the postal road to Ayan. The young nobleman had fulfilled his duties so satisfactorily that he was intrusted with the execution of a more important project : the settlement of peasants on the banks of the Lower Amur.

Muravioff was not unduly elated by the victory at Petropavlofsk, and wisely foresaw the necessity of preparing for a more serious attack during the continuance of the war, which promised to be a long one. The military operations in the Far East were carried on under exceptional circumstances of a very curious nature, which gave rise to many strange incidents. The Russian forces concentrated in Transbaikaila were at a great distance from the points liable to be attacked : Kamchatka and the coasts of the sea of Okhotsk, and the gulf of Tartary. On the other hand, the more rapid sea communications of the allies were rendered useless by the fact that, owing to the severity of the climate, navigation is impossible along these coasts for many months. We have thus the curious spectacle of Muravioff, at Irkutsk, almost in the centre of Asia, studying the preparations of the allied fleet, and leisurely providing measures for baffling their attacks. He is first warned from St. Petersburg that the allies have decided to revenge their repulse at Petropavlofsk by renewing the attack in great force next summer; then later (in a letter of February 25, 1855), he remarks that the papers report the preparations for the attack, and the appointment of a new French admiral who was still at Brest on January 15; he therefore calculates that the fleet probably will not appear on the coast before the end of June or beginning of July. These circumstances, skilfully utilised by Muravioff's activity and prompt decision, together with the enemy's ignorance of the coast, rendered the naval operations of 1855 as inglorious for the allied squadron as those of the preceding year.

The winter suspension of hostile operations allowed Muravioff to attend to the principal objects which required his attention: the safety of Petropavlofsk and of the Russian squadron; the preparations for a second and larger expedition down the Amur, able to repulse any landing of the allies; the selection and equipment of a body of peasants willing to settle on the banks of the Amur between Mariinsk and Nikolaiefsk.

As soon as Muravioff was informed from St. Petersburg of the preparations for a more formidable attack on Petropavlofsk, he recognised the impossibility of a successful defence before the arrival of powerful reinforcements, which unfortunately could not be despatched in time. He therefore took a decision, heroic in his case, as it entailed the sacrifice of his cherished plan—one of the first he had conceived when he arrived as Governor-General in Siberia; he ordered the abandonment of the naval port in the bay of Avacha. He readily judged that as Petropavlofsk could not be successfully defended, the garrison being also short of provisions, it must be forthwith abandoned. The decision, promptly taken, had to be rapidly executed, as the delay, even of a day, might cause the destruction of the Russian squadron. There was no time to consult St. Petersburg, and Muravioff assumed the heavy responsibility of issuing orders, on his own authority, to Admiral Zavoiko to evacuate Petropavlofsk and remove the garrison and even the civil population. The order was given to Martynoff, his aide-de-camp, who, starting in the beginning of December, travelled the most inhospitable region of Siberia in the depth of winter.

On October 30, 1854, Muravioff had addressed a despatch to the Chinese Foreign Office, in which, after drawing attention to the fact that Colonel Zaborinski had not been allowed to proceed to Peking, he requested that a place should be appointed for the plenipotentiaries to meet and settle the frontier question. He also announced his intention of descending the Amur next summer, with an armed force for protecting the sea-coast against the attacks of England and France.

Great preparations were made during the winter for the second expedition down the Amur, which was to be on a far larger scale than the first. The military force alone was to consist of about 3,000 men, besides the settlers and their families, recruited by Volkonski. A thousand men were employed on the Shilka in building about 130 barges, capable of transporting over 7,000 tons of cargo. For the defence of the coast and the mouth of the Amur, Muravioff intended to bring down fortress artillery with a large supply of ammunition. The transport of this heavy material illustrates the natural capacity of the Russians in coping with the difficulties of land carriage across immense distances. The artillery was brought all the way from Tobolsk and Yekaterinburg, a distance of 4,000 versts, as many as sixty horses being harnessed to the guns, the roads, especially in the hilly country of Transbaikalia, presenting great difficulties.

Volkonski, in the meanwhile, was busy in choosing peasants and providing for their comfortable settlement in the desolate region of the lower Amur. At last fifty-one families, consisting of 481 individuals, were selected, and, besides a large supply of provisions, they were provided with cattle, seed, and agricultural implements : the Buriats generously offered 500 head of horned cattle to these pioneer settlers on the Amur.

Martynoff, who had left Irkutsk in the beginning of December, 1854, proceeded by Yakutsk, Okhotsk, and the wild coast land of the Okhotsk sea in dog sledges, reached Petropavlofsk on March 3, 1855, having covered the distance of 8,000 versts in the unprecedentedly quick time of three months. The defenders of Petropavlofsk, though they had only a scanty stock of provisions, were prepared to die at their posts ; they were, therefore, greatly surprised at the unexpected order to evacuate the place, arm the ships, and remove the inhabitants and all movable property. Admiral Zavoiko carried out the orders with great alacrity, and by March 30 he had shipped over 1,400 tons of various goods, and had his seven vessels armed and ready for sea. As the harbour of Petropavlofsk was not yet free, a passage was sawn through the ice into the larger Avacha bay, and on April 5 the whole fleet sailed for De Castries. The English vessels ' Encounter ' and ' Barracouta ' were cruising about, watching the entrance of the bay ; but a fog enabled the Russians to elude their vigilance. The small force left at Petropavlofsk was placed under the command of Martynoff, with orders to retreat inland at the approach of the allied squadron. To preserve communications with Kamchatka, a small vessel was stationed at Bolsherietzk [1] with a chain of Cossack pickets extending up to Petropavlofsk.

The allied squadron in the Pacific was as unsuccessful in 1855 as in the preceding year : the French admiral had died and had been succeeded by Admiral Fourichon; the supreme command, however, devolved on the English admiral, Bruce, who decided to collect a powerful force for the destruction of Petropavlofsk and the Russian fleet. The rendezvous of the scattered vessels was fixed at the southern extremity of Kamchatka, and there was a steeple-chase in the Pacific, all the English and French ships converging to the appointed spot. The combined squadron consisted of five French and nine English vessels, with a total of 450 guns ; a force quite sufficient to achieve its object. Unfortunately, a great mistake had been committed in choosing a point too far from Petropavlofsk for the concentration of the fleet, which thus could not observe closely the movements of the enemy.

Two vessels, as we have seen, had been sent to watch Avacha bay on April 2 (14), but three days later the Russians succeeded in slipping away in a fog. A month later, on May 2 (14), Admiral Bruce arrived at the rendezvous and immediately sailed with the whole squadron to Petropavlofsk, but when he arrived on May 8 (20), the Russians had left more than a month before, and he found the place deserted, the American flag flying over the houses of a few foreign traders.

Admiral Bruce started in search of the Russian fleet, and as vessels from the China squadron had been ordered to search in the gulf of Tartary, he sailed for Alaska, reaching Sitka on July 1 (13), 1855. Again he was

[1] On the opposite (west) coast of the peninsula, almost on the same parallel as Petropavlofsk.

disappointed, as the Russian fleet was not there and the settlement was not worth destroying, because the few traders demanded to be taken on board in case their defences against the natives were dismantled. We must now return to the Russian squadron, which by the rapid execution of Muravioff's orders had escaped destruction.

Admiral Zavoiko's squadron transporting the garrison and refugees from Petropavlofsk, consisted of the following vessels: the frigate 'Aurora;' the corvette 'Olivutza,' which arriving too late to take part in the defence of Petropavlofsk had remained there for the winter; the transports 'Dvina,' 'Irtysh,' 'Baikal,' and a boat. The navigation was difficult and tedious along the coasts of Kamchatka and in the sea of Okhotsk, taking up the greater part of the month: the frigate 'Aurora' arrived at Imperatorski bay on April 25, and on the following day was joined by the corvette 'Olivutza.' They found at anchor the frigate 'Pallada,' which had not been able to get over the bar of the Amur, and had been obliged to winter at Imperatorski bay : as she was old and unfit for active service, an officer and ten men had been left on board with orders to set fire to the ship if the enemy approached.

The commander of the 'Olivutza,' on his way from Petropavlofsk, had met an American whaler and was informed that an allied fleet of seven sailing vessels and a steamer had left Honolulu for San Francisco on January 26, to purchase stores and prepare for an early attack on Petropavlofsk. This was very serious news, because, unless unexpectedly delayed, the allies ought to have already reached the coast of Kamchatka, and on finding the Russian fleet had escaped, they must have sailed in pursuit with the indications they were sure to obtain from the whalers in the sea of Okhotsk. Admiral

Zavoiko therefore held a council of war, which decided it was unsafe to remain at Imperatorski bay, and urged the necessity of retiring further north. The 'Aurora' and 'Olivutza' sailed at once, and on May 1 anchored in De Castries bay, where they found the transports 'Dvina' and 'Irtysh.'

The small Russian squadron was still in a very dangerous situation. Nevelskoy came to De Castries overland, and announced that the mouth of the Amur would not be free from ice before the end of May or beginning of June. On the other hand it was known that a portion of the English China squadron had been detached to blockade the sea of Okhotsk and the gulf of Tartary. An overpowering allied force might therefore arrive at any time from the broad southern entrance of the gulf of Tartary, before escape was possible through the narrow northern part of the gulf, where the sea, owing to the proximity of the coasts and the cold currents from the sea of Okhotsk, remains ice-bound much later.

The Russians, in constant expectation of being attacked, cleared their ships for action and kept a vigilant watch. They had not long to wait, for on May 8,[1] the same day that Admiral Bruce arrived at Petropavlofsk, an English squadron composed of a frigate, a steam corvette, and a brig, hove in sight. Towards evening the steam corvette entered the bay, took soundings, and, after exchanging a few shots with the Russian vessels at anchor, withdrew, joining the rest of the squadron outside the bay. Admiral Zavoiko expected to be attacked on the following morning, but the English squadron retired to some distance, and on May 11 was no longer visible from De Castries. The rest of the naval operations were so

---

[1] Here Du Hailly gives the same date, May 20 (May 8, Russian style); probably after cruising on the coast of Japan he had found the true date.

curious, and the English commander was so severely blamed for the measures he adopted, that a circumstantial explanation is necessary.

The Russian force consisted of the 'Aurora,' 16 guns, the 'Olivutza,' 16 guns, besides the transport 'Dvina,' with probably a few more guns, and three other transports. The English commander, Sir Charles Elliott, had the 40-gun frigate 'Sybille,' the 17-gun screw-corvette 'Hornet,' and the 12-gun brig 'Bittern;' he was therefore blamed for not having attacked at once the Russian squadron with his three vessels. But it must be borne in mind that at that time the discoveries of Nevelskoy about the geography of Eastern Asia were unknown out of Russia : it was generally supposed that Saghalien was a peninsula with an isthmus joining it to the mainland, south of the mouth of the Amur, where now the straits of Cape Lazareff are known to exist. Commodore Elliott therefore judged that, as the Russians could not retreat further, being confined in the narrow extremity of the gulf of Tartary, it would be sufficient to watch them at a distance, to prevent all escape southwards until reinforcements arrived. He preferred this safer course to the risk of attacking with his small squadron the six Russian vessels, anchored in a little-known bay where an accident on a shoal or rock might have disabled one of his ships. He could not know at the time that, owing to the necessity for transporting the whole garrison and inhabitants of Petropavlofsk, besides a large cargo, even the guns of the 'Aurora' were unserviceable. He despatched the brig 'Bittern' to Admiral Stirling on May 11, and remained with his other two vessels to prevent the escape of the Russian fleet.

A council of war was held by Admiral Zavoiko with Nevelskoy and the commanders of the other vessels, in which it was decided to fight to the last in case of attack. But on May 14 an officer sent to reconnoitre came back with the welcome news that the ice had broken up and the sea was free up to Cape Lazareff. On May 15, under cover of a fog, the whole squadron sailed out of De Castries and steered north. On the 18th Zavoiko met the American brig 'William Penn,' with a part of the crew of the Russian frigate 'Dvina,' which had been destroyed by a seismic wave on the coast of Japan. These shipwrecked men had first come to Petropavlofsk, and finding it abandoned had returned to De Castries in time to meet the Russian fleet. Fogs, fresh winds, and the strong current in the narrow channel, rendered the progress of the Russians very slow, and not till May 24 did they reach Cape Lazareff. Here, according to the arrangements made by Muravioff, they began to fortify their advantageous position. The straits are only four miles broad, and the navigable channel still narrower. On shore there were 200 men, formerly belonging to the 'Pallada,' working hard to erect fortifications, and on May 28 they had eight guns mounted ready for service. Telegraph stations were also established on all the headlands. But on the morning of May 27 a messenger arrived from Muravioff, who had come down the Amur, with orders for the fleet to retreat further north and take shelter in the Amur.

In the meanwhile Commodore Elliott, anxious to keep watch on the Russian vessels, returned to De Castries on May 16, and was amazed to find they had disappeared. Landing parties[1] were sent ashore, but they only found the personal effects of a Kamchatka apothecary. As the

---

[1] Even this landing would not have been possible if Muravioff's orders had been strictly carried out, as the commander of the Kizi post should have proceeded to defend De Castries; but he was sick, and had not been informed by Zavoiko or Nevelskoy of the approach of the English.

imaginary isthmus precluded all possibility of escape to the north, the English vessels immediately sailed south, in the opposite direction to Cape Lazareff, where Zavoiko was preparing his defence, and carefully explored the whole gulf of Tartary, in the vain hope of finding the Russians concealed in some bay. The French vessels in the China Sea were not able to give much assistance, as they had been damaged by running aground and their crews were suffering from scurvy; only one was able to join Commodore Elliott. After a long, fruitless search in the gulf of Tartary, the allies concluded that the Russian squadron must have passed unperceived in the fog, have circumnavigated Saghalien, and sought refuge in the sea of Okhotsk. This was also a very little known region, but some vague reports mentioned Ayan as the new naval station in that sea, and it was chosen for the next attack.

Muravioff, as early as February 18, 1855, had forwarded another despatch to Peking. After describing the unsuccessful attack of the allies on Petropavlofsk, he declared his intention, in accordance with instructions from his sovereign, to proceed down the Amur as soon as the river was open for navigation, and lead a second expedition with artillery and provisions to the mouth of the Amur to repulse the probable attacks of the allied fleet. This second expedition, which was much larger than the first, was unable to start as early as Muravioff had intended. He had fixed April 16 for the day of departure, in order to be at Kizi on May 6, even before the mouth of the Amur would be free from ice. The arrival of the squadron of Commodore Elliott at De Castries bay on May 8 shows with what careful foresight Muravioff timed his arrangements. Muravioff, with his usual alacrity, was at Nertchinsk on April 6, but he found the preparations for the coming embarkation in a very backward state, and he blamed his subordinates for their slowness. In his anxiety to inspect the preparations lower down the river, he proceeded on horseback by dangerous mountain paths with a single Cossack guide.

To avoid the confusion which had been experienced in the first expedition, the second was divided into three sections. They were to start separately, some days after each other. The first was to consist of twenty-six barges, carrying half a battalion of Cossacks, under the command of Muravioff himself; the second, of fifty-two[1] barges, was to convey the 15th line battalion; and the third, of thirty-five barges, half of the 14th line battalion; about 3,000 men in all. Most minute instructions were issued in advance, ordering the men to become acquainted not only with their several boats, but with all the cargo which was to be embarked. Notwithstanding Muravioff's foresight and activity, there was some confusion, and he was able to start only at the beginning of May with thirteen barges, leaving some of his staff to bring down the remainder of the boats of the first section.

In the meanwhile the Chinese had sent a despatch proposing that the Russian and Chinese plenipotentiaries should meet at Urga, and proceed to Gorbitza and settle the frontier question. Muravioff, while descending the Amur, sent an answer on May 8, stating that, as he had announced on February 18, he was at present engaged in leading reinforcements to the mouth of the Amur. He would remain there until September and be ready to treat this important question with the plenipotentiaries that should be sent for the purpose. A few days later, on May 12, Muravioff met four junks with Chinese

---

[1] Barsukoff states 64 barges.

officials proceeding to Gorbitza to erect posts and delimit the frontier. He repeated to them the same arguments, requesting that they should return to Aigun and wait further instructions from Peking. The mandarins dared not disobey the orders they had received, and continued their voyage up river provided with passports from the Russian authorities.

When Muravioff reached Aigun he forwarded a despatch to the Chinese governor, informing him that he was proceeding to the mouth of the Amur to protect it against the English; that 104 large boats, including a steamer, were to follow, transporting 300 horses, 300 cattle, and over 8,000 persons of both sexes, besides cannon, rifles, and war material. He requested that the vessels should not be detained. This information greatly surprised the Chinese, as from the numbers of the expedition and the presence of cattle they perceived that the Russians intended to establish permanent settlements on the Amur.

When Muravioff reached the lower Amur he at once issued orders that Admiral Zavoiko should take command of the vessels and men which had been serving under Nevelskoy, while the latter was appointed chief of the staff of Muravioff, who as commander-in-chief of all the land and sea forces established his headquarters at the post of Mariinsk, which by the convenient waterways of the Amur and Lake Kizi could communicate readily with Nikolaiefsk and De Castries. As we have seen, the vessels composing the squadron from Petropavlofsk, men-of-war and transports, had been ordered to retire at once into the Amur at Nikolaiefsk, whither fortress artillery had been brought for their protection. The defence of De Castries, abandoned by the fleet, was intrusted to a detachment of 500 Cossack infantry.

During these active military preparations to repulse the possible attacks of a formidable enemy, Prince Volkonski was quietly occupied in establishing his settlers on the banks of the lower Amur, as if the profoundest peace reigned in the country. The settlers, on twelve barges, formed part of the second section of the expedition, and started on May 14, 1855. They suffered much during the voyage, some boats running aground in the shallow rapid Shilka; the cattle dying from want of food, which could not be obtained from the other boats that had continued their course. On the Amur navigation was more pleasant, as the great increase of water enabled them to float over islands and their submerged trees; but typhus broke out and spread rapidly. The disease, however, was not of a very serious character, as only two deaths occurred, and this loss was more than compensated by the four births that took place during the voyage.

When the settlers reached Mariinsk on June 13, they were informed that places for their future villages had already been chosen by Nevelskoy; but Prince Volkonski sagaciously surmised that the choice had been dictated by purely military considerations, without taking into account the necessities of men obliged to cultivate the soil for their sustenance. He therefore persuaded Muravioff to allow a committee of the oldest peasants to survey the banks of the lower Amur and select the most appropriate places for establishing agricultural settlements. The results of their exploration fully justified the measure proposed by Prince Volkonski, for only one of the places indicated by Nevelskoy was found fit for the purpose for which it was intended. Four settlements were thus formed on the right bank [1] and one on the left

[1] Irkutskoe, Bogorodskoe, Mikhailofskoe, Novo Mikhailofskoe.

bank [1] of the Amur. A colony of Cossacks was also established on an island opposite to the post of Mariinsk.

While the Russians had withdrawn their vessels to Nikolaiefsk and were busy fortifying and colonising the lower Amur, the allied fleet was cruising about in the fruitless search for the Russian squadron which had so mysteriously disappeared from Petropavlofsk and De Castries. On June 27 an English frigate appeared at Ayan, and found it in the same condition as Petropavlofsk and De Castries—no ships in harbour and the inhabitants withdrawn into the interior; she therefore left on July 9.

On the same day Archbishop Innocent, the friend of Muravioff and the strenuous supporter of his schemes for the development of Eastern Siberia, arrived at Ayan. He immediately commenced comforting the inhabitants, who had retired to the woods at twelve versts from the town, christening their infants and celebrating divine service. On July 21 an English frigate again appeared, and was followed by another on the 22nd, when the officers landed. A curious incident then took place. The English officers, being informed of the presence of an Archbishop, proceeded to his house, but found he had gone to church. On their arrival there they found Innocent, in the imposing dress of the Orthodox Church, on his knees, earnestly praying for the success of the Tsar against his enemies. The officers patiently waited until the end of the service, when they informed the Archbishop (probably as a joke) that they were compelled to take him prisoner. Innocent, however, entered into the humour of the situation, declaring that he was not a military man and could be of no use, and added, ‘You see, you will have to feed me.’ The English officers then

[1] Serghiefskoe.

invited the Archbishop on board, drank his health with champagne, and released a Russian pope who had been made prisoner when the allied squadron had captured on July 22 (Aug. 3) a Bremen ship with 300 Russian sailors, the remainder of the crew of the 'Dvina.'

The English made another attempt to capture Zavoiko's vessels in October, when Admiral Stirling ordered Commodore Elliott to sail up the gulf of Tartary. Hopes were entertained that at this advanced period of the year the Russians would be obliged to retire to their winter quarters, and could be surprised taking shelter at De Castries bay. The commander of the 500 Cossacks who had been stationed for the defence of this place by Muravioff, having waited in vain to be attacked until the beginning of October, had in the meanwhile retired to Mariinsk, leaving only a detachment of seventy men,[1] with two mountain guns. On October 3 (15) a frigate and two screw-corvettes appeared at De Castries, to the great surprise of the small garrison ; a courier was sent at once to Mariinsk for reinforcements, while the Cossacks occupied an advantageous position on the skirts of the wood which fringes the bay. The English landed about 400 men, who were at once exposed to a heavy fire from the Russians concealed in the forest. The English replied with grape-shot, but as they could not discover the force of the enemy, and the experience of Petropavlofsk had taught the danger of venturing rashly into an unknown country, they retired to their boats.

During the afternoon the vessels shelled the shore, doing, however, little damage, as the Russians had only one man killed and one wounded. The shelling from the ships continued for several days, but the slender

---

[1] Barsukoff states 120 men.

chances of success the English might have had on the first day were rapidly diminishing as reinforcements successively arrived. On October 4 the Russian commander came back from Mariinsk; on the 5th a company of Cossacks arrived, and was followed by 200 more on the following day. On October 17 the English squadron set sail, thus putting an end to all warlike operations for 1855. In the following year Commander Elliott, resuming his cruise in the gulf of Tartary, accidentally discovered Imperatorski bay, till then unknown to all except the Russians, and found there the burnt hull of the ' Pallada.'

The naval operations of the allies in the Far East were uniformly unsuccessful owing to their ignorance of the country and to the rapid measures of defence taken by Muravioff. The operations in 1854 were terminated by the disaster of Petropavlofsk, and the following year was spent in long fruitless cruises around the supposed peninsula of Saghalien in search of the Russian fleet, which had quietly retired through the straits, where the imagination of geographers had placed an isthmus.

Muravioff, besides superintending the defence of the coast, had in the meantime commenced negotiations with the Chinese about the frontier question. In compliance with his request, Chinese plenipotentiaries had been sent down the Amur, and on September 8 they reached his headquarters at Mariinsk.

The first conference was held on September 9. Muravioff, being sick, was represented by Admiral Zavoiko, who, after repeating the usual arguments about the necessity of protecting the mouth of the Amur against the aggression of foreign powers, made the following proposals:

1. That all the places which had been occupied for

the above purpose, as well as all the coast, should definitely belong to Russia.

2. That to secure uninterrupted communications, both in winter and summer, between the troops and fortresses at the mouth of the Amur and the inland provinces (as communications by land over the mountains had been found practically impossible), it was necessary to have a chain of settlements on the left bank of the Amur, which would thus constitute the best natural frontier between the two empires. By this means Eastern Siberia would be protected from naval attack, and all cause of future disagreement between Russia and China would be removed.

The Chinese plenipotentiaries asked that the proposal should be made in writing, and at the second meeting, which took place on September 11, they read to Muravioff, who had recovered from his illness, the note of the Russian Senate of June 16, 1853—the foolish document by which Nesselrode had compromised the whole question of the Amur. Muravioff, however, skilfully eluded the effects of the weak despatch by remarking that the earnest desire of the Russian Government was the permanent maintenance of peaceful relations between the two great neighbouring empires of China and Russia. He then requested the plenipotentiaries to communicate to the authorities of Peking his intention of sending another expedition down the Amur, and of establishing permanent communications between the troops and fortresses at the mouth of the river and the inland provinces.

After giving instructions for the construction of three powerful forts, mounting fifty-three guns, to defend Nikolaiefsk, which had now become the centre of the Russian forces and the shelter of the fleet, Muravioff started for Irkutsk, choosing, as on former occasions, the route by Ayan. He embarked on the American vessel 'Palmetto,' the first foreign ship to reach the Amur by the southern passage discovered by Nevelskoy. Leaving Nikolaiefsk on October 1 he narrowly escaped capture by an enemy's ship, and after a very rough passage reached Ayan on October 18. He arrived at Irkutsk towards the end of December, nearly three months after his departure from Nikolaiefsk.

From Irkutsk Muravioff issued instructions for a third expedition down the Amur in the following summer. The Chinese merchants trading on the frontier then spread the report that their Government intended to prevent any further navigation on the Amur, a large army being concentrated for this purpose in Southern Mongolia. Though such rumours deserved little credit, it was necessary to obtain accurate information on a subject of such importance, and on January 12, 1856, Volkonski was sent in the severe Mongolian winter with forty-one degrees of frost to Urga. After a very friendly conversation with the Amban, or Mongolian official, it was discovered that the Chinese were making no military preparations for sending an army to the Amur.

Freed from all apprehensions on this account, Muravioff —— saw the expediency of proceeding to St. Petersburg to communicate directly with his Government, especially as great administrative changes were probable in the new reign of Alexander II., who had succeeded his father Nicholas at the beginning of 1855. A number of experienced officials had now been chosen and trained during several years for the special work on the Amur, and they could be trusted to carry out their instructions during their chief's absence. Colonel Korsakoff and Lieut.-Colonel Busse were appointed to superintend the preparations and command the coming expedition down the river.

The conditions of the Russian forces on the lower Amur during the winter were satisfactory, thanks to the extraordinary activity and intelligence displayed by the commanders. It is necessary to bear in mind that in the spring of 1854 the posts of Nikolaiefsk and Mariinsk contained lodgings only for thirty-eight men, and that by the arrival of the successive expeditions down the Amur in 1854 and 1855, by the sudden evacuation of Petropavlofsk, and by the retreat of the fleet in the Amur, about 7,000 people of both sexes were concentrated in those places. Warm houses and provisions were provided for all this large population, notwithstanding that the whole coast was blockaded by the allied fleet, and that through the absence of Russian posts on the Amur all communications with the interior were impossible.

As Muravioff had foreseen, his presence in St. Petersburg was much needed. The Chinese Government had complained about his occupation of places on the Amur, and the Russian Foreign Office, with the self-satisfied consciousness of scoring a diplomatic success of the highest order, intended to demand the right of navigation on that river, and permission to establish on its banks certain stations for storage of provisions and fuel. But Muravioff, who had now become fully aware of the visionary nature of the Chinese claims to sovereignty on the left bank of the Amur, justly considered these demands insufficient and dangerous to the true interests of Russia in the Far East. He therefore applied for and obtained his appointment as plenipotentiary for the negotiation of a new treaty with China.

Having secured this important appointment, which gave him the means of settling the future interests of that

Eastern Siberia which he loved so well, Muravioff was able to attend to his health again, much impaired by hard work and the severity of the climate. After sending minute instructions to Korsakoff about the next navigation on the Amur, advising him to avoid all collision with the Chinese, and even to bear threats with patience, he retired to his favourite German health resort.

The war in Europe had been concluded by the treaty of Paris, but as the third military expedition was already organised, it started down the Amur in the middle of May 1856. It was composed of 110 boats and rafts conveying 1,636 men and 24 officers of the 13th and 14th line battalions; on May 21 it had reached Aigun, and Korsakoff went ashore to confer with the Chinese mandarins. He explained that a large number of vessels would proceed up and down river during the summer, and that provisions and garrisons would be stationed on the left bank of the Amur. The Chinese answered that, although they had received no instructions about the navigation of the river, still they would not restrict the free movements of the Russian vessels; but they objected to the establishment of garrisons and storehouses on the left bank. Korsakoff answered that he was obliged to carry out the instructions of the Governor-General Muravioff, and requested the mandarins of Aigun to report the matter to Peking. The Chinese were very anxious to know the number of Russian troops at the mouth of the river, and Korsakoff told them there were about 10,000, and 5,000 more were expected. They were still more disagreeably surprised when they heard that 500 men were going to be stationed at the mouth of the Zeya opposite to Aigun.

In consequence of the negotiations of Korsakoff, Lieut.-Colonel Busse was able to proceed down river with the third expedition without any opposition, and to found four posts on the left bank : Kumarski, opposite the mouth of the Kumara, with 25 men ; Ust-Zeiski, at the mouth of the Zeya, with 50 men ; Khinganski, at the commencement of the mountain-chain of the Little Khingan, with 24 men ; and Sungariiski, opposite the mouth of the Sungari, also with 24 men. Thus, a few months after the treaty of Paris, the Russians were already established on the whole course of the Amur, with a series of well-chosen posts on the left bank. The Amur had virtually become a Russian river, and it was only necessary to obtain the sanction of the Chinese to what had already been accomplished. This was a question which required only a little time and patience, and it was settled by Muravioff with his usual tact and firmness.

The brilliant achievements of the period 1854–56, the successful defence against the allied fleet, the three expeditions down the Amur, the occupation of the Pacific Coast, and the establishment of posts on the left bank of the Amur had been effected with very little loss of life, even the victory of Petropavlofsk having been cheaply won. But a blind adherence to orders given conditionally, and intended to be interpreted with discretion, marked the end of 1856 with a sad catastrophe, the terrible details of which are still remembered on the Amur. Muravioff, from St. Petersburg, had given instructions that on the conclusion of peace the greater part of the troops stationed on the lower Amur should return to Transbaikalia. General Korsakoff, who was Military Governor in the absence of Muravioff, issued orders to this effect about the middle of April, and at the same time made preparations for forwarding provisions to all the newly established posts on the Amur to revictual the troops as they journeyed up the river. Three transports started successively on June 4, 9, and 12, carrying provisions for 2,700 men to be distributed in the following order:—five days' rations at Ust-Strielk and Kutomanda,[1] ten days' rations at Kumarska and Ust-Zeya, and twenty days' rations at Ust-Sungari.

These prudent measures were absolutely necessary, because the distance to be traversed by the homeward-bound troops from Mariinsk to Ust-Strielk, over 2,300 versts, was at that time a barren waste, where it was difficult and in many places impossible to obtain even a scanty supply of food. The navigation against the stream, and in a late season of the year, was also difficult ; the current of the Amur is very swift, and, unless favourable winds allow the use of sails, vessels can only slowly advance by tracking when the banks are suitable ; if these are swampy or rocky, rowing becomes the only means of propulsion, and progress is still slower. When the waters of the Amur are low and the current less impetuous, it is possible always to keep in the main stream, but it becomes extremely difficult even to distinguish it when the waters rise. From its mouth up to the confluence of the Zeya, a distance of 2,000 versts, with the exception of the rapids of the Little Khingan, where for over 100 versts the bed is confined between hilly banks, the Amur has often a width of 30 versts, and it is hard to discover the main course of the river in the immense expanse of surging waters. In the long toilsome journey, rowing and tracking among islands and along the sinuous banks, mistakes were often made—an affluent being taken for the main river ; thus a whole day was spent in tracking up the Kumara until its direction due

---

[1] This name is not found on the maps ; it must have been near Albazin, judging by the distances from Kumarska and Ust-Strielk.

south revealed that it could not be the Amur. The Cossacks and soldiers were unaccustomed to these difficulties, as in their navigations down the Amur the current itself infallibly indicated the course to the sea.

The troops ordered to return to Transbaikalia were composed of Cossacks and infantry; the former, stationed among the Ghiliacks, were able to purchase native boats and were soon ready to start; the latter encountered greater difficulties, having to wait for the arrival of vessels, or even being obliged to build boats themselves. The homeward-bound expedition was divided into three detachments.

The first, commanded by Colonel Seslavin, numbering about 1,000 men, started about the middle of June, only a few weeks after the official notification of the conclusion of peace had reached the lower Amur. After surmounting great difficulties it reached the Russian borders in good condition at the commencement of winter, the different parties arriving at Ust-Strielk between September 25 and October 8.

The second detachment, commanded by Major Yazykoff, numbering over 800 men, started somewhat later, about the end of June, and was less fortunate; many of the men had contracted fever in the lower Amur, and were too weak to withstand the continuous hard work. Heavy mortality broke out among the troops, especially between the stations of Kumarska and Kutomanda, a distance of 400 versts, which should have been covered in ten days, but which took up fifteen, and in some cases twenty, days. The men, having received only ten days' rations at Kumarska, suffered great distress for want of food, and many perhaps would have died of starvation if they had not luckily found, at 50 versts from Kutomanda, a barge laden with provisions, which had run aground during the preceding summer.

The third detachment, commanded by Colonel Oblenkhoff, numbering nearly 400 men, started very late, as it received orders while conveying cargo on the river, and had to proceed first to Mariinsk, and then prepare for the long, fatiguing homeward journey. Notwithstanding the utmost despatch, their preparations could not be finished before the end of July, a month after the departure of the second detachment. Admiral Kazakievitch strongly dissuaded Oblenkhoff from starting so late in the summer, advising him to postpone his departure to next year and to winter at Nikolaiefsk. The orders given by Karsakoff were conditional, Oblenkhoff being instructed to start only in case he were able to do so early; but the latter was anxious to return to Transbaikalia, and he hoped to distinguish himself by accomplishing the arduous journey even under the most unfavourable conditions.

The ill-fated detachment left Mariinsk on July 27, and arrived at the appointed time on October 8 at Kumarska without having suffered from scarcity of provisions; but on resuming the journey, at only five versts from that post, ice appeared on the river in such quantities as to render it impossible to proceed in boats. The troops had to return to Kumarska and wait, in roughly built huts, nearly three weeks until the ice on the river was sufficiently thick. On October 28, as soon as the river was frozen hard, without the slightest delay, the troops hurried on their march with the terrible consciousness that death was at their heels and that their only safety lay in a swift advance over the long distance before them.

Unfortunately long marches were impossible for the attenuated men with worn-out shoes and threadbare coats. The 400 versts to Kutomanda, reckoned as a ten days' march, was only covered in twenty-two days. The winter days were short, and at night the soldiers were obliged to huddle together around the fires. The cold was intense, twenty degrees (Reaumur) below zero,[1] and was felt more severely as the daily allowance of food was reduced in the vain attempt to make ten days' rations suffice for the whole distance. From November 3 only half the usual quantity of sugar was issued, and on November 6, all the supply of tea having been exhausted, the men were reduced to boil straw and the bark of trees. On November 9 stragglers from the advanced guard began to lag behind. They had the appearance of walking skeletons, and were obliged to gnaw the leather straps of their knapsacks to prolong their wretched existence. Death by starvation with all its terrible accompaniments now seemed to be the doom awaiting the small exhausted column slowly dragging itself forward on the frozen Amur. It was known that a barge laden with provisions had been abandoned near Kutomanda, and the hope of reaching it in time raised the drooping spirits of the men. Many days were passed in alternate hope and fear lest the provisions had been devoured by the preceding detachments. Starvation began to claim its victims, and terrible scenes were enacted among the survivors. At last, on November 15, Cossacks arrived with six horses laden with provisions sent from Kutomanda; the starving men recovered a little strength, and on the 19th were able to reach their destination.

After a few days' rest at Kutomanda the march was resumed. Though no longer menaced by actual starvation, provisions were not abundant, and the intense cold caused even worse sufferings to the ill-clad soldiers, whose worn-out shoes and clothing hardly covered their bodies. On December 12 twenty-four men with frozen feet were abandoned on the way, most of them to die on the icy

---

[1] Equal to 13° Fahrenheit below zero.

expanse of the Amur amid the winter silence of its desolate banks. At last, on December 16, the unfortunate detachment reached Ust-Strielk after a journey of 143 days, in which it lost 102 men—nearly a third of its force.

The terrible experience undergone by this detachment recalls the sufferings of the expeditions under Buza, Dejneff, and Poyarkoff in the seventeenth century, and shows the indomitable energy displayed by the Russians in their struggle against the inhospitable climate of those northern regions which they have chosen for the expansion of their race.

Muravioff remained in Russia until the beginning of December, and, as on his former visits, he obtained the imperial sanction for important measures affecting the welfare of Eastern Siberia. The important posts occupied on the gulf of Tartary and the mouth of the Amur were officially recognised as Russian by the administrative creation of a new province—the Primorskaya, or Coast Province—comprising, besides Kamchatka and the shores of the sea of Okhotsk, also the coast around the mouth of the Amur. Muravioff had already ordered that communications should be kept up during the winter between the posts on the lower Amur, and postal stations had been built between Mariinsk and Nikolaiefsk, with four horses attached to each station. Besides these regular postal communications, the first journey from Nikolaiefsk to Transbaikalia on the frozen Amur with horses and dog-sledges was accomplished during this winter.

In the beginning of 1857 Muravioff began his usual preparations for an expedition down the Amur, which had now become a yearly habit; this time he intended to settle Cossacks with their families on the left bank. As the establishment of these military colonies required the sanction of the Tsar, he forwarded a report to the War Office, and obtained the necessary authorisation.[1]

In the meanwhile events in China attracted the attention of the Russian Government. It was known that England and France were preparing a powerful force for service in the China seas, and intended to send diplomatic residents to Peking. Russia, which had inaugurated official relations with the Celestial Empire nearly two centuries before by the treaty of Nertchinsk, was resolved to participate in the new movement. Admiral Putiatin, already favourably known by the Foreign Office for his successful conclusion of a treaty of commerce with Japan, was appointed Minister at Peking, with instructions also to settle the frontier question.

This nomination at first alarmed Muravioff, as he feared that Russian interests on the left bank of the Amur might be sacrificed in imprudent negotiations with the subtle mandarins of Peking. But after an interview with Putiatin on his arrival at Irkutsk on March 21, 1857, he became convinced that his alarm was unfounded, and that the interests of Russia on the Pacific were in safe hands. In fact he had soon to assume the unwonted and uncongenial part of moderator, and to curb the impetuosity of the bluff sailor.

Putiatin left Irkutsk on March 29, and in April arrived at Irkutsk, where he informed the Chinese frontier authorities of his arrival, and asked permission to proceed to Peking through Mongolia. Muravioff had taken great care to impress the Chinese with the special importance of the embassy; he had sent his band to Kiakhta, had ordered that the town should be illuminated, and the

---

[1] Muravioff's energy and activity had introduced such rapid communications between Irkutsk and St. Petersburg that the report was forwarded on February 28, and the imperial sanction followed on March 19.

troops paraded to receive Putiatin with noise and pomp. But the Chinese, pastmasters in such arts, were not dazzled by the display. With their usual dilatoriness they delayed answering until May, when they informed Putiatin, with covert sarcasm, that as they had no special business to discuss with Russia, it was not necessary that a person of such importance should undertake the long fatiguing journey to Peking.

Putiatin, incensed at the treatment he had received, wrote to the Foreign Office proposing the occupation of Aigun, and on May 15 left Kiakhta to join Muravioff, who, with two battalions of infantry and some field artillery, was proceeding down the Amur. They reached Aigun on June 5, and Putiatin proposed—without waiting for instructions from St. Petersburg—to occupy the town until he obtained permission to go to Peking through Manchuria. But Muravioff was averse from taking such an important step without the authorisation of his Government. He was faithful to the traditional Russian policy of pacific absorption without unnecessary violence. The occupation of the mouth of the Amur and the establishment of posts on the left bank had been effected in territory where China had never exercised any real sovereignty, and her opposition was purely formal. The occupation of Aigun, on the other hand, would have been a manifest act of aggression, arousing just fears for the safety of the whole of Manchuria.

The objections of Muravioff were not based on military motives; he was quite ready for war, had formed his plan of campaign even for an advance on Peking if necessary; and on June 4, at Ust-Zeya, opposite to Aigun, had given Putiatin a statement of the forces disposable on the frontiers of Manchuria and Mongolia. He had ready 16,000 infantry, 5,000 cavalry, 1,000 artillery with forty pieces, besides a reinforcement of 1,000 men which could be sent over the frontier from Irkutsk and Yenisseisk; a force sufficient at that time, when China was desolated by the Tai-ping rebellion and threatened by England and France, to take Peking and dictate terms of peace. But Muravioff had no desire for a war of conquest; he only wished to secure for Russia an outlet to the sea through territory which had never been occupied by the Chinese, and which they had thus tacitly recognised as useless.

Putiatin asked the Chinese authorities at Aigun for permission to proceed to Peking through Manchuria; but it could not be granted, as no instructions had been sent from the capital. Finding it therefore impossible to reach his destination by land, he resolved to make an attempt by sea, and, leaving Muravioff at Ust-Zeya, he descended the Amur. Putiatin started from Nikolaiefsk on July 1, and, after inspecting some new harbours on the gulf of Tartary, on July 24 reached the mouth of the Peiho.

The Chinese had been informed of his intended visit by sea, and had forwarded a despatch stating that Tientsin, near the mouth of the Peiho, was not a fit place for negotiations. This despatch in due course of time was answered from St. Petersburg by a fresh request that the Russian Minister should be received in the capital. In the meanwhile Putiatin was engaged in a fruitless diplomatic contest with the obstinate Chinese mandarins at Tientsin. At first they refused even to receive his despatches; but, though they finally yielded on this point, they would not allow him to proceed to the capital, and complained to St. Petersburg about his pertinacity, stating that only foreign envoys, bearers of tribute to the Emperor, were admitted in Peking.

Putiatin, after remaining some time at the mouth of the Peiho, went to Shanghai, where he attentively followed the military operations of the French and English, who were then preparing to attack Canton. He communicated much valuable information to his Government about the internal conditions of China, and the terror pervading the maritime provinces at the arrival of the Russian vessels in the gulf of Pechili. The local knowledge acquired on the coast enabled him to suggest the most effective plan for overcoming Chinese obduracy. He proposed to blockade the mouth of the Peiho and prevent the junks carrying grain to Peking from discharging their cargo. As his diplomatic mission had failed, at the end of December 1857 he was appointed admiral of the detached squadron in the China seas, and Imperial Commissioner, with instructions to watch the operations of the Western Powers during the war.

After Putiatin had left Ust-Zeya, Muravioff remained on the Amur the whole summer, attending to administrative and diplomatic business with his usual activity. A series of Cossack villages, comprising 450 families, were established on the left bank of the river from Ust-Strielk to the rapids of the Little Khingan, and a camp was formed at Ust-Zeya for the 14th line battalion and a detachment of artillery. Strict orders were given to live on friendly terms both with the aborigines and Chinese; but, on the other hand, in case of unfriendliness or concentration of troops at Aigun, the Russians were instructed to cross the river and disarm the Chinese, and even to occupy the town.

The Chinese commander at Aigun addressed a protest to Muravioff against the constant navigation of the Amur and the permanent settlement of troops and colonists on the left bank of the river, declaring this conduct to be injurious to the continued friendship of the two countries, and insinuating that it had not been authorised by the

Russian Government. But the protest came too late—
the Russians had discovered the imaginary nature of
the Chinese sovereignty, and the little value attached to
the region ; besides, the Chinese, through excessive fear
and obstinacy, had recently given just cause for offence.
Muravioff quickly availed himself of these facts ; in
his answer he referred to the previous correspondence
between the two Governments, and declared that as a
Russian envoy had been appointed for Peking, and was at
present in the gulf of Pechili, all questions should be
settled with him ; he therefore returned the despatch to
Aigun.

On his return from the Amur, Muravioff left Irkutsk
for St. Petersburg, but, after a short residence there, was
obliged to go abroad on account of his health.

In the meanwhile the newly settled Amur region was
progressing rapidly. During the summer of 1857 seven
foreign vessels entered the river, and the following winter
a road for postal communications between Nikolaiefsk and
Ust-Strielk was completed.

In the spring of 1858 Muravioff, after having restored
his health in Europe, had returned to Irkutsk, and was
preparing for his usual yearly expedition down the Amur.
He had intended it should have been far larger than any
of the preceding, a whole brigade of Cossacks with their
families—about 12,000 persons of both sexes—being
destined as colonists in the new region. But the outstanding questions with China rendered it necessary to postpone
this great exodus.

Putiatin had vainly tried to persuade the Chinese to
send plenipotentiaries to Shanghai to treat with him, and
it now became evident that Muravioff, who had already
occupied the Amur, was the man best qualified to obtain
the official recognition of the accomplished annexation.

The Chinese Government, at that time, was engaged in a dangerous struggle with the Taiping rebellion, and with England and France. It could not consent to treat either at Peking or at Shanghai about the alienation of territory or the renunciation of sovereign rights, without losing prestige in the eyes of its own subjects and of the foreign enemy. It preferred to relegate such negotiations to a little-known region, on the unfrequented banks of the great northern river of the Black Dragon.[1]

Muravioff, having decided to start as soon as the ice broke up on the river, sent in advance a courier to Ust-Zeya with instructions to communicate to the Chinese authorities at Aigun his speedy arrival, but to add that he would stop only a short time, as he was in haste to reach the mouth of the Amur. Therefore, if the Chinese wished to confer with Muravioff, they had better put off the meeting until his return voyage. Muravioff was really anxious to reach Nikolaiefsk, as he hoped to receive there news from Putiatin; but he also wished to convince the Chinese that he had no special desire to enter into negotiations. The ruse produced the expected effect.

On April 26, Muravioff left Strietensk, and on May 6 he reached Ust-Zeya; but at eighty versts before that place he had been met by Chinese mandarins, requesting him to delay his departure and confer with Prince T-shan, the commander-in-chief of the forces on the Amur. Muravioff had at last brought the Chinese to the point he wished, and the negotiations were forthwith commenced, and pushed on with his usual alertness.

On May 11 the first conference was held at Aigun. Muravioff proposed that the river Amur should be the frontier between the two empires, and showed its necessity—especially at a time when England, being at

[1] The Chinese name for the Amur.

war with China, might seize the mouth of the Amur and the coast to the south by right of conquest. The Chinese general repeated the arguments, already often adduced by the Peking Government, that all the preceding treaties had settled the frontier along the rivers Gorbitza, Uda, and through an undetermined region along the coast. After a very long discussion Muravioff ended the sitting by producing the draft of a treaty already prepared, and on which he demanded the views of the Chinese plenipotentiary on the following day.   It consisted of the following articles :

1. The frontier of the two empires to be : (1) the river Amur, the left bank to the mouth to belong to Russia, the right bank up to the river Ussuri to belong to China. (2) The course of the Ussuri to its sources, and thence the frontier was to go south to the peninsula of Corea.

2. Navigation on the rivers marking the frontier to be allowed only to vessels of the two empires.

3. Free trade to be allowed on the above rivers.

4. Chinese subjects living on the left bank to remove to the right bank within a period of three years.

5. The revision (by persons specially appointed for that object by the two empires) of preceding treaties, in order to fix new rules for all matters concerning the profit and glory of both empires.

6. The present convention to be considered as supplementary to preceding treaties.

The first conference had shown that the Chinese were very anxious to preserve friendly relations with Russia, but they seemed also obstinately bent on adhering to their own views about the frontier. The negotiations, therefore, promised to be long and difficult. Muravioff was determined, on the other hand, that they should be brief. To attain this object, he again concealed his impatience, and, alleging sickness, on May 12 he sent his interpreter Pero to continue the negotiations.

As after several long sittings the obstinate Chinese showed no signs of yielding, Muravioff again changed his tactics, assuming a more resolute tone. Pero was instructed to inform the Chinese that only the magnanimity of the Russian Tsar had preserved peace between the two countries after the late unjustifiable affronts; that they had no right to quote on every occasion the treaty of Nertchinsk concluded in 1689, because on that occasion they had acted with bad faith, sending their envoys with an army, and threatening offensive operations, while the Russian plenipotentiary had come only with a simple escort. Besides, the Chinese had been the first to violate that treaty by levying tribute in places not within their frontier. They had also lately given serious offence by refusing to receive Putiatin, and by burning a Russian factory. This energetic remonstrance produced a great impression on the Chinese, who at last consented to conclude the convention.

On May 16, 1858, the convention of Aigun was signed; it had been concluded with Muravioff's usual rapidity, the negotiations lasting only six days. A few concessions were made to the Chinese. The Manchu inhabitants on the left bank of the Amur near the river Zeya were allowed to remain under the Chinese authorities, and the region between the Ussuri and the sea was declared to belong in common to Russia and China until the frontier should be permanently fixed. In granting the last point, Muravioff probably had in mind the treaty of Nertchinsk, which likewise left undetermined the territory adjacent to the sea. Russia had waited 170 years to settle the vague frontier of Golovin. It took only two years to complete the frontier of the convention of Aigun.

The terms exacted by Muravioff were very moderate, considering the military power at his disposal and the conditions of the Chinese Empire at that time. Nevelskoy had urged the necessity of claiming the whole basin of the Ussuri, advancing the frontier to the mountain chain of the Little Khingan, which runs between that river and the Sungari.

On his return to Ust-Zeya, Muravioff was received with great enthusiasm, and a few days later, on May 21, a solemn religious service was celebrated by Archbishop Innocent in a church which had been specially constructed and consecrated in the name of the Holy Annunciation.

At the church parade Muravioff addressed the troops with a few impressive words such as he knew so well how to choose on all important occasions : 'Comrades, I congratulate you ! We have not laboured in vain ; the Amur now belongs to Russia ! The prayers of the holy Orthodox Church and the thanks of Russia are for you ! Long life to Emperor Alexander II., and may the newly acquired country flourish under his protection ! Hurrah ! '

The post of Ust-Zeya was also at the same time re-christened with the name of Blagoveshtchensk,[1] the Annunciation.

The final solution of the question of the eastern frontier of Siberia caused great satisfaction in St. Petersburg, and Muravioff received the title of Count Amurski.

After this brilliant diplomatic success Muravioff did not relax his unremitting exertions ; he prosecuted his voyage down the Amur to Nikolaiefsk, settling Cossacks and troops in the most convenient places.

At the mouth of the Ussuri, near the place where Khabaroff repulsed the attacks of the Manchus, an

---

[1] It is now the most flourishing city on the Amur.

important post was established and named Khabarofsk[1] in honour of the bold Cossack explorer. On his return voyage, in the steamer 'Amur,' he ascended the Sungari, and inaugurated Russian navigation on the river, asserting the rights granted by the convention of Aigun.[2]

It was the third time that Muravioff descended the whole course of the Amur to its mouth, and it is remarkable that on each occasion important results were achieved.

In 1854 he opened the Amur and saved Petropavlofsk; in 1855 he saved the Russian fleet; and in 1858 the Amur was confirmed to Russia. On his return to Irkutsk his attention was directed to the Ussuri country. He planned the settlement of Cossacks on that river, and urged the necessity of light-draught steamers.

He resolved to visit the coast next year, and ascertain the requirements of the new frontier. From a conversation with the Chinese officials at Aigun, on his return voyage, Muravioff had ascertained that mandarins had been sent on the river Sui-fun to mark the frontier. But this was incompatible with Russian interests on the Pacific, which required the coast a hundred versts to the south, as far as Possiet bay on the Corean frontier.

The convention of Aigun had been followed at a week's

---

[1] It is now the seat of the Governor-General of the three provinces of Transbaikalia, Priamurskaya, and Primorskaya.

[2] The First Article granted the Russians the right of navigation on the Sungari river, and it was confirmed by the Fourth Article of the Treaty of Peking and the Eighteenth Article of the Treaty of 1881. Notwithstanding these repeated sanctions the Russians have been unable to practically enforce their rights. In 1859 Maximoff went up the Sungari as far as the town of San-Sin, but was obliged to return; in 1864, steamers sent to explore the Sungari reached Ghirin, but met with great difficulties, the mandarins forbidding the inhabitants to sell provisions to the Russians; in 1866 the Russian Government sent an expedition to buy grain, but the mandarins prevented the inhabitants from trading; in 1869 other unsuccessful attempt to open trade was made by Russian merchants.

interval by the treaty of commerce concluded at Tientsin on June 1, 1858, by Putiatin, whose perseverance had been at last crowned with success. Perceiving that the Chinese were beginning to yield to foreign pressure, and allow approach to the capital, the Russian Government in January 1859 decided to appoint General Ignatieff political agent at Peking, with instructions to settle the frontier question on the Ussuri. Muravioff approved the measure, and suggested that Ignatieff should be appointed full Minister in order to be of equal rank with his British colleague, Minister Bruce. On the arrival of Ignatieff, Muravioff accompanied him to Kiakhta on April 17, 1859, but the Chinese delayed granting permission to proceed to Peking, and Muravioff was obliged to leave him on May 2, in order to attend to affairs on the Amur.

Shortly after Muravioff's departure, General Ignatieff received instructions to proceed to Peking, where, however, his desire for a speedy arrangement of the frontier in the Ussuri region met with the usual obstructive dilatoriness on the part of the Chinese.

Muravioff, in the meanwhile, was busy collecting information about the region which was to be delimitated. A party was sent to reconnoitre the country and draw up maps, and Muravioff, after his arrival at Nikolaiefsk at the end of May, started for a long cruise on the Pacific coast. He visited Japan, arrived at the mouth of the Pei-ho shortly after the unsuccessful attack of the Taku forts by the English and French fleets, and then went to Wei-hai-wei, where he remained some time. But the most important result of this expedition was the survey of the coast of the Ussuri region ; Muravioff carefully examined the vast gulf near the Corean frontier, giving it the name of Peter the Great bay (Victoria bay), and selected the harbour of Vladivostok and Possiet bay as sites for future settlements. His mind was always ready to grasp new facts, and to modify his views as his knowledge expanded and circumstances altered. His fixed plan of extending Russian influence in the Pacific had led him, on his first arrival as Governor-General of Eastern Siberia, to select Petropavlofsk in 1849 as the future site of the great Russian naval station ; later the discoveries of Nevelskoy and the experience of the war with the allies had shown the superior advantages of Nikolaiefsk and De Castries ; now the convention of Aigun, and the troubles of China with the Tai-ping rebels and the Western Powers, gave Russia the opportunity of securing more southerly ports, and Muravioff recognised that the bay of Peter the Great was destined to become the centre of Russian naval power in the Pacific.

The preliminary steps for the execution of this plan were carried out in the following year, when a party of forty men occupied Vladivostok on July 20, 1860, and a company of infantry about the same time occupied Possiet bay. The effective occupation of the region soon received diplomatic sanction by the Treaty of Peking, concluded on November 2 by General Ignatieff ; the Chinese were forced to abandon their procrastination and to yield to the persistent demands of Russia, when they were humbled by the Western Powers. The frontier desired by Muravioff was granted, and Manchuria lost all access to the sea on the east.

By the annexation of the whole Ussuri region Russia acquired a fertile territory with a relatively mild climate and several fine harbours. The measures adopted for the colonisation of the left bank of the Amur were now employed on the right bank of the Ussuri and on the sea-coast ; Cossack settlements and peasant colonies were established in the most appropriate places for practising agriculture and maintaining communications with the

Amur. In the first years, however, Russia suffered from the same troubles which have more recently afflicted France and Japan in Tonkin and Formosa; bands of Chinese outlaws overran the country lightly ceded by their Government, and persistently harassed the new foreign masters. In 1868 these brigands increased in numbers and boldness; they formed bands 1,000 strong, attacking and burning the Russian settlements; the scanty Russian forces, scattered in small detachments over the extensive region, were in several cases surprised and defeated. But the arrival of reinforcements from the Amur, and the rapid concentration of the small garrisons in the Ussuri region, soon enabled the Russians to take the offensive, disperse the brigands, and restore tranquillity in the country.

The last plans of Muravioff were carried out eleven years after his departure, in 1872, when the Russian naval station in the East was transferred from Nikolaiefsk to Vladivostok. This port, situated at the south-eastern extremity of the Russian Asiatic dominions, near the Corean frontier, is more favourably situated than its predecessors—Petropavlofsk and Nikolaiefsk; it is closed by ice only during a few months, and even then, owing to the latest improvements in ice-breakers, it can be artificially kept open for navigation during the whole winter. The aspiration for an outlet on the open sea, which had become part of the national policy since the time of Peter the Great, had at last been realised on the Pacific at the terminus of the great eastward expansion, which had been proceeding intermittently for nearly three centuries.

This new naval station in the Far East, securing access to the ocean, offered compensation for the long enforced exclusion from the land-locked Black Sea. The Russians, probably influenced by this reflection, were led to notice the resemblance of the natural features of their

new port to those of Constantinople. The city of the Byzantine Cæsars had fascinated the mind of the race from the time of Oleg's famous raid, and the marriage of Ivan III. with Sophia Paleologus had strengthened this feeling by raising dynastic claims to the inheritance of the fallen Greek Empire. These thoughts recurred to the Russians at the end of their long eastward advance, when they named the sinuous channels of the sea at Vladivostok, and thus on the former shores of Manchuria we now find the eastern Bosphorus and the Golden Horn.

The possession of the Amur and of the sea-coast up to the frontier of Corea completed the Russian expansion in Northern Asia; Muravioff finished the work commenced by Yermak. The Cossack ataman had shown the way across the Ural, and the impulse given by his powerful individuality sufficed to bring the Russians to the Straits of Behring by the middle of the seventeenth century, but the want of support from Moscow had rendered fruitless the daring exploits on the Amur. While in the north a natural frontier had been found on the shores of the Pacific, in the south cramped boundaries had been accepted through fear of the military power of China. This abrupt and unnatural termination of the glorious process of conquest which had given Russia the northern part of the continent, had been acquiesced in for 160 years, until the energy and activity of Muravioff overcame the obstacles raised by bureaucratic indolence and diplomatic timidity.

This long period of inactivity need not seem strange if we reflect on the general slow advance of the Russian race, originally weak in numbers, expanding over the enormous extent of the northern plains; it can be paralleled in the European history of the nation. The heroic but premature victory of Kulikovo in 1380 required a century to unfold its consequences in the overthrow of the Tartar domination. On the banks of the Amur, in the Far East, the daring exploits of Khabaroff and Tolbuzin effected no permanent results in the seventeenth century; they bore fruit only in the nineteenth century, when the Russian race, grown more numerous, had already established settlements beyond the Baikal.

The parallel can be carried further. As the overthrow of the Tartars was due to a double process, the gradual increase of the power of Moscow and their slow decline through misgovernment and internecine warfare, so in the Far East we have similar factors working to bring about a reversal of conditions. In the period following the Treaty of Nertchinsk the Russian Empire had grown enormously in power, the population in Siberia had increased considerably, and numerous settlements had been founded in Transbaikalia, forming a convenient base of operations on the Amur. On the other hand, events of an opposite nature had taken place in the Great Empire of Eastern Asia. The warlike Manchus, scattered among the enormous population of China, had gradually lost their military virtues; their warlike reputation, become a mere tradition, was dispelled by the rude attack of the English in the first China war; the Tai-ping rebellion which followed threatened to overthrow the Government.

Besides this general weakness the local conditions on the Amur were still more unfavourable; Manchuria, the original seat of the dynasty, had gradually become a neglected province in the distant north; a part of its hardy population had emigrated to gather the fruits of victory in the fertile regions of the south, and had been replaced by Chinese immigrants of a quiet, peaceful character. To secure Russian supremacy and recover the long-lost Amur it was sufficient to recognise the altered conditions and to utilise the forces accumulated during two centuries. Muravioff had the merit of discarding preconceived opinions founded on historical precedents obliterated by time, and of resolutely carrying out the clear views formed by personal observation. As soon as he had ascertained the weakness of the Chinese on the Amur, and had organised the Cossack army in Transbaikalia, the annexation of the new provinces depended simply on the time necessary for overcoming the sluggishness and timidity of the Russian Foreign Office.

Muravioff had also the merit of imparting a new direction to Russian expansion in Eastern Asia. The general north-eastern tendency of the race has been sufficiently shown ; the sea alone stopped the Cossacks in the seventeenth century, and even this obstacle was insufficient at the beginning of the present century, when the Russians continued their advance, crossing to the American continent and occupying Alaska. Muravioff considered that the American possessions should be ceded to the United States under favourable conditions, and his advice was followed, and Alaska was sold. He thought that Russia should limit her activity to the old continent. Here, however, the sea, which had been already reached during the seventeenth and eighteenth centuries, precluded all expansion to the east. It became, therefore, necessary to follow the shores and expand in an opposite direction to the south-west. The places successively chosen for naval stations in the brief period of Muravioff's administration, Petropavlofsk, Nikolaiefsk, Vladivostok,[1] clearly indicate the new direction.

---

[1] The naval station was transferred to Vladivostok some years after Muravioff had left Siberia, but he had already indicated the advantage of its position.

The annexation of the Amur having been effected to obtain access to the Pacific, the possession of open ports now became a necessary consequence of that policy. Each successive port chosen, though superior to its predecessors, raised the desire for another further to the south, freer from ice during the winter. After the transfer of the naval station from Nikolaiefsk to Vladivostok, close to the frontier of Corea, the south-western expansion of Russia along the coasts of Asia was checked for a considerable time. Though the disordered internal conditions of the Corean peninsula, a prey to party intrigues and civil war, invited intervention and offered a good field for the administrative ability of the Russians, which has established order in so many regions of Asia, the rival interests of China, Japan, and Great Britain rendered any advance in that direction extremely dangerous.

For a long time Russia was suspected of having designs on a Corean port, but these fears were exaggerated and could only refer to a remote contingency. Russia has been uniformly cautious, and has only absorbed countries neglected by owners and neighbours. Besides, her maritime requirements always have been moderate; Vladivostok sufficed as a naval station in the Pacific, and it remained the most southern port of Asiatic Russia for thirty years. When a further advance was made it was not due to Russian initiative, but was brought about by a rapid succession of unexpected events, and by the necessity of counterbalancing the acquisitions of other Powers.

The wants of Russia in the Far East, after the annexation of the Amur province and the Ussuri region, though less urgent, were similar to those felt at the time when Muravioff began his brilliant administration in Eastern Siberia. An outlying part of the Empire, now in the south instead of the north, required to be connected by a more direct route ; Vladivostok, the centre of naval power in the Pacific, could only be reached by a long detour by the Amur and Ussuri rivers. Far more important than the acquisition of a port further south was the question of securing rapid and easy communication with Vladivostok. As long as steam navigation on the rivers was the most rapid available means of communication in the Amur region, the circuitous route presented no inconvenience, but its disadvantages became evident when the Russian Government conceived the gigantic project of extending the Siberian railway to the shores of the Pacific.

CHAPTER VI

THE SIBERIAN RAILWAY

THE great rivers of Siberia and their numerous affluents, which facilitated the work of conquest, served also as the readiest means of communication for commerce and news in the early period of the Russian occupation. But these natural highways soon required to be supplemented, especially when the Russians, increasing in numbers, were able to extend southward and conquer the warlike natives of the more fertile regions. The climate and the nature of the soil in the south are favourable to the establishment of a large settled population, while the affluents of the great rivers do not approach so closely as in the north, where in several cases a portage of a few miles is sufficient to connect two river-basins. The Russian colonists therefore settled principally in the south, forming in time a chain of towns and villages, which it was found necessary to connect by roads.

The sovereigns of Moscow continued in northern Asia the mission they had pursued in Russia : the suppression of disorder and violence, and the establishment of a strong peaceful government, in regions hitherto desolated by tribal feuds, and by raids of the nomads of the steppes. They knew the violent, undisciplined character of the Cossack founders of the Asiatic Empire, and recognised the necessity of exercising control by a system of regular communications. The opening of postal roads,

the construction of stations, the settlement of postilions
in the distant region, were among the first cares of the
Government.

As early as 1601, yamshtchiks or postilions were settled
at Tiumen, a frontier town of Siberia, and their number
increased steadily ; in the year 1710 it was reckoned that
they amounted (with their families) to about 7,000, out of
a total population of 250,000 souls. The distances between
the principal towns were also carefully measured, and
mile-posts erected : in 1715 this work was accomplished
between Yakutsk and Okhotsk, and in 1721 it was
carried out between Krasnoyarsk and Irkutsk. In the
year 1712 orders had been issued to widen the roads in
Western Siberia to a breadth of twenty-one feet.

All these measures were necessary for the work of the
Government, for the rapid conveyance of despatches and
officials, and were similar to the methods adopted by
founders of empires in extensive thinly peopled regions
in all ages. Cyrus in Western Asia, and Charlemagne in
Central Europe, had recognised in remote times the
necessity of building roads, and of organising a special
service of government couriers. But as soon as the
Russian domination was established in Siberia, the
Tsars of Moscow adopted also measures for the general
benefit of their distant possession and its inhabitants :
their enlightened policy was far in advance of the age.

The postal roads, and their regular succession of
stations with relays of horses and postilions, served for
the general use of the public, as well for the conveyance
of travellers as for the transmission of letters. The rates
charged for these services were extremely moderate.
The price charged for post-horses in Western Siberia at
the beginning of the eighteenth century was from two- to
three-tenths of a kopeck per verst. In Scotland, in 1603,

the charge for post-horses was $2\frac{1}{2}d$. for a mile. The charge for letters was also very moderate ; it was reckoned per *zolotnik* (about a sixth of an ounce), and from Moscow to Verkhatur, Tobolsk, and Tjumen, an average distance of over 2,100 versts, the tariff was 18 kopecks per *zolotnik*. From Moscow to Berezof, Surgut, Tomsk, Yenisseisk, and Krasnoyarsk, an average distance of over 3,700 versts, the rate was 30 kopecks. From Moscow to Ilimsk, Yakutsk, Irkutsk, and Nertchinsk, an average distance of over 6,500 versts,[1] 40 kopecks were charged. This tariff prevailed in 1682 and in 1696.

These charges will appear wonderfully low if we compare them with those levied nearly a century and a half later—in the first half of this century—in the most advanced nations of Western Europe. In England as much as $14d$. could be charged on a letter, and in France for $7\frac{1}{2}$ grammes (less than two *zolotniks*) 1 franc 20 centimes were charged for a maximum distance of 900 kilometres, about a ninth of the Russian maximum distance to Yakutsk. In the United States up to 1846, 10 cents were charged for distances over 300 miles. In the convention of 1836 between France and England the postage across the frontier was fixed at $10d$. or 1 franc. It is, indeed, very strange that while even in England (the nation most advanced commercially) up to the beginning of this century the postal system was based on the most narrow-minded fiscalism, and had for its sole object the extortion of money from the public, in Siberia more than half a century before, the Russian Government was inspired by the enlightened views inaugurated by Palmer, and now prevailing throughout Western Europe, that the

---

[1] All these distances have been given according to the *Russky Kalendar*, where there is a table of the distances of all Russian towns from Moscow.

primary object of the postal service should be the convenience and advantage of the public.

The postal communications in Siberia were rare and slow in the early times. In 1724 there was only a monthly service to Tobolsk from Moscow; later, in 1731, it became fortnightly; but from Tobolsk to Yenisseisk and Yakutsk it was only monthly, and from Yakutsk to Okhotsk only once every two months. It required half a year for news to travel from Kamchatka to Moscow in the eighteenth century. These slow, interrupted services appear strange now, but they cease to cause surprise when we compare them with the old postal communications of the most advanced nations of the West. Before 1633 there was only a weekly mail between London and Antwerp and Brussels; in 1667 there were only two posts a week between Edinburgh and Aberdeen, and one to Inverness; in 1702 there was only a fortnightly service between New York and Boston. The delivery of letters in the British Isles was also very slow. Before 1635 letters were carried on foot, and two months were required for an answer to a letter from London to Scotland or Ireland. Before Palmer's plan (1784) the average speed of the post was only three and a half miles an hour.

These comparative figures show that Siberia was not very backward in postal communications in the early period; and when we consider the extent of the country, its rigorous climate, scanty population, and the peculiar conditions of Russian history, which up to the time of Peter the Great prevented all influence of the progressive nations of the West, we must give full credit to the Government of Moscow for the attention it paid to its distant possessions.

In Western Siberia, on the flat uniform plains, the construction and maintenance of the roads offered no difficulties except at the crossing of the rivers and water-courses, where, however, by an ingenious system of ferry-boats,[1] the traffic suffered little interruption. But in Eastern Siberia the natural conditions of the country were not so favourable ; the huge Lake Baikal, stretching from north to south for over 400 miles, and surrounded by lofty mountains, presented great difficulties ; further east the Yablonoi, with their steep slope on the Pacific, offered great obstacles to the construction of the road to Okhotsk indispensable for easy communications with Kamchatka. The Baikal at favourable times was easily crossed, and its waters became the highway for the trans-port of goods and travellers into Transbaikalia. But when traffic increased, especially with the development of the China trade through Kiakhta, the inconveniences of the route across the lake became evident. The Baikal is subject to violent storms, and as it is frozen for several months in winter, there are intervals in spring and autumn when it is impossible to cross, as the ice, though too weak to bear sledges, is sufficient to impede naviga-tion. These various causes often stopped all traffic, and goods accumulated on the shores without means of trans-port.

Towards the end of the eighteenth century these facts were brought to the knowledge of the Russian Govern-ment, which authorised the expenditure necessary for the construction of a road around the southern extremity of Lake Baikal for alternate use whenever the direct passage across the lake, either by sledges or ships, was impossible. By this means uninterrupted communications were secured along the great postal road traversing the Russian

[1] The *samoliots* which, fixed by long cables to anchors in the middle of the stream, swing across from bank to bank like a pendulum under the influence of the current.

possessions in Asia from west to east. The road stretched as far as the Russian dominions up to the boundaries fixed by the treaty of Nertchinsk ; but when Muravioff's bold action advanced the frontier to the Pacific Ocean, the road was extended along the course of the Amur and the Ussuri up to Vladivostok. Then a portal was erected at Irkutsk, at the commencement of the eastern extension of the great highway, some thousand miles from the sea, bearing the simple inscription, ' Road to the Pacific Ocean.' These appropriate words briefly summarise the object of Muravioff's policy in the Far East.

The road along the Amur and Ussuri was supplementary, and only used when the winter frosts rendered impossible the steam navigation which Muravioff had introduced from the beginning of the Russian occupation.

About the middle of the present century the most important applications of science to the wants of life began to penetrate Siberia and profoundly influence its economical development. The first steamer appeared on the Ob as early as 1843,[1] and another, the ' Constantin,' entered the mouth of the Amur in 1846; and in 1863 steam navigation commenced on the Yenissei. At present steamers are running on all the Siberian rivers and their more important affluents, and the traffic is increasing yearly.

The introduction and development of steam navigation in Siberia many years before the construction of railways forms a curious parallel to the ancient expeditions of the Cossacks in the sixteenth and seventeenth centuries, when they advanced on the northern rivers long before using the roads to the south. Steam has

---

[1] After several failures, the first successful steamer appeared on the Volga only in 1842.

penetrated and spread through Siberia almost in the footsteps of Yermak and his successors.

Before examining the construction and future of the Siberian railway, it will be useful to cast a hasty glance on the development and present state of steam navigation on the rivers, as both systems of communication are bound to interact mutually.

The navigation on the splendid water-ways of Siberia is handicapped not only by the climate, but also by the fact that the great rivers flow into unfrequented seas and through thinly peopled districts. The Ob, Yenissei, and Lena flow northward into the Arctic Ocean, until lately considered ill adapted for regular navigation ; and though the general course of the Amur is eastward, as soon as it receives its full complement of waters from the Sungari and Ussuri, it also runs northward for 5 degrees of latitude and debouches into the bleak inhospitable sea of Okhotsk. The population throughout Siberia is still so scanty that in many regions there is only a fraction of an inhabitant per square mile.

Among the great rivers in the north, the Ob, lying further to the west, is most favourably situated ; it flows into the Arctic Ocean at a lower latitude than either the Yenissei or the Lena, and the districts through which it passes are more populous. Western Siberia, containing the greater part of the Ob basin, has three million inhabitants on about one million square miles— quite a dense population for Siberia. Moreover, the vicinity to European Russia offers a great transit trade—exports of raw produce and imports of manufactured goods.

In consequence of these favourable conditions steam navigation on the Ob and its affluents has progressed rapidly. The following table, compiled from two independent sources, Dolgorukoff and ' Siberia and the Siberian

Railway,' which agree in the main, will show at a glance the steady increase in the number of steamers during half a century:

Year	Number of Steamers, according to	
	Dolgorukoff	'Siberia,' &c.
1846	2	—
1854	—	3
1859	5	—
1860	12	10
1864	16	—
1866	26	—
1870	—	22
1875	—	32
1880	36	37
1883	50	—
1885	—	57
1887	—	60
1889	—	64
1890	65	65
1891	—	69
1892	—	90
1893	—	102
1895	120	—

As early as 1846 the first voyage from Tomsk to Tiumen, now the principal line, was accomplished, and in 1853 regular trips between those towns were established. In 1860 a monthly line was inaugurated between Tobolsk and Tiumen, and the first voyage to Berezof on the lower Ob accomplished. In the following year steamers went up the Irtysh as far as Semipalatinsk, and next year (1862) steam navigation commenced on the Tavda and its affluents, the Sosva and Lozva. In 1865 the first steamer went up the Tchulym to Atchinsk.

In the river system of the Ob, covering over three and a half million square versts (more than one and a half million square miles), with a length of 5,300 versts and with regular navigation for 15,000 versts (10,000 English miles), there are at present [1] four principal lines of steamers:

[1] According to the *Guide to Siberia* of 1897.

1. Tiumen—Tobolsk—Tomsk ;
2. Tiumen—Tobolsk—Omsk—Semipalatinsk ;
3. Tomsk—Barnaul—Biisk ;
4. Tomsk—Tchulym.

The first and most important line is 2,178 versts long (over 1,400 miles), and runs on the rivers Tura, Tobol, Irtysh, Ob, and Tom ; the steamers cover the distance in about eight or ten days. The second is 2,684 versts long (about 1,780 miles), and runs on the rivers Tura, Tobol, and Irtysh. The third and fourth are simply branch lines from Tomsk, running in the first case for over 1,000 versts on the upper Ob and river Bii, and in the second for about the same distance on the Ob and river Tchulym.

To understand the functions performed by these lines it is necessary to examine the economical condition of Siberia, especially of its western part and the pre-existing trade-routes. Owing to the scanty population and absence of manufacturing centres there is little local trade in Siberia. Commerce is represented by the exchange of the mineral and agricultural produce of Northern Asia with the manufactured goods of European Russia. This traffic has been carried on principally along the route first traced by Yermak and the early conquerors of Siberia by the rivers Volga, Kama, Tchussovoya, Serebrianka, Taghil, Tura, Tobol, Irtysh, and Ob, passing from the eastern water-ways of Russia to the western ones of Siberia.[1]

The introduction of steamers has simply developed trade on the old routes : the line from Tiumen to Semipalatinsk serving for the trade of the region watered by the Irtysh, and the line from Tiumen to Tomsk for that

---

[1] The lines of steamers and railways follow so closely the old routes of the Cossacks that the small maps of Chap. ii. serve also for this chapter.

watered by the Ob. The third and fourth lines bring to the important commercial centre of Tomsk the traffic of the upper affluents of the Ob. The common terminus, therefore, of all the lines is Tiumen, a town on the river Tura not far from the ancient portage, now rendered obsolete by a short railway, leading to the basin of the Kama and thence to the great Volga.

The distribution of trade along the rivers is accomplished in the following order and proportion. European goods coming from Tiumen descend the Tura and Tobol, a small quantity branching off up the Tavda and Sosva. At the mouth of the Tobol an important division takes place : 25 per cent. of the goods go up the Irtysh (by the second line of steamers) to Omsk and Semipalatinsk ; the remaining 75 per cent. descend the Irtysh to its confluence with the Ob, where a small quantity is sent down the lower Ob to Berezof and Obdorsk, while the greater part go up the Ob to Surgut, Narym, and Tomsk, even branching off by the Tchulym and Bii. From the above it is clear that in the transit of European goods the Ob plays a more important part than the Irtysh. Siberian produce follows the same routes, but in an opposite direction.

The lower courses of the Tura and Tobol are of the highest commercial importance, forming a junction of the small and large water-ways bringing goods from Russia and Siberia.

The navigation on the Ob is subject to many difficulties arising from climatic causes and want of proper appliances. The rivers are frozen for many months, and at low water steamers cannot reach even such important places as Tomsk and Tiumen ; judging from the timetables the navigation lasts only about four months. Want of beacons, of proper observations on the rise and fall of the rivers, and of telegraphs to rapidly communicate these observations, increases the dangers and difficulties of navigation.   All these inconveniences will disappear when the increase in the volume of trade will pay for the employment of dredgers and the establishment of a telegraph line along the banks of the Irtysh and Ob to signal the variations in the level of the waters.

Trade is steadily increasing, especially since the opening in 1884 of the railway from Perm to Tiumen, which joins the basins of the Volga and Ob in lieu of the old portage.   The movement of the traffic in goods on the rivers Tura and Tobol, which forms, as we have mentioned, the junction of all the water-ways, has increased as follows :

In the year	1886	3	million poods	(about 50,000 tons).
„	1888	7	„	(about 115,000 tons).
„	1890	8	„	(about 133,000 tons).
„	1895	16	„	(about 266,000 tons). [1]

The second great river of Siberia, the Yenissei, is less favourably situated ; its mouth on the Arctic Ocean is further north ; the population on its banks is much scantier, 950,000 inhabitants on about 1,500,000 square miles contained by the governments of Yennisseisk and Irkutsk, and there is little transit trade from and to Europe.   Steam navigation consequently commenced later and has developed more slowly.   Steamers began to run in 1863, and in 1888 there were only four, transporting a total cargo of 129,000 poods (little over 2,000 tons) ; in 1890 the steamers had increased to six with a cargo of 260,000 poods (little over 4,000 tons).   The important affluent of the Yenissei, the Angara, flowing from Lake Baikal and joined by that sheet of water with the Selenga, unfortunately presents great difficulties to regular naviga-

---

[1] The book *Siberia and the Siberian Railway*, 2nd edition, 1896, says *now*, and probably refers to the figures of the preceding year.

tion; on a total course of 1,705 versts from the Baikal to its confluence with the Yenissei, only the upper 600 versts to the Bratski *ostrog* are navigated by steamers; below the latter point, for over 1,000 versts, a series of rapids presents great difficulties. Sibiriakoff obtained, in 1885, a monopoly of the navigation for five years, and built steamers for the purpose, but his attempt in 1888 was unsuccessful, and the lower course of the Angara will probably remain closed to steam navigation still for many years to come.

The obstacles to navigation on the Angara greatly lessen the value of the water-way of the Yenissei, depriving it of all the traffic from Irkutsk, Transbaikalia, and even Mongolia. The lines of navigation are therefore few and short: from Krasnoyarsk to Yenisseisk and Minusinsk on the Yenissei, and from the Baikal to Balagansk on the Angara.

The idea of uniting the two river basins of the Ob and Yenissei by a canal attracted the attention of the Russian Government at an early period. At the end of the last century a project was presented to Paul I. to connect the Tym affluent of the Ob with the Sym affluent of the Yenissei; other projects were presented later, proposing canals joining other affluents of the two rivers; the flat nature of the country, and the numerous streams intersecting it, offering a variety of solutions to the problem. These projects were not taken up at the time, and the question has only lately been practically settled. In 1875 Phuntusoff, a Siberian merchant, conceived the idea of joining the Ket (affluent of the Ob) with the Great Kas (affluent of the Yenissei), and undertook at his own expense local investigations which proved the feasibility of the project. The attention of the Government was then drawn to the work, and a canal $7\frac{1}{2}$ versts long and

42 feet wide at the bottom was finished; it is very favourably situated, because the Great Kas flows into the Yenissei near the mouth of the Angara.

At present only light-draught vessels, during a short period, can traverse the Ob-Yenissei canal, which, however, can be much improved whenever the increase of trade may render it necessary. Steam navigation on the Yenissei is still insufficient to justify a considerable outlay for that purpose, and its development, as we have seen, greatly depends on the successful solution of the problem of the navigation of the Angara; therefore the future of the Ob-Yenissei canal ultimately rests on the steam navigation of the Angara. When these problems shall have been solved, there will be an immense water-way of 5,000 versts from Irkutsk to Tiumen, from the Baikal almost to the Ural.

The third great river, the Lena, is even more unfavourably situated; near its mouth, far in the north, it forms an enormous delta difficult of access. The population in the adjacent regions is very scanty; the Yakutsk province has only 272,000 inhabitants on an area of over 1,700,000 square miles. It lies remote from European Russia, and is not connected with the Yenissei by canals. Steam navigation exists between Tarasofskaya and Yakutsk, a distance of 2,160 versts (1,440 miles), but only one trip a year is made to Yakutsk.

The Amur, of all the great rivers of Siberia, is the most favoured by nature; its course lies in lower latitudes, and it debouches into a sea which has always been frequented by ships; its permanent occupation by Russia commenced in fact from the sea. Notwithstanding the scanty population of the neighbouring country, and the brevity of the Russian occupation, steam navigation has developed rapidly. It commenced under the direction of the Government: the first steamer, 'Constantine,' penetrating into the estuary in 1846 on an official expedition. The second steamer, the famous 'Argun,' proceeded in an opposite direction, having been built by Muravioff on the Shilka, and formed part of his first famous navigation of the river in 1854. At first only Government steamers navigated the Amur, and they had increased to twelve in 1870, when the first private company started conveying mails and passengers on the river. In 1885 the private steamers had increased to forty-four, belonging to a variety of companies and private undertakings.[1]

There is a regular mail line almost along the whole course of the Amur, from Strietemsk to Nikolaiefsk, 3,074 versts (over 2,000 miles), with a branch line up the Ussuri of 820 versts (about 540 miles). Another line of steamers also performs the same service, without, however, carrying the mails, and there are besides many other steamers running up the Zeya (for 1,000 versts) and the Bureya, principally for the gold-washing camps on those rivers.

Steam navigation will increase steadily on the Amur as the population increases in the adjacent regions, and as the general internal communications of Siberia improve. The Amur is the only river which flows into a sea never entirely frozen, and the growing importance of the Pacific as an international highway of trade will also raise its importance in the future.

This brief sketch of the navigable condition of the Siberian rivers will suffice to show their defects. The Amur alone has of late years, thanks to its eastward direction, been entirely available for rapid steam communication, and has served as a part of the great highway traversing from west to east the northern part of Siberia. All the other great rivers are only utilised in their middle course; a zone bounded by the 50th and 60th parallels of north latitude comprises almost all the portions of their

---

[1] In 1897 two companies alone had forty steamers running on the river.

courses traversed by regular steamers. In this region the peculiar conformation of the Siberian rivers, formed by the junction of two considerable streams, one of which has an extensive lateral deviation, constitutes a series of river communications from east to west which serve to convey the traffic to and from European Russia. The lower courses of the rivers, running almost due north into the unfrequented Arctic Ocean, are at present little used, and serve simply for the insignificant local trade. Persevering attempts have been made to remedy these defects, and to open the splendid river systems of Siberia to ocean steamers; but the lack of commercial advantages has counterbalanced the scientific success of a series of daring navigators.

Although in the sixteenth century Russian vessels frequented the Kara Sea, and were met there by the early English navigators,[1] in the present century an opinion, supported by some scientific authorities, had prevailed which maintained the impossibility of maritime communication between Europe and Siberia through the Arctic Ocean. This opinion was first challenged in 1853 by Sidoroff, an enterprising Siberian, zealous for the progress of his country. His arguments, based on the constant intercourse of the inhabitants of the mouths of the Petchora and Ob, received no attention; but, not discouraged, he continued to urge his views and succeeded, after many years, in demonstrating practically their correctness. The series of bold navigations in the Arctic Ocean, culminating with the famous voyage of the ' Vega,' were ultimately due to the initiative and self-sacrifice of Sidoroff.[2]

[1] See Chap. ii.

[2] In this century Siberia has been lucky in possessing many public-spirited citizens, such as Sibiriakoff, Sukacheff, &c., who have spared no efforts in developing all the resources of their country.

Only after many years, in 1862, did Sidoroff succeed in giving practical execution to his plans, and prevailed on Kruzenshtern to undertake a voyage to the northern coasts of Siberia. The voyage was unsuccessful, but it proved that the Kara Sea was free from ice. Sidoroff, finding no supporters in Russia, went to Sweden, where he became acquainted with Nordenskjöld and converted him to his ideas of the possibility of a sea route to Siberia. In 1869 Sidoroff started with the steamer 'Georgii,' but he lost valuable time at the mouth of the Petchora in saving the English steamer 'Norfolk,' and was obliged to return without having effected his purpose. He then published in 'Petermann's Journal' the offer of a reward of 2,000*l.* sterling to any vessel reaching the mouth of the Yenissei from Europe. This offer attracted the notice of Captain Wiggins, who, in 1874, reached the mouths of the Ob and Yenissei, and returned to England.

This first practical proof of Sidoroff's theory gave an impulse to northern navigation, and in 1875 the mouth of the Yenissei was reached by Wiggins and Nordenskjöld. Sidoroff himself was not so lucky, because the vessel he sent in 1876 was shipwrecked; his perseverance, however, finally triumphed in 1877, when a vessel built to his order at Yenisseisk sailed down the river and reached St. Petersburg. The same year a steamer went up the Ob and Irtysh, discharging her cargo at Tobolsk, and another arrived at the mouth of the Yenissei.

The year 1878 was the most remarkable in the history of Siberian navigation. Two steamers arrived at the Ob; the s.s. 'Tzaritza' and the 'Moskva' reached the Yenissei, the latter proceeding up as far as Yenisseisk; and Nordenskjöld also started with the 'Vega,' 'Lena,' 'Fraser,' and 'Express.' The two last ascended the Yenissei; the 'Lena' went up the river of the same name for 2,700 versts (about 1,800 miles) to Yakutsk, and the famous 'Vega' almost reached Behring straits before she was stopped by the ice. The following summer the 'Vega' reached the Pacific, and Nordenskjöld had the glory of effecting that north-eastern passage which English and Dutch navigators had striven to accomplish in the sixteenth century.

This famous voyage conclusively proved the possibility of reaching all the great northern rivers of Siberia by sea, and in the following years two English companies were successively formed for developing the sea trade of Siberia, but both failed. The commercial advantages of the sea route depend on the increase of population and improvement of the internal communications of Siberia, as well as on a better choice of steamers and goods required for the trade, and greater facilities for discharging and loading cargo. In the meantime attempts are continually made to provide Siberian buyers by sea with the few articles in general request. In 1897 a cargo of brick-tea was shipped at Shanghai for London for transhipment to Siberia. The opening of a portion of the Siberian railway has already increased the sea traffic of the northern rivers.

The imperfect communications afforded by the Siberian rivers and the difficulty of finding a common outlet for them in the sea naturally directed public attention to the necessity for railways, both as an independent system of communications and as supplementary to the existing water-ways. This double object is important, and must be borne well in mind in what follows.

The first projects of railways in Siberia appeared at the time when Muravioff's activity infused a new life in the hitherto neglected region. The occupation of the Amur and the study of its lower course had revealed the advantages of De Castries bay, only separated by a narrow strip of land from Lake Kizi, which communicates with the river. , In 1857 Colonel Romanoff drafted the project of a carriage road, to be transformed later into a railway, between Sophiisk and De Castries ; it was thus intended that traffic should proceed direct to the gulf of Tartary, avoiding the détour north and the difficult entrance to the Amur estuary. Want of funds prevented the execution of this project, but Muravioff appreciated its importance, and later, in a letter to his brother, on April 3, 1858, he alluded to the necessity of railways for facilitating the communications to the coast ports near the mouth of the Amur.

In the same year, 1857, an English engineer proposed — a horse railway from Nijni-Novgorod, *via* Kazan and Perm, to one of the ports on the Pacific Ocean. Though the idea of this gigantic tramway seems strange at present, it must be remembered that rapid transit is only a want of advanced commercial conditions and of thickly peopled countries, and that the first trains in Siberia have been very slow. Considering also that there are four million horses in Siberia, and that very little coal has been extracted, the project had a practical character and was perhaps the only one possible at that time for such a long line. The proposal, however, was not accompanied by estimates, and therefore received no attention from the Government.

An American, Collins, presented at the same time a — less ambitious scheme for the construction of a short railway line from Irkutsk to Chita, thus joining the capital of Eastern Siberia with the upper waters of the Amur. He proposed to found a company and raise the necessary funds in Siberia. Muravioff favoured the project, probably because it facilitated communications with the newly acquired territory, but it was rejected by the Government as premature.

In 1858 the idea of a gigantic railway traversing the whole region again came up with the project of Morrison, Horn, and Sleigh, who proposed to join Moscow with the Pacific. No assistance was asked from the Government, but such important privileges were required that they constituted a real foreign monopoly, for a prolonged period, of the whole trade of Siberia. This project was therefore also discarded, especially as the Government at the time had no intentions to favour such extensive schemes.

In 1858 another project, on the same vast scale, was presented by Sophronoff, who proposed to build a railway from Saratof through the Kirghize Steppe to Semipalatinsk, Minusinsk, Selenghinsk to the Amur and Peking. This project had also the fate of its predecessors, but it attracted considerable public notice, and in the polemical literature which appeared on the subject an important opinion gained strength: the necessity for following the direction of the already existing great postal road from Nijni-Novgorod to Kiakhta [1] in the construction of the Siberian railway. This theory also deserves to be remembered in what follows.

All the above projects were compiled by men working at their desks, trusting to their imagination rather than to practical knowledge of the country, its configuration and requirements. The next ten years brought fewer projects on more moderate lines, but based on local knowledge and inspired by practical views. It was no longer sought to connect Russia with the Pacific, but to build a line for the use of existing commerce.

---

[1] At that time the prolongation to Vladivostok did not exist; the construction commenced that very year.

In 1862 Kokoreff & Co. proposed a line joining the basins of the Volga and Ob, based on the project of Rashet, an engineer intimately acquainted with the intervening Ural country, where he had been employed for many years. The railway was to start from Perm and proceed *via* Nijni-Taghil to Tiumen, a distance of 678 versts (about 450 miles) with a short branch of 13 versts to Irbit. This project naturally enlisted the support of the owners of the mining and metallurgical establishments in the Ural country, through which the proposed line was to pass. This popularity encouraged Colonel Bogdanovitch, in 1866, to propose another similar line from Perm, through Yekaterinburg to Tiumen, which, he added, might be prolonged to the Chinese frontier for strategical and commercial purposes. All Siberia now became interested in the question, and a third line was proposed by the merchant Liubimoff in 1869, which, starting also from Perm and passing through Yekaterinburg, was to reach the river Tobol at a point 49 versts (about 32 miles) north of Kurgan.[1] The total length was to be 711 versts (about 472 miles), and a branch line from Yekaterinburg of 131 versts (about 87 miles) was to traverse the Ural country.

All these three projected lines had for common starting-point Perm on the Kama : the first two had for terminus Tiumen on the river Tara, and the third a point on the river Tobol, 49 versts below Kurgan. They thus terminated on the lower courses of the Tura and Tobol, which play, as we have seen, such an important part in the river navigation of Western Siberia. These short lines had therefore the great practical advantage of joining the river Kama with the most frequented affluents of the Irtysh, of connecting by the most direct route the basins

---

[1] Where the Great Siberian Railway now crosses the Tobol.

of the Volga and Ob, the most important navigable rivers of Russia and Siberia. The lines also followed an old well-known route which had served for Yermak's conquest, for the early Russian immigration of the first centuries, and for the growing trade between Europe and Northern Asia in later times.

— The attention of railway projectors was next directed to connecting these lines with the general network of Russian railways, and in the years 1872–74 several plans to that effect were proposed.[1] The line from Perm to Tiumen thus assumed a new aspect, as it became part of the general railway system of the empire, and would serve for the future transit of goods from and to Siberia, when railways should be extended far into the region. But at that time the local interests of the flourishing mining industry in the Ural were far more important than considerations affecting the great line intended to be built across Siberia. Therefore, in 1875, the Government decided to adopt the line of Bogdanovitch, without any connection with the general system of Russian railways, to serve for the local wants of the Ural, and for connecting the river traffic of the Volga and Ob.

The work commenced at once, and in 1878 the line from Perm had reached Yekaterinburg, and in 1884 it was finished as far as Tiumen.

The adoption and early construction of this line gave rise to other projects on a larger scale, but similarly utilising the Siberian rivers. In 1880 the engineer Ostrofski proclaimed the theory that to develop the resources of Siberia and its commercial relations with

---

[1] Three lines were proposed: 1st, Kineshma-Viatka-Perm-Yekaterinburg, 933 versts ; 2nd, Nijni-Kazan-Krasnouphimsk-Yekaterinburg, 1,172 versts; 3rd, Alatyr-Ufa-Tchelabinsk, 1,173 versts. This last line has been adopted and connects with the Siberian railway.

Russia, it was advisable to improve the internal communications of Siberia before prolonging the Russian railways beyond the Ural. He thought it was premature to build a continuous railway through Siberia, and suggested the following partial lines:

1. A line of 800 versts from Perm to Tobolsk, joining the rivers Kama and Irtysh. This was an improvement on the line then in construction, as it had its terminus on the Irtysh, always navigable, while Tiumen on the river Tura is inaccessible to steamers during the low-water season.[1]

2. A line of 560 versts from Tomsk to Krasnoyarsk, joining the rivers Ob and Yenissei. With these two lines and with the existing river navigation he secured communications between the Baikal and the Volga.

3. A line from Omsk to Barnaul, joining the Irtysh and the Ob to shorten the long river route to Tobolsk for the products of the rich Altai district. This line might also be extended to the Chinese frontier.

Ostrofski maintained that the only practicable plan of joining Irkutsk, the centre of Siberia, with Moscow, the centre of Russia, was by largely employing the existing steam communications on the rivers. The construction of an uninterrupted railway was a later question depending on the more or less rapid development of Siberia. This future line he, however, roughly sketched out, remarking that it must pass through ' Riazan, Spask, Ufa, and thence further to Zlatoust, Tchelabinsk, Petropavlofsk, Omsk, Kainsk, Tomsk, Mariinsk, Atchinsk, Krasnoyarsk, Kansk, Nijni-Udinsk, Balagansk, up to Irkutsk, meeting the most important administrative and commercial towns of Siberia, never leaving the zone of maximum population,

---

[1] The steamers were obliged to stop at Yevleva, distant 246 versts from Tiumen.

and traversing almost exclusively the fertile black earth
zone from the Volga to the Yenissei.' This line, traced
out by Ostrofski, has been almost entirely followed in the
construction of the present Siberian railway.

Engineer Sidensner, who had been a member of the
expedition to study the construction of the Ob-Yenissei
canal, and who was probably biased by his special
studies, evolved another project in which the railway
played a still less important part. He showed that the
completion of the Ob-Yenissei canal, and the artificial
improvement of the lower course of the river Angara,
opened a vast water-way of 5,000 versts from Tiumen to
the Baikal. Moreover, this system of river communication was separated from the course of the Amur, leading
to the Pacific, only by a distance of 950 versts. Even
this distance, from the Baikal to Strietensk, could be
traversed in great part by water, leaving but a very short
portage. He reduced the land tract in the following
way. On the west, 150 versts could be traversed on the
Baikal and river Selenga, on the east 350 versts could be
performed on the rivers Shilka and Ingoda. The remaining 450 versts were still further shortened by improving
the navigation of various minor streams, until the distance
by land dwindled down to 18 versts necessary for crossing the crest of the Yablonoi. This portage was to be
effected by railway, a short line thus sufficing to secure
easy communications throughout the whole length of
Siberia, from the Pacific to the Ural, where the line in
construction would extend them to the Volga and the
Caspian. The project, though favourably received, was
not carried out for want of funds.

Many other projects were presented by private persons,
and several Governors in Siberia proposed partial lines of
railway for their provinces, but the time was not yet ripe :

it was a work reserved for the last decade of the century.

In the year 1890 the Russian railways had stretched eastward in three lines, abruptly stopping near the Ural. In the north there was the so-called Ural railway with its terminus at Tiumen; in the centre there was the Zlatoust-Mias railway with its terminus at the last-named station; and further south there was the Orenburg railway terminating at the town of that name.

The old project of a railway traversing the whole length of Siberia now again attracting attention, the question arose which of the three existing lines on the Ural should be used as the western terminus of the immense railway destined to have its eastern terminus at Vladivostok on the Pacific. By adopting the first line, that from Perm to Tiumen, the Siberian railway would proceed by Yalutorofsk, Kainsk, Mariinsk, Krasnoyarsk, Nijni-Udinsk. This plan was exposed to many objections. Owing to its northerly course it was forced to leave aside the important town of Omsk; and its length was 3,474 versts. Moreover, as the Perm-Tiumen line was a detached, independent one, serving exclusively for the use of the Ural mining district, and for joining the rivers Kama and Tura, it would be useless for the transit between Siberia and Europe, unless another 1,000 versts of railway were constructed from Perm to Nijni-Novgorod connecting with the general network of Russian railways. The line from Mias could be prolonged through Kurgan, Kainsk, Mariinsk, Krasnoyarsk, to Nijni-Udinsk, with a total length of 2,683 versts—791 versts shorter than the former. The third line would have to be prolonged from Orenburg through Omsk, Atbassar, Akmolinsk, Pavlodar, Biisk, Minusinsk to Nijni-Udinsk, a total length of 3,400 versts. Besides being also long, this third route presented serious difficulties : the western part passed through steppes without water, and exposed to violent winds and snowstorms in winter, and the eastern part passed through a mountainous country offering serious technical difficulties.

These reasons naturally led to the adoption of the second line as the western terminus of the Siberian railway. On February 21, 1891, the Government decided that the Zlatoust-Mias line should be extended to Tchelabinsk, which was to become the first station of the future Siberian railway. The views expressed by Ostrofski eleven years before had now triumphed ; the direction of the new line had for its primary object the development of the resources of Siberia ; strategical considerations and the desire to open new markets for Russian goods became secondary objects.

The construction of the Siberian railway was finally decided by an imperial rescript of March 17, 1891. This measure was made known to the public with the solemnity befitting its importance. It was promulgated on the shores of the Pacific, at Vladivostok, the future eastern terminus of the immense line, on May 12, 1891, by the Tsesarievitch, now Tsar Nicholas II., who on May 19 laid the first stone of the gigantic work.

For the smooth working of this great undertaking it became necessary to cut up the great line into a variety of sections corresponding to natural divisions. This plan allowed the work to be carried on simultaneously at different points, securing administrative independence for each ; it was moreover useful on account of the great difference in the work dependent on geographical conditions. These sections, seven in all, which it will be necessary to bear in mind, are the following, proceeding from west to east :

1st Section.—Western Siberian line, from Tchelabinsk to the river Ob, 1,328 versts (880 miles).

2nd Section.—Central Siberian line, from the river Ob to Irkutsk, 1,754 versts ($1,162\frac{1}{2}$ miles).

3rd Section.—Circumbaikalian line, from Irkutsk to Mysovaya (around the lake), 292 versts (194 miles).

4th Section.—Transbaikalian line, from Mysovaya to Strietensk, 1,009 versts (669 miles).

5th Section.—Amur line, from Strietensk to Khabarofsk, about 2,000 versts (1,326 miles).

6th Section.—North Ussurian line, from Khabarofsk to Graphska, 347 versts (230 miles).

7th Section.—South Ussurian line, from Graphska to Vladivostok, 382 versts (253 miles).

Total : 7,112 versts ($4,714\frac{1}{2}$ miles).

The first section, the Western Siberian, is of the easiest construction ; it passes through a flat country, and the only obstacles are the rivers : the Tobol, Ishim, Irtysh, and Ob, especially the two latter, which require respectively bridges spanning 700 and 840 yards. The country through which it passes, especially the Ishim and Barabinsk steppes, is fertile.

The Central Siberian encounters greater natural difficulties ; the country, at first hilly, gradually becomes mountainous ; the inclination of the road, never exceeding 0·0074 ($=\frac{1}{135}$) in the Western Siberian, now reaches 0·015 ($=\frac{1}{66}$) beyond Nijni-Udinsk. Many rivers have to be crossed—some, such as the Yenissei and Uda, requiring bridges with a span of 930 and 350 yards. This part of the line, starting from the Ob in about 55° N. lat., runs north-east to Mariinsk and Kansk in 57° N. lat., and then turns to the south-east up to Irkutsk in 53° N. lat.

The Circumbaikalian line offers enormous difficulties ;

it has to run along the shore between the lake and mountains, often steep and rocky; numerous torrents have to be crossed by strong bridges; and when the country becomes flat, it is often marshy. Great détours have to be taken, as may be perceived by the fact that in one case the road could be shortened 30 versts by cutting a proposed tunnel of 4,170 yards. But Russian engineers are not familiar with tunnel-making, and avoid the task if possible. — The Transbaikalian line, though to a less extent, also offers great difficulties. After crossing the Selenga on a bridge 700 yards long, it has to go up the valleys of various rivers—the Uda, Briana, &c.—until it reaches the Yablonoi crest at a height of 3,412 feet above sea-level. Then it descends the Pacific slope down the valleys of the rivers Chita and Nertcha. The latter also requires a bridge of 350 yards. The climatic conditions are also most unfavourable; on the Yablonoi crest in June and July, while the temperature rises to 77° Fahr. by day, it falls to 23° Fahr. by night. Owing to the almost complete absence of snow, the ground is frozen to a great depth. From a series of experiments made in the valley of the Chita, at a height of 2,380 feet above sea-level, it has been found that in winter the ground is frozen to an average depth of 24 feet 6 inches, and though during summer it thaws to a depth of 12 feet 10 inches, there remains a stratum of 11 feet 8 inches continually frozen. — The Amur line has been imperfectly surveyed, but enough is known to show that it will present enormous difficulties. It will require numerous long bridges on the tributary rivers and a gigantic one of 2,000 yards across the Amur itself. The climatic conditions, through want of snow, are about as bad as in Transbaikalia, but there will be additional difficulties owing to the scanty population residing only along the banks. Whenever the line recedes from the river, it crosses an uninhabited region, thickly wooded, where, owing to want of communications, it is impossible to get the necessaries of life and to transport railway materials.

The North and South Ussurian sections are much less difficult, but the route, running up the narrow valley of the Ussuri, meets numerous tributaries intersected by the spurs of a mountain chain. The rivers Khor, Bikin, and Iman require bridges spanning from 180 to 460 yards, and the Ussuri one of 280 yards. After passing Lake Khanka, the line descends into the valley of the Sui-phun down to the Golden Horn at Vladivostok.

This rapid sketch suffices to show the difficulties existing in the eastern part of the Great Siberian Railway, between Irkutsk and Khabarofsk, a distance of over 3,000 versts. It is, however, necessary to remark that the greatest difficulties are to be found around Lake Baikal and along the Amur, where steam navigation for many years has afforded a rapid means of transit. This fact had an important influence in the distribution of the work necessary for the completion of the entire line. Though the ultimate object of the undertaking was to secure continuous railway communication from the Ural to the Pacific, from Tchelabinsk to Vladivostok, it could not be ignored that the entire accomplishment of this object involved the labour of many years. In the meantime it was highly desirable to achieve as early as possible such a railway development that, together with the existing river navigation, a system of rapid steam communications could be attained.

For this purpose the seven sections of the work were distributed in three groups, to be undertaken successively, the most important naturally preceding. The following order was adopted:

GROUP I

1st Section, Western Siberian.
2nd   ,,   Central Siberian.
7th   ,,   Southern Ussurian.

A supplementary line from Tchelabinsk to Yekaterinburg was also to be constructed to join the Great Siberian with the Ural railway.

GROUP II

6th Section, North Ussurian.
4th   ,,   Transbaikalian.

GROUP III

3rd Section, Circumbaikalian.
5th   ,,   Amur line.

The first group was to be commenced at once, and finished not later than the year 1900. The work was to commence at both ends, and to gradually converge towards the centre. The gaps in the line were more apparent than real, and corresponded with the plan proposed of securing rapid communications as early as possible. With the completion of the first and second groups, the only parts of the line left unfinished would be those around Lake Baikal and along the Amur, where steamers ply incessantly and fulfil the functions of a railway for the time. This temporary plan of securing continuous steam communications, either by river-boats or railway across the whole length of Siberia, received further support in 1895,[1] when it was decided to push on simultaneously the work of both the first and second groups, which were to be finished by 1898.

This acceleration of the programme has been carried

---

[1] It is not irrelevant to note that it was the year marking the end of the war between China and Japan which produced such important changes in the Far East.

out almost entirely; in August 1898 the first train reached Irkutsk, and in the same year the railway was also opened to Khabarofsk. The work in the Transbaikalian section was retarded by exceptional meteorological conditions; unusual rains in the summer of 1897 caused an extraordinary rise in the upper waters of the Amur, the Chita, and Shilka, such as had not been recorded for over a century. Besides devastating many villages on the banks, the floods destroyed the railway which had been completed for about 80 versts from Strietensk. Along the banks of the Shilka, where service trains had been running, a deplorable scene was presented in 1897—engines overturned, rails torn up, embankments washed away.

The third group was left in abeyance even in 1895, — when such haste was displayed for the early completion of the other groups. The causes of this neglect were twofold : the existence of steamer communications and difficulties of construction. Postal and commercial communication between Irkutsk and Transbaikalia are generally carried on across the lake on steamers in summer and on sledges in winter; only when the water is freezing or the ice thawing, the postal road around the southern extremity of the lake comes into requisition. The construction of the Circumbaikalian section along this latter route entails, as we have seen, great difficulties, especially for Russian engineers who never have had occasion to construct lines in a rough mountainous country. Even the construction of the postal road was only accomplished at the end of the last century. On the other hand, the old method of carrying goods, passengers, and their carriages, across the Baikal in steamers from Listvinitza to Mysovaya, was not practicable in the case of the passengers and goods of the Siberian railway; the expense and loss of time in shipping and landing at the two ends would remove the advantages of the long continuous railway. The Baikal was therefore the first serious difficulty met by the Siberian railway.

The solution proposed for this difficulty was the employment of steam ferries, similar to those used on Lake Michigan, capable of carrying a whole train and of breaking the ice in winter. This plan presented the advantages of shortening the distance—66 versts from Listvinitza to Mysovaya instead of over 200 around the southern end of the lake—and of diminishing the expenses: 15,000,000 roubles were estimated sufficient for the steamers, instead of 24,000,000 for the Circumbaikalian line. The proposal was so plausible that a steamer has been purchased, and in 1897 a wharf was in construction at Mysovaya to enable the steam ferry to come alongside and land the train.

Lately, however, serious objections have been raised to this plan, and the Circumbaikalian line is again coming into favour. Lake Baikal is subject to violent storms and thick fogs, which stop navigation ; such events and the consequent accumulation of trains on both shores would disorganise the traffic of the whole line. It is doubtful whether the ice-breaking steamers will be able to cut a way through the thick ice formed during the severe Siberian winter. Moreover, the reduction in the expenditure is called in question and rendered doubtful by appropriate arguments. The saving was evident when the cost of only a few steamers was reckoned ; but to carry across five trains daily from each end, it is calculated that seven or even eight steamers (keeping one in reserve) will be required. Seven steamers will cost about 17,500,000 roubles, and wharves, docks, &c., will require 8,000,000 more. The saving has already disappeared, while the

A RUSSIAN SENTINEL

cost of working the seven steamers is reckoned to be slightly in excess of the working expenses of the Circumbaikalian line. Of course any increase in the number of the daily trains would require additional steamers, turning the balance still more in favour of the railway. Sanguine supporters of the Siberian railway trust in a great development of trade, and expect that even twenty trains a day at both ends will be required.

It is therefore probable that the Circumbaikalian line will be constructed, at least for alternate use, together with the steam ferries.

The other section of the third group—the Amur line—presents still greater difficulties. It has not even the compensation of being short like the Circumbaikalian, which is only 292 versts. Here we have about 2,000 versts to be constructed through dense forests, across big rivers, often away from all population, under rigorous climatic conditions, with a frozen soil requiring to be laboriously broken up. Moreover, the local conditions do not warrant the heavy expenses necessary for the work ; the population of the Amur province amounts only to 115,000 inhabitants, and the country is mostly uncultivated ; many years must pass before the trade of the people, all living on the banks of the river, and already provided with regular steamer service, will require a railway. The only use of the Amur line is, therefore, to connect the railway from Moscow arriving at Strietensk with the railway from Vladivostok at Khabarofsk. And to achieve this purpose 2,000 versts of railway have to be constructed on a circuitous line following the irregularities of the course of the river Amur.

To understand the circumstances of the case and the events which ensued, it is necessary to bear in mind the geographical position of the Russian possessions in the

Far East. By the treaty of Peking, Russia had acquired the Ussuri territory, a long tract of country stretching south of the Amur to the frontier of Corea; her eastern frontier thus became an irregular curve sweeping right round Manchuria on the north and east. Almost at the extremity of this curve Vladivostok had been chosen as the naval stronghold of Russia in the Pacific, and now it was destined to become the terminus of the Siberian railway. To reach it the railway must follow the long frontier on a useless détour which increased the distance by about 1,000 versts.

At the end of the century Russia was confronted with similar difficulties to those she had met nearly fifty years before. Her naval base on the Pacific, Vladivostok, was situated at the southern extremity of a detached portion of the empire, which could only be reached by a long circuitous route. Muravioff, when he assumed the Governor-Generalship of Eastern Siberia, had found the Pacific naval base of that time, Petropavlofsk, cut off from the rest of Siberia, the only communication lying far in the north by a circuitous route leading to the detached peninsula of Kamchatka. The conditions at present were not so unfavourable; the loss of time entailed by the détour did not require weeks, but, thanks to the railway, only about a couple of days; yet, with the changed conditions of modern life, even this delay was important. The former difficulties had been overcome by Muravioff during his brilliant administration, profiting sagaciously by the political events of the time. | The Crimean war secured the right of navigation on the Amur; the little value attached to the country on the north of that river by the Chinese Government, its internal trouble with the T'ai-p'ings, and the war with England and France had successively secured the Amur and Ussuri regions. Political events of a similar nature furnished the opportunity to Russia of removing the difficulties encountered in the eastern part of the Siberian railway.

The war which broke out between China and Japan in 1894, and continued for the first months of 1895, deeply interested Russia ; the military operations were mostly carried on in Corea and Manchuria, regions relatively near to the eastern terminus of the Siberian railway ; the results of the war, it was feared, might injure her future interests. When, by the treaty of Shimonoseki, China was obliged to cede a portion of Manchuria, Russia felt the necessity of interfering and of preventing the establishment on that continent of a new political factor, which might hinder her free development on the Pacific ; the successful intervention also afforded the basis for a future demand of compensation. This followed rapidly, and Russia obtained the permission from China to extend her railway through Manchuria to Vladivostok. The détour along the Amur now became unnecessary, except for local requirements which, as we have seen, are not urgent. The increased influence acquired by Russia in Peking, the activity of her surveying parties in Manchuria, and the fact that Vladivostok is only artificially kept open by ice-breakers during the winter months, favoured the suspicion that her ultimate aims were directed to Port Arthur, which is free from ice during the whole winter. At any rate, there was no haste or abruptness in carrying out these plans ; Russia waited until the German occupation of Kiao-chou forced her to claim some equivalent compensation. The lease of Port Arthur and Ta-lien-wan, and the right to connect these ports by branch lines with the main Siberian railway, secured another nearer outlet on the Pacific. It is even probable that the commercial terminus of the railway will be closer, at Newchwang, or, as the Russians more accurately call it, the port of Ying-tzù.

These important concessions obtained from China profoundly affected the construction of the eastern part of the Siberian railway. The permission to extend the line straight through Manchuria to Vladivostok rendered superfluous the Amur section and even portions of the Transbaikalian and Ussurian sections, which were not required for the continuous communication with the Pacific. The problem to be solved by the Russian engineers was now to find from which point of the Transbaikalian section the Manchurian line should commence, and on which point of the Ussurian section it should terminate. Surveys for this purpose were undertaken in 1897, and, after several routes were rejected, it was decided that the line should start from Kaidalovo on the Transbaikalian section and terminate at Nikolskoe on the South Ussurian section. By this means 806 versts of the first section and 100 of the second would be utilised for the great trunk line, *i.e.* the greater part of the one and only a small portion of the other. This projected Manchurian line, officially designated as the East Chinese section, has to overcome serious difficulties ; its route is intersected by two chains of mountains, the Great and Little Khinghan, which further north cross the course of the Amur. A convenient passage has been found over the Great Khinghan, but the Little Khinghan presents more serious obstacles and requires fresh surveys. These technical considerations suggested a different direction and terminus to the Siberian railway; a southerly direction towards the gulf of Liao-Tung to Newchwang or Port Arthur was advocated instead of the easterly direction to Vladivostok in the sea of Japan.

The route now projected starting from Kaidalovo [1] passes south of the Adun-Tchelon chain, through the valley of an affluent of the Mutnaya (south of Abaguitui), and then, crossing the Great Khinghan by the portage between the rivers Tchin-ho and Jol-Tchol in a country offering slight difficulties, reaches the watershed between the rivers Sungari and Lao-ho, where a cart road leads from the basin of one river to the other. This part of the country is so easy that the Emperor K'ang-hsi projected a canal of fifty versts for joining the two rivers. The valley of the Lao-ho then leads to the sea, where Newchwang offers an excellent commercial centre open to navigation for the greater part of the year. A branch line to Port Arthur would secure uninterrupted access to the sea even in winter. This line would be shorter than the East-Chinese section.

Other projects have appeared, and it is even proposed to shift the origin of the East-Chinese section further west on the other side of the Yablonoi, at Taidut, a station on the river Khilok. This route would bring a further reduction in the total distance of 160 versts. As this line would leave the Transbaikalian section before the latter crosses the Yablonoi, another passage over that chain would have to be made, but even this is alleged to be an advantage, for while the Transbaikalian section accomplishes it in thirty-nine versts, this last project would effect the passage from the valley of the Khilok to that of the river Ingoda in 104 versts, allowing gentler slopes across the mountain ridge.

The routes, either from Kaidalovo or Taidut to Newchwang, would have the merit of considerably shortening the total distance. It is interesting to notice the persistent and successful efforts to diminish the

---

[1] Between Chita and Nertchinsk, nearer to the former.

enormous distance; according to the original plan including the Amur section, more than 9,000 versts of railway separated Moscow from Vladivostok; by substituting the East-Chinese section through Manchuria the distance was reduced to 8,000 versts ; and by rectifying some short lines in Russia, and by choosing Newchwang as the terminus on the Pacific, it is further reduced to 7,280 versts. In a commercial sense Newchwang is preferable to Vladivostok as a terminus, being nearer to China with its rich markets, but it is probable that the line to Vladivostok will also be pushed on rapidly, as it will be useful for the Japan trade.

The great railway shortly to be completed, joining the Atlantic and Pacific eastwards, as the American and Canadian railways do westwards, fulfils two great purposes. It will develop the resources of Siberia—the object for which it was constructed—and it will constitute a new commercial route for rapid travel and for exchange of the products of East and West. The second object, far more dazzling, especially on account of the great decrease in the time necessary for reaching the Far East, thus apparently bringing those distant regions closer, has attracted far more public attention.

The first and most important result following the completion of the Siberian railway will be the more rapid conveyance of mails and passengers to the Far East. Passenger trains in Western Siberia at present run at the average rate of twenty-two versts an hour, including stoppages ; at this moderate speed it will take about fifteen days to reach Vladivostok from Moscow, and fourteen to reach Newchwang. If we take as starting-point London, the great commercial centre of the world, we must add about two days' journey to Moscow.[1] Then to

<hr>

[1] At present there is no rapid train from London to Moscow as there is

reach Shanghai, we must add five days from Vladivostok, and about three from Newchwang, giving a total of twenty-two days *via* the first port, and nineteen *via* the second. There is a considerable saving of time over the sea route through the Suez Canal, which takes over a month ; if we choose Hong Kong for comparison, we must add three days for the Siberian route and deduct the same for the sea route, still leaving a balance in favour of the former. Even to Japan there will be a saving of time, as compared with the Canadian route, if a proper service of rapid steamers be established between Vladivostok and one of the nearest Japanese ports.

We have assumed for our comparisons the minimum speed, such as is used at present on the lines of Western Siberia, which are purely for the local use of thinly peopled districts; but when the whole line is completed to the Pacific, its importance for international transit will require higher speeds. It is confidently expected that there will be passenger trains running at the rate of 35 versts an hour, and perhaps express trains at the rate of 45 versts. The latter would save a week on the whole journey, reducing the time from London to Shanghai and Hong Kong to about twelve and fifteen days respectively. To show the future possibilities of the Siberian railway, it will be sufficient to state that a train travelling at the rate of the Nord express—90 versts an hour—would employ less than four days to cover the distance from Moscow to Newchwang or Vladivostok, reducing the time from London to Shanghai to about nine days. Of course such trains will not be required and will not run for a long time, but the rate of travelling is increasing so fast at present that young and

to St. Petersburg, but there will certainly be one as soon as the Siberian railway is completed.

perhaps middle-aged persons may live to see such trains running to the Pacific, at least weekly.

The Siberian railway will compete favourably with the sea route also in cheapness. The Russian Government, faithful to the broad-minded policy pursued for centuries, in securing cheap conveyance of mails and travellers through Siberia, will reduce the fares on the railway to figures which seem ridiculous in other countries. Tickets from Moscow to Vladivostok, including sleeping accommodation, will cost by first, second, or third class 100, 60, or 40 roubles respectively. If we add the fare from London to Moscow 125 roubles, from Vladivostok to Shanghai 80 roubles, and food expenses for seventeen days at 85 roubles, we get a total of 390 roubles from London to Shanghai, instead of 772 roubles *via* Brindisi by the sea route.[1]

The difference in price is so considerable that there is room for other incidental expenses, which might occur on the journey.

The Siberian railway, like the Canadian-Pacific, would offer, especially in summer, better climatic conditions than the Suez route, which traverses the Indian Ocean and the Red Sea. These several advantages acting conjointly will render the Siberian route the most convenient for passengers to the Far East.

Only a few of the most evident facts have been moderately stated in favour of the Siberian railway, but the sanguine supporters of the route claim far more.

[1] In these calculations it is generally overlooked that most of the passengers from London to Shanghai are either residents of the Far East or persons on business that will detain them for a considerable time ; they therefore generally carry a quantity of luggage, which is liberally treated and seldom charged by the steamer companies. We must therefore add about a hundred roubles to the cost *via* Siberia : this amount would allow each passenger over 3 cwt. of luggage besides 36 pounds free and hand-luggage, a total of nearly 4 cwt., sufficient for average requirements. This addition would still leave a large balance in favour of the Siberian route.

They contend that passengers from Europe for the Dutch Indies will prefer this route, and that passengers from New York and the Eastern States will find it cheaper and quicker to reach China and Japan by crossing the Atlantic and traversing the old continent by railway. The calculations on which these assertions are founded are rather nicely poised, but they will be based on more practical foundations as soon as the speed of the Siberian railway has been considerably increased.

It will be more difficult for the Siberian railway to compete for the conveyance of goods from and to the Far East: the low freights prevalent at present by the Suez route will render it preferable for the trade between the seaports of Europe and those of China and Japan. The only goods to and from the Far East which will be able to bear the tariff of the Siberian railway are those that are liable from their value to high freights by steamer, or are apt to be damaged by heat and moisture on the long sea-voyage. The Siberian railway may also absorb the trade coming from the interior of Russia. It is calculated that the total cost from Moscow to Vladivostok by railway and steamer, *via* Odessa and Suez Canal, is slightly in excess of what will be charged by the Siberian railway, travelling direct to the same destination. The conditions will be still more favourable for the districts in the east of Russia, further removed from the sea and nearer by rail to Vladivostok.

The principal object of the Siberian railway, and from which it will derive its largest profits, will be the development of the country it traverses: a country possessing much natural wealth, hitherto little available owing to the want of easy communication. Not only will it supply this want, but it will contribute powerfully to increase the steamer traffic on the Siberian rivers; already the

short line from Perm to Tiumen has given a great
impetus to navigation on the Ob, and the completed
sections of the Siberian railway have attracted a larger
number of ocean steamers to the Arctic Ocean.)While
the railway is proceeding, the Government is undertaking
works for the improvement of the navigation of the
Tchulym and the Angara, the most important eastern
affluents of the Ob and the Yenissei. Success in this
work will extend eastward the network of fluvial communications as far as Transbaikalia, almost within reach
of the navigation of the Amur. European Russia
possesses a system of canals affording uninterrupted
water-communication between the Caspian, the White
Sea, and the Baltic, and the problem of endowing Siberia
with a similar system will probably be solved when the
new railway has quickened the life of the immense
region.

The Siberian railway will be the last and most important measure in the great work of slow pacific conquest, which has been proceeding for many centuries, as
it will afford the readiest means for the eastward expansion of the race. Of late years the eastward drift of the
population has been very remarkable in European Russia,
eastern towns like Samara and Saratof having developed
with extraordinary rapidity. Emigration to Siberia is
steadily increasing: while it amounted to about 5,000 a
year from 1860 to 1880 (110,000 for the whole period),
it increased to nearly 10,000 yearly between 1879–85
(55,000 for the six years). In 1892, owing to famine in
Russia, emigration rose to 90,000.[1] The southern part
of Siberia offers a fertile soil, similar to the best of
European Russia, which is much sought after by the

---

[1] Kraefski gives 600,000 for the year 1894, but I suspect this high
figure must be a misprint for 60,000.

peasants. The railway will enormously increase the European emigration, attracting labourers and facilitating the journey of the peasants desirous of settling on unoccupied lands.

It will act in a far higher degree than can be conceived in other countries, owing to the special tariffs on Russian railways which favour long journeys, the charges for long distances being relatively much lower than those for short ones.[1] Thus, taking for instance the third class, the most generally used, and the most adapted for peasant emigrants : the passenger fare

for 100 versts is roubles 1·44
„   500   „   it is „   5·20
„ 1,000   „   „   „   8·40
„ 2,000   „   „   „ 12·80
„ 4,000   „   „   „ 20·80

It will be seen from the above figures that 4,000 versts, a distance of over 2,640 English miles, can be travelled for about 20 roubles, or less than 42s. : the cost is only a little over a fifth of a penny per mile.

Russian railways are administered for the convenience of the public and not for private speculation : every comfort is provided, and unless the carriages are over-

---

[1] The price of tickets on Russian railways is charged per verst only up to a distance of 300 versts; greater distances are charged according to zones

of 25 versts for distances from 301 to 500 versts
„ 30   „   „   „   501 „   710   „
„ 35   „   „   „   711 „   990   „
„ 40   „   „   „   991 „ 1,510   „

For distances above 1,510 versts, the zones are of 50 versts. Above 325 versts the price of each zone is 20 kopecks third class, 30 kopecks second, 50 kopecks first class. As the zones increase, the cost therefore relatively decreases : thus to travel 1,000 versts (over 660 English miles), from 1,510 to 2,510 versts in first, second, and third class costs respectively 10, 6, and 4 roubles.

crowded, passengers of all classes, without any extra charge, have suitable sleeping accommodation. The tariffs are inspired by principles similar to those with which Rowland Hill revolutionised the postal service : though it is impossible, at least at present, to adopt a uniform charge, it diminishes relatively for great distances.

The cheap travelling afforded over the whole breadth of Northern Asia will open the country to all classes of Russians : as soon as the railway is completed, Siberia will cease to be considered the land of convicts [1] and exiles ; it will become effectively a part of the empire, contributing to the maintenance of the population and to the development of manufactures.

The cost of the Siberian railway has been estimated at 350,000,000 roubles (nearly 40,000,000*l*.), and though it is hoped to reduce this sum by the abandonment of the expensive Amur section, it is probable that, as in most cases, the actual expenses will surpass the estimates. To appreciate fully the extent of the sacrifices incurred by the Government, it must be remembered that in late years 20,000,000 roubles have been spent yearly in Eastern Siberia, while the revenue only amounts to 6,000,000 : even the revenue of all Siberia is inferior to the expenditure of recent times. The large sums continually spent by Russia for the improvement of her distant possessions have been heavily felt by the thickly peopled central provinces. But the Government was actuated by motives of a broad far-seeing policy ; it has definitely adopted the view of Muravioff that Siberia is destined to absorb the surplus population of Russia for over a

---

[1] Already in the towns and more populous districts there is strong opposition to the deportation of convicts, and whilst this page is passing through the press there comes the news that the Tsar has appointed a commission to devise other means of dealing with convicted persons.

century, and it has rejected the narrow view of Nesselrode, who valued the country only as a convenient land for the deportation of criminals. The Siberian railway, which is responsible for the heaviest expenses, will probably bring the reward of these prolonged sacrifices. The immense country it traverses will become, what is indicated by its geographical position, an extension of Russia, where population will flow gradually, shifting eastward the centre of the empire and developing a new civilising power of unknown possibilities in the old continent of Asia, in regions of unexplored wealth. It will complete pacifically the work undertaken amidst hardships and difficulties by Yermak and the Cossacks.

CHAPTER VII

CONCLUSION

THE Russian Empire, extending from the Baltic to the Pacific, resembles by its size and geographical position the huge empire formed by Genghiz Khan and his successors. It is situated further north, the Mongols hardly touching the forest regions of northern Russia and Siberia, but this fact may be considered as a particular case of a general historical law—the centre of political power shifting steadily northward from the banks of the Euphrates and Nile to Greece and Rome, and thence later to the higher latitudes of Europe. There is, however, a striking difference in the means and time employed in the formation of the two empires, as well as the direction of the expansion. The Mongols achieved their conquests with unexampled rapidity and great ferocity, advancing westwards in a few years to the frontier of Germany, marking their triumphs with the indiscriminate slaughter of the vanquished. The Russian Empire has been the slow, regular growth of many centuries; the race has gradually expanded eastwards, employing probably ten centuries to cover the distance from the Danube to the Ural, and three more to secure firm footing on the Pacific. The movement has been so regular that centuries serve to mark its rhythmus. After the Mongol conquest had crushed the nation for nearly a century and a half, Demetrius Donskoi destroyed the prestige of the conquerors at the battle of

Kulikovo in 1380 ; a century later, in 1480, the Tartar yoke was finally thrown off. After another century, the Tartar states of Kazan and Astrakhan having been conquered, and the Ural reached, Yermak started in 1581 for the conquest of Siberia. The eastward expansion in Asia continued for another hundred years, until it was stopped by the treaty of Nertchinsk in 1689. A long halt of over a century and a half then followed, when the movement was again taken up by Muravioff and is now steadily proceeding.

The process, except in rare cases, has been eminently pacific, the aboriginal races being either absorbed, or isolated into sporadic groups by the surging mass of the expanding Slav race. The principal object desired and achieved by Russia has been the establishment of order; when a struggle has been necessary for this object, the vanquished have generally recognised the advantages of the conquest.

The Grand Dukes of Moscow gradually displaced the khans of the Golden Horde, and secured for Russia a strong government and the abolition of wrangling feudalism. The Tsars of Russia now propose to offer rapid and secure transit across Asia, such as prevailed in the most flourishing period of the Mongol empire.

The rich countries of Eastern Asia have been accessible at various historical periods either by sea or by land : [1] the latter route was especially preferred in the thirteenth century, when the strong government of the Mongols secured a safe passage throughout their vast empire. Then merchants from the Mediterranean could reach the Yellow Sea through Sarai, Central Asia, and Mongolia. In a few years merchants from the North Sea and the

---

[1] This is shown by Colonel Yule in his usual lucid way.

Baltic will be able to reach the Yellow Sea through Moscow and Siberia. The great railway, now fast completing, may therefore be considered the commercial concomitant of Russian expansion on the Pacific: the consolidation of the empire of the Tsars reopens the land route across Asia abandoned for nearly six centuries, since the break-up of the Mongol power produced disorder and lawlessness throughout the continent. The movement commenced by Yermak and completed by Muravioff has led irresistibly to the land route, which in the nineteenth century has become a railway.

The expansion on the Pacific of the vast empire now steadily progressing in internal development, and the opening of a new commercial route, are events which will produce great and lasting consequences on the neighbouring countries of the Far East, and it will be necessary to examine their probable nature in the future.

China is the country most directly affected, on account of the long common frontier with Russia, and because the eastern part of the Siberian railway runs through the northern province of Manchuria. If the experience of the past is the surest foundation on which to base previsions for the future, China has little to fear from her northern neighbour; the two empires have been in contact for over three centuries, and notwithstanding frequent frontier trouble there has never been war. It is difficult to find elsewhere such a peaceful record.

After the treaty of Nertchinsk, the Chinese, inflated by their success, subjected the Russians to numerous humiliations, often capriciously stopping the trade at Kiakhta which had been sanctioned by treaty. These annoyances were quietly endured, and Russian patience cannot be ascribed to prudence, because even in later years, when China was no longer considered formidable, similar annoyances [1] have been inflicted and have not provoked retaliation. The annexation of the Amur and Ussuri regions was achieved pacifically, and acknowledged by the Chinese in the convention of Aigun. This quiet transfer was due more to the internal troubles and foreign wars of China than to the shadowy nature of the sovereignty in the disputed territory.

After the treaty of Nertchinsk the Chinese had taken no measures to secure effectual possession of the reconquered territory; they were content it should remain a kind of 'no man's land.' This fatal omission led them to relinquish it as soon as the Russians were willing and able to advance. The real cause of their loss was so apparent to the Chinese themselves, that after the treaty of Aigun they began to colonise Manchuria and to increase its garrisons. Even after these measures, the right bank of the Amur, which has belonged to China for centuries, remains almost uninhabited, except in a few places; presenting a striking contrast with the left bank, thickly studded with towns and villages, though it has been occupied by Russia less than half a century.

The Russians have had the greatest toleration for the customs of the Chinese and for their local self-government, even when it was prejudicial to their legal sovereignty. Russian annexation therefore has been favourable to the Chinese people, opening new fields for their trading enterprise: all the Russian towns from Vladivostok to Chita have Chinese quarters, with a numerous population of shopkeepers and workmen; there are far more Chinese living on the Russian banks of the Ussuri and Amur than on their own. Away from the river, in the interior of the Ussuri region, Chinese villages are governed by their own elders and headmen. The relations between the Chinese

---

[1] The obstacles to Russian navigation on the Sungari river.

traders and the aborigines have continued as they were before the treaty of Aigun : the former artfully supplying the hunters with tobacco, spirits, etc., hold them always in debt, which passes from father to son, constituting a veritable commercial bondage. Besides swindling the natives with their commercial ability, the Chinese in outlying districts even collect tribute, as in the time of their domination.[1] The toleration of the Russians, extended even to such flagrant acts, gives the Chinese far greater advantages than in the pre-Russian period : this is evinced by their growing numbers in regions where before they scarcely appeared.

Russia has never entertained ideas of conquest of China : this would be contrary to the ancient traditions of her policy, which has always aimed at occupying thinly peopled lands affording room for her surplus population. The conquest of a thickly peopled country like China would be a new departure for which Russia is not prepared. The spirit of the government and the character of the people are averse from pride of race : the only feeling on which to base such conquests. The sentiment of race-equality has succeeded well in the Russian Empire, because the ever-increasing number of the prolific Slav race has rendered it possible to neglect heterogeneous elements gradually and irresistibly absorbed or smothered. But this principle would be fatal in the government of the millions of China.

For many years there was mutual distrust and suspicion between the two countries. China, after the cession of the Amur and Ussuri regions, feared further encroach-

---

[1] This happened in the unfrequented Daban district, situated at the portage between the upper waters of the Khor and Bikina (right tributaries of the Ussuri), where the Russians were not allowed to approach by the jealous Chinese traders.

ments and made considerable military preparations in Manchuria. The latter measures alarmed Russia, who feared a reconquest of the Amur she had already lost two centuries before. These fantastic apprehensions went so far as to lend foundation to the theory that China was the ally of Great Britain in a possible war with Russia, the pivot of her Eastern policy. The Japanese war dispelled these visionary schemes—it showed the military inefficiency of China and changed the position of Russia. The latter stepped into the place of Great Britain, and, after the intervention to recover the Liao-tung peninsula, assumed the rôle of protector of the tottering empire. For her valuable services Russia only obtained the permission to prolong her railway through Manchuria.

The reluctance of the Russian Government to hasten expansion in the Far East, and a certain superstitious respect for the mysterious Chinese Empire which still lingered in the European Foreign Offices, would probably have prevented all occupation of Chinese territory for an indefinite period had not unforeseen events precipitated matters. The bold action of Germany at Kiao-chao forced Russia to occupy Port Arthur: her ancient relations with China and the future interests of the Siberian railway compelled her to seek some equivalent for the new acquisition of the upstart rival.

The lease of Port Arthur and Ta-lien-wan, and the Siberian railway through Manchuria, will probably lead to further annexation, but the condition of China at present is so critical, that a slight shrinking of the frontiers is a question of relatively little importance. The feeble empire, threatened by external enemies and by internal dissolution, may well consider with indifference the entire loss of the surrounding subject territories, provided the eighteen provinces of China proper can be saved from impending disintegration. Never in the whole course of her long history has China been confronted by such terrible dangers as at present : the crisis requires great sacrifices, which should not be grudged if they avert complete ruin. Though Russia certainly needs further annexation in Manchuria, she is as much interested as Great Britain, if not more, in the independence of China.

Russia became a neighbour of Corea in 1860, when after the treaty of Aigun Muravioff ordered the occupation of Vladivostok and Possiet bay. Though the distracted condition of the country, with its bitter political parties, offered frequent occasions for intervention, and though the southern position of the peninsula with its fine coasts offered ice-free ports for the future needs of her navy, Russia has, during forty years, abstained from continuing that southern expansion down the eastern coasts of Asia inaugurated by Muravioff. She was, however, always suspected of aiming at the occupation of a Corean port. These suspicions were based on the fact that her surveying parties had been active on the eastern coast of the peninsula, and that suitable ports were to be found in that locality. These facts, however, were only sufficient to indicate the wishes and future wants of Russia, not the practical bent of her policy, averse to violence and consistently pacific.

Russia for over twenty years paid no attention to her new neighbour. Though crowds of Corean immigrants flowed across the border to escape the extortions of the officials and the horrors of civil war and of famine, the Russians made no attempt to encourage this movement and to acquire influence in the peninsula. They even went so far as to negotiate by letter with the Corean frontier authorities to obtain a full pardon for those Coreans who by leaving their country had become amenable to capital punishment. The hopes of the return of the emigrants to their mother-country were frustrated, because the Corean exiles had no faith in the promises of their vindictive officials and preferred to remain under the protection of the White Tsar. It was only after Japan, the United States, Great Britain, and even Italy, had concluded treaties, and Corea had been opened to the whole world, that Russia entered into relations with her southern neighbour in the Far East.

To understand the true nature of Russia's policy in the early times, it is necessary to bear in mind that for over fifteen years Russia was the only nation in contact with Corea. Up to 1876 China was separated by a broad belt of uncultivated land known as the Neutral Zone, and Japan was too busy with the great internal questions preceding and following the Restoration, the great political transformation which brought back the Mikado and created modern Japan.

Russia, in the brief period mentioned, was in the same position as regards Corea as she had been for over a hundred and fifty years, from the treaty of Nertchinsk to the treaty of Nanking with respect to China—the only country with a common frontier. In both cases Russia took no advantage of her exceptional position to forestall other nations.

Russia has been equally indifferent to the nominal sovereignty claimed by China and to the practical control of the country assumed by Japan at the time of the war : she was satisfied with the voluntary guarantee of the independence of Corea frankly offered by Japan. Only after the collapse of the Japanese régime, consequent on the assassination of the Queen of Corea, Russian influence became paramount in the country, and there seemed some foundation for a future policy of gradual absorption. But the Russians soon recognised what had been dearly learnt by their predecessors—the Japanese—the irreducible character of the Corean problem : a nation plunged into the deepest degradation and unwilling and unfit to free itself from the miserable bloody feuds which distract it. Luckily, about the time the Russians perceived their false position, in which they risked the implacable enmity of Japan for the sake of the momentary favour of a paltry party unable to steer the same course even for a few months, the German occupation of Kiao-chou gave the long-wished-for opportunity for securing a port free from ice during the winter. The occupation of a Corean port, which had never been a practical object, ceased even to be a desideratum of Russian policy in the Far East.

The southward expansion, inaugurated by Muravioff, had taken a sweep westward, clearing at a bound the Corean peninsula, which ceases, as it deserves it should do, to be of any importance in the Far East.

The Siberian railway, with its two termini at Vladivostok and Port Arthur, by its enormous commercial and political consequences, would be of incalculable benefit to Corea if its degrading internal condition did not render it incapable of all progress.

The Russians came in contact with the Japanese at an early date, when they occupied Kamchatka and the Kurile islands, which form a chain between Japan and the continent. At the time of Peter the Great a school of Japanese was founded in St. Petersburg, and later in 1739 a Russian expedition for commercial purposes was sent to Japan. At the beginning of this century another attempt was made to conclude a treaty of commerce, but it also failed. These disconnected events led to no lasting consequences. It was only about the middle of the present century that relations between Russia and Japan grew more important and became permanent. Russia had not only to follow the example of other European nations who were hastening to conclude treaties of commerce with Japan, opened to the world by Commodore Perry, but she had also to settle frontier questions. In 1853 Nevelskoy had founded several posts in Saghalien, and as the Japanese also claimed rights over that island, it became necessary to delimit the possessions of the two countries. The treaties of 1855 and 1858 left the question undecided, as it was only stipulated that Saghalien should belong to both empires. The local authorities of both nations repaired this omission, and by tacit agreement the river Kusunai was chosen as the common frontier : a Russian post being established on one bank and a Japanese post on the other. The Russians had already attempted in 1858 to obtain entire possession of the island, and in 1865 they renewed the attempt, offering in exchange for the southern part of Saghalien the group of the Kurile islands. This proposal was not accepted, and on March 18, 1867, a convention was concluded to explain the joint ownership of the island : it was defined as 'the common right of Russians and Japanese to occupy unoccupied places all over the island.'

This strange definition gave rise to a colonising steeple-chase, in which the Russians were no match for the alert Japanese, who, in their usual systematic way, began organising the settlement of the country. The populous Japanese islands were near, and readily furnished colonists, while the Russians had to draw settlers from Europe with the inducement of great privileges, or to found settlements of unmarried soldiers, utterly valueless for peopling the country. The Russians crossed the Kusunai and went south to found a port at Aniva, and the Japanese in their turn went north of the Kusunai, hunting for unoccupied places. As the Russians had not sufficient soldiers to occupy all desirable places, they erected posts with inscriptions to denote that an occupation had taken place. This ingenious scheme was quickly adopted by the Japanese.

This keen competition occasioned many disputes between the local officials of the two countries, but it is remarkable that the confusion caused by the extraordinary diplomatic definition gave rise to no collision between rival detachments. This mutual forbearance was probably due to the good temper of the two races. The good relations of the two peoples went further than mere politeness, as on two occasions outlying Russian posts were saved from starvation by the assistance of the Japanese. It is useful to bring to light the grateful Russian record of the generous deeds performed over thirty years ago amid the snows of Saghalien, as it will show that the humane treatment of the Chinese prisoners during the late war arose not from the wish to pose favourably in the eyes of the world, but from the chivalrous character of the Japanese nation.

The Saghalien question became of great importance to Russia when she established penal settlements and commenced developing the coal mines of the island. The entire control of Saghalien had now become a necessity, and, after prolonged negotiations, on April 25, 1875, a treaty was concluded by which the desired exchange of the Japanese part of Saghalien for the Kuriles was effected.

Twenty years passed in friendly relations when the war with China again brought Japan in conflict with Russian interests. At the outbreak of hostilities Russia was alarmed for the independence of Corea, which had been rapidly occupied by the Japanese troops; but these fears were removed by the spontaneous declaration of Japan that she was striving to secure the effective independence of the peninsula. The brilliant military successes of Japan, her determination to humble China, but, above all, the prudent secrecy maintained regarding the conditions of peace aroused the watchfulness of Russia, who had to guard the interests of her great future railway and secure a convenient terminus on the Pacific. When the conditions of the peace imposed at Shimonoseki became known, Russia felt obliged to interfere and prevent the cession of the Liao-tung peninsula. There were many reasons to suggest this action: Japan was at that time already in virtual possession of Corea, and a further extension by the occupation of the strategical position of Port Arthur would render her the dominant power in the eastern part of the Asiatic continent. The future Siberian railway, flanked by the continental possessions of the new formidable power, would lose much of its importance, and would be deprived of a short route to the sea. On the other hand the intervention would establish claims for compensation from China—the extension of the Siberian railway through Manchuria, perhaps even the terminus to a Chinese port on the Yellow Sea, were already foreseen. But it is doubtful whether the most sanguine Russian statesman even dreamt that in less than three years they would be in possession of Port Arthur.

The Japanese statesmen who had negotiated the treaty of Shimonoseki probably foresaw they would have to reduce their claims, and purposely exacted the double cession of the Liao-tung peninsula and the island of Formosa, either of which could be relinquished according as the pressure of rival nations was stronger in the north or south. But the great body of the nation, innocent of these diplomatic tactics and flushed by success, felt annoyed and mortified at the sudden and unexpected loss of the fruits of victory. Dreams of future vengeance haunted the minds of the people and led them to approve unhesitatingly the expensive schemes for the increase of the army and navy proposed by the Government.

On the other hand, in Russia mistaken notions prevailed both in official circles and in the public mind; Japan was suddenly and without any justification considered as the natural enemy of Russia; all her movements were watched suspiciously, as it was considered necessary to stop her dangerous rapid expansion. An unfortunate incident increased these sentiments of mutual distrust and dislike.

After the conclusion of peace with China, Japan continued to exercise effective control in Corea for the laudable purpose of establishing order and progress in the country. But the task soon proved to be beyond even the subtlety and patience of the Japanese; they became entangled in the ceaseless intrigues of the wretched parties of the peninsula, and, far worse, they were degraded to the low level of the Corean factions. Through the fatal negligence or connivance of a Japanese official the Queen of Corea was assassinated, and this dark deed, though quite in unison with a long series of crimes perpetrated by the various Corean parties, deprived the Japanese of the moral authority to continue their self-imposed task. The weak imbecile king had at last sufficient intelligence to apprehend possible danger to his insignificant person, and fled for protection to the Russian Legation.

From this moment Russian influence became paramount in Corea, and the Japanese were quietly supplanted. The Russian party, unfavourable to Japan, now enjoyed its triumph and emphasised the fact by a series of measures calculated to diminish Japanese influence in the peninsula; military instructors were sent to train

Corean soldiers, and a financial adviser was appointed to Seoul. It seemed for a moment as if the Japanese were destined to fail in the object for which they had undertaken the war—the neighbouring peninsula rescued from China was falling under the protection of Russia. It is probable that the Japanese felt more deeply this second intervention than the first, which had deprived them of Port Arthur. The great mass of the Japanese people attach an exaggerated importance to Corea, not so much based on strategical considerations of vicinity as on historical reminiscences of former wars and conquests in the country. Until lately Corea represented the whole foreign policy of the nation. There are, besides, practical reasons which justify their interest in the country : large Japanese settlements exist in all the Corean ports, and most of the trade is in their hands.

The action of Russia was also unprovoked and not required for the protection of her interests. Japanese statesmen had recognised the motives which obliged Russia to interfere in Liao-tung, but her success there should have prevented all further intervention in questions not directly concerning her. If Russia had continued in her forward policy in Corea, it is probable that war with Japan could not have been indefinitely averted. But the mistake was gradually recognised and rectified; the Russians perceived they were playing China's game, unconsciously revenging her vanished suzerainty. Moreover, as soon as the Japanese had been supplanted, the Russians, now no longer necessary instruments for the intrigues of the Corean factions, began to encounter the difficulties, vexations, and disappointments which had fallen to the lot of all who have attempted the hopeless task of reforming Corea.

The occupation of Port Arthur, which has completely

diverted the attention of Russia from Corea, has removed the greatest cause of dissension between Japan and Russia ; the latest conventions between the two empires have settled all outstanding difficulties. But though the principal cause of conflict has ceased to act, it will take some time to allay national feeling, which has run very high, and has driven the two countries in the last few years to make incessant military preparations for what was generally considered an inevitable struggle.

A war between the two great military powers of the Far East would be a great misfortune. The struggle between the vast continental empire with its base of operations far away in Europe, and the compact island empire close to the field of conflict, would be highly interesting to the military student, but it would be most barren of results. The most complete success on either side, highly improbable if we take into account the tried bravery of the two armies and their different conditions, would achieve very little. The triumph of Russia could never bring her armies on the soil of Japan, untrodden by conquerors since the advent of the race : it was a task beyond the power of the Mongols when their empire was at its zenith. The victory of Japan would not enable her to conquer the Russian possessions on the Pacific, protected by their rigid climate and present barrenness. The country cannot support its scanty population, and the invading army would have to be provisioned from Japan ; the inhabitants could not be conquered, as they consist mostly of garrisons and military colonists. The failure of the allies during the Crimean war showed conclusively the natural strength of the Russian position on the Pacific at a time when her forces were much less numerous.

The only object attainable by a successful war might be the conquest of Corea, a poor country torn by factions, utterly insufficient to requite the loss of blood and treasure entailed by such a desperate conflict. The only stake worthy of such a gigantic struggle would be the crumbling empire of China; but at present Russia and Japan could only claim a small portion, as there are many candidates for the eventual partition. It might have been different only a few years ago.

If Russian diplomatists had been more alert and enterprising, they might have secured a secret understanding with Japan at the time of the war in 1894–95 for the joint partition of the Far East; no other combination of powers could have been formed at the time sufficiently interested to exert the force necessary to withstand the formidable coalition of the only two nations who possess considerable military force in that region. At the end of the century Russia missed her chance in the East as she had missed it in the West at the beginning of the same period. The failure to understand the true consequences of the French Revolution and to accept the frank offer of Napoleon prevented the conquest of Constantinople and retarded the expansion in Central Asia. The revolution brought about by Japan in the Far East, an event transcending the limits of routine diplomacy, was equally misunderstood, and Russia failed to secure the aid of this unexpected political factor in her own interests. In both cases, instead of bargaining separately for a satisfactory compromise, she preferred to become entangled with the shrewder European diplomacy and to work more for the interests of others than for her own. The enmity of Japan, incurred through hasty action in Corea, rendered Russia's position in the Far East extremely precarious.

The dangers arising from the tension of popular feeling are luckily diminished by the intense sentiments of loyalty prevalent in both countries : the word of the sovereign is a law joyfully accepted by the whole nation. If the Tsar and Mikado desire peace and friendship, no conflict can arise between Russia and Japan, and the decisions of enlightened rulers are more far-seeing than those of an impulsive, irresponsible people.

The Japanese are remarkable for their self-control and reticence, even when their passions are most excited, and it is therefore difficult to judge the motives that will inspire their future policy. But they are also very intelligent, and they will probably abandon idle thoughts of revenge and adopt the policy most beneficial to their growing interests. The expansion of Russia in the Far East, the completion of the Siberian railway, its commercial complement, will be found to confer the greatest benefits on the island empire. Count Okuma, one of the most broad-minded statesmen of Japan, speculating on the future of his country, remarked that the growing wealth and population of Canada and Siberia would increase its importance as the centre of the new world activity arising in the Pacific.

[Viewed in this light, Russia will be one of the most powerful factors of Japan's future greatness : the opening of Siberia and Manchuria by the new railway, the development of their natural resources, and the consequent increase of population, will give rise to an enormous trade with Japan, so near, yet subject to such different natural conditions.] The northern island of Yesso, hitherto so scantily colonised by the Japanese, will probably rapidly increase in importance, thanks to the development of the neighbouring mainland.

The war with China must have taught Japan that her strength by sea is even greater than by land. If she wishes to become the Great Britain of the Pacific, she must borrow a lesson from English history, and abandon the continent and take to the ocean. She must forsake the mediæval policy limited to Corea and act on a wider field, directing her efforts to become the centre of maritime commerce between the new countries fast arising on the shores of the Pacific. She has no time to lose in altering her course, as the rate of historic change is increasing fast, and already by irreflective adherence to traditional policy and prejudiced attachment to questions which have lost their significance, she has neglected a precious, perhaps irrecoverable, opportunity to assert her power in a new direction, and to keep open the way for her future expansion.

England is not a neighbour of Russia in the Far East, all her colonial possessions are far away, yet she may be considered the nation most affected by the impending changes. Her empire is essentially on the sea, and every country that has a coast may consider she has England for her neighbour. She is, besides, the greatest commercial power, owning the majority of shipping on the ocean, and she has preponderating interests in the trade of China. The near inauguration of a new trade-route, especially one exclusively by land, must attract the attention of a people whose best activity for several centuries has been devoted to commercial exploration all over the world, of the people that now commands the great highways of the sea.

Above all, England is a great world power, keenly observant of the expansion of other nations, especially of Russia, the only other great world power.

English interests in China are essentially commercial, and they are in no danger, either from Russian expansion or the new land route. As long as Great Britain possesses the largest share of the shipping and capital of the world, and business intelligence and enterprise to utilise these powerful factors, her trade cannot be in danger anywhere. It cannot be affected even by protective tariffs, as they exist in most countries of Europe where British trade flourishes. It is a mistake to suppose that Russian influence is fatal to the trade of foreigners, as in Vladivostok and other Russian towns of Eastern Siberia there are many flourishing German firms. It has been shown that the Siberian railway cannot compete for the carriage of goods from Europe to Eastern Asia, therefore it will only affect shipping beneficially, opening up new markets hitherto inaccessible, and English merchants and ship-owners with their usual alertness will be sure to profit by the new trade. The new railway which will confer such benefits on Japan, situated at its eastern terminus, will confer still greater ones on Great Britain, for she has interests everywhere, both in the East and in the West.

The present expansion of Russia on the Pacific affects Great Britain as a world power, and the question in China is only a particular instance of the general rivalry prevailing between the two countries for the last half-century. This antagonism produced the Crimean war, and has often since threatened to bring about another conflict. A struggle between the two great expansive races of Europe, the Slav and the Anglo-Saxon, would be a misfortune, especially as it could produce no lasting results.

The hostility between the two races is mainly founded on errors and misconceptions. The conditions of Russia and England are so different that most writers who have not thoroughly studied the subject fail to grasp the main facts. They judge Russia by the aspirations of Peter the Great, who first brought her to European notice, and they ignore the natural tendencies existing before, and which are ever resuming their influence in directing the development of the country. Englishmen, naturally biased by the influence of sea power in their own history, are led to attach too much importance to the dazzling projects of Peter the Great, the creator of the Russian navy. They are apt to suspect that the possession of a port or a coast is only preliminary to the development of a navy for challenging the command of the sea. They overlook the fact that Russia is a vast continental empire and that her maritime wants are moderate. In her huge territory she contains a large part of what geographers call continental drainage, and is almost a world to herself with the large inland seas and lakes like the Caspian and Aral. For her internal commerce she has means proportionate to her size. While the sea shipping of Russia is inconsiderable, there is an enormous tonnage on her rivers unknown to the outer world; [1] this immense disproportion is a clear proof of the continental aims of the nation. Russia only needs a few outlets to the sea, just as England requires coaling stations all over the globe, as subsidiary aid for the real power which the former wields on land and the latter on the sea.

There are also widespread prejudices in England against Russia on account of the autocratic form of government, which is supposed to be constantly bent on aggression, proceeding steadily on a secret fixed plan of universal conquest. Englishmen are so satisfied with their constitution, and have derived such advantages from it, that they are convinced it is the only good form of government. But the merits of a political constitution are not absolute ; they depend on times and circumstances. Representative government, which has succeeded so well

---

[1] According to the *Russki Kalendar*, 1899 (Suvorina), the tonnage of the river vessels amounts to 8,850,000 tons, a third of the tonnage of the whole ocean shipping of the world !

in England because it is the slow indigenous growth of centuries, has been a miserable failure on the continent, where it has been violently transplanted to nations not historically prepared for the advent of such radical changes. The violent scenes in the Austrian Parliament, and the scandalous agitation of rival parties about Dreyfus in France, are instances of the evils of liberty conferred on peoples not trained to self-control. Russia has shown singular good sense in not blindly following the universal fashion prevalent in Europe, and in adhering to the form of government evolved historically on her own soil.

The terrible Mongol invasion finally showed the evils of disunion which had afflicted the race for so many centuries. Later the dangers of popular government in Novgorod, and of an elective monarchy in Poland, convinced the Russians that the despotism of Moscow was necessary for their future greatness. In the long struggle against Asiatic nomadism, on the shelterless plains without defensive hills, with the broad rivers bridged over by the winter frost, the solitary Russian race, abandoned—nay, even attacked—by the Christian brothers of the West, had to take to heart the stern military duty of discipline. The leader of this vast camp, of this nation of soldiers, the Tsar of later times, was the true Roman Imperator, the absolute military chief charged with the defence of his country, of Europe, of Christendom, against the Asiatic hordes. That the form of government was required by historical conditions is proved by the fact that the small fief of Moscow, the appanage of the junior son of Alexander Nevski, now extends to the straits of Behring and to the Pamir. That it is not incompatible with social progress is evinced by the fact that the great reform measure—the emancipation of the serfs—was effected without bloodshed and even without friction. The absolute power of the Tsar is essentially military in its character, as is shown by the easy familiarity it allows : the Emperor greets his soldiers at the reviews and embraces Tolstoi.

The supposed aggressive policy of Russia is also not borne out by facts, at least as far as her European neighbours are concerned. She has never been at war with Austria, seldom with Prussia : the conquest of Poland was undertaken in accord with her neighbours, and was provoked by the disorders of the corrupt Polish aristocracy. The Slav race has retreated rather than advanced in Europe, abandoning the country on the Elbe and Danube.

Prussia, the kernel of the modern German empire, was originally Slav, and Berlin and Vienna were anciently also Slav towns. Rather than engage in long wars for small territories, the Slavs have preferred to advance in the north-east to lands neglected by all on account of the rigid climate ; they have preferred to undertake a struggle against nature rather than against their neighbouring European races.

This expansion in the north-east has been the irresistible tendency of the nation, and not the execution of a plan of the rulers. The Government has uniformly checked and retarded the advance of the people ; Yermak was recalled by Ivan the Terrible, and Muravioff was constantly hampered by Nesselrode.

These few facts ought to be considered by a section of the British public, always ready to suspect dark schemes of the Russian Government, and equally ready to counsel violent means to thwart them. They will find that Russian expansion is a far more serious phenomenon than they lightly suppose, and that opposition is far more difficult. They then may pause and ascertain whether opposition is at all necessary or desirable.

To measure accurately the difficulty of arresting the natural irresistible expansion of a nation of 130,000,000 increasing at the rate of considerably over a million a year, we can refer to history. The most serious attempt to check Russian advance in the East culminated in the Crimean war, when a formidable coalition was formed for the purpose by England, France, Turkey, and Sardinia: Austria also lending indirect support. It is generally known that the results of the long victorious war waged by the allies were not lasting; in less than twenty years Russia had recovered her position in the Black Sea. But long before that event she had found compensation in Asia for her losses in Europe: the Crimean war itself had given Muravioff the opportunity of opening the way to the Pacific, and the years of European peace which followed enabled Russia to annex the Caucasus and Central Asia.

When Gortchakoff expressed the policy of his Government by the memorable expression, 'La Russie se recueille,' he unconsciously coined a plausible phrase for the ignorant Western public; it only expressed the rest of diplomacy, not the true state of the nation which had resumed its work in Asia.

The negative results of the Crimean war are slight encouragement for a repetition of the attempt, especially as the relative power of Russia has increased, and promises to steadily increase in the future. At the time of the Crimean war the total population of the allied powers exceeded that of Russia: it is the reverse at present. Moreover, a coalition against Russia is improbable, as most of the continental nations are averse from the measure. France is her ally; Germany, on account of the tradition of the House of Hohenzollern and the advice of Bismarck, wishes to preserve friendly relations with her powerful neighbour, while Austria, weakened by the internal war of races, could not lightly embark in a war against the champion of that Slav race which forms the majority of her population.

England, thanks to her insular position and command of the sea, possesses greater independence and can lightly risk an adventurous policy, but she could achieve nothing in a war with Russia. Her matchless navy, perhaps more relatively powerful than at any former period, is a formidable weapon against every nation that has a coast subject to attack and shipping to be destroyed; but it is powerless against Russia, wanting in these weak points. The continental character of the Russian Empire now comes out in full force: its defects become a safeguard. During the Crimean war the fleet was unable to effect anything, and it would be in a worse position now, as the experience of Japanese and Americans in the late wars has shown that the progress of artillery has given the superiority to land defences. A general blockade of the Russian ports suggested by some would also be ineffectual, as, owing to the increase of the traffic on the rivers and railways, the country is becoming less dependent on the sea, and a blockade might even act as a stimulus to internal trade.

The forces of Russia and England are, to use an apt mathematical expression, incommensurate—there is no common term to express their relative value—and thus they should remain. All attempts on either side to meet the other on its own ground are doomed to failure, as they do not correspond with national conditions. Russia can never launch a fleet able to meet the squadrons of England, and the latter can never put in the field an army able to stand against the huge forces of Russia. The two great races of Europe are separated by the

nature of their empires. The Anglo-Saxons have taken
for their dominion the ocean, its islands, favoured
coasts, and shipping; the Slavs have conquered the
continent, with its great rivers and inland seas. A
conflict under these conditions is objectless. Bismarck, in
his usual trenchant way, put the question in a popular
form by saying that it was a struggle between the
elephant and the whale.

There is besides no adequate motive for hostility
between the two races. Russia is not a rival of Great
Britain for the dominion of the sea or commercial
supremacy—the foundations of her greatness. In the
next fifty years England has far more to fear from Germany
and the United States, and if ever she incurs loss from
their competition she will regret the years wasted in vain
hostility born of foolish prejudice. Russia has never
annexed any territory. England intended to occupy all
that was fit for her colonisation. The latest acquisitions,
Ta-lien-wan and Port Arthur, are situated in a region
that has never been coveted by England, and, though it
may sound strange, it is an undoubted fact that their
possession by Russia is an advantage to Great Britain.
In English hands they would only be an insignificant
addition to the numerous British naval stations all over
the world, while in Russian hands they become the
terminus of the great railway, and the centre of a
great coming trade which certainly will benefit British
shipping.

The progress of Russia need not awaken the jealousy
of Great Britain. It is a narrow-minded policy to imagine
that the depression of other countries is indispensable to
national prosperity. Of course there are cases when the
ruin of one country is necessary even for the existence
of another, but luckily they seldom occur; in most

instances the prosperity of each nation contributes to the general welfare. The vast colonial empire of Great Britain is certainly a benefit to France, as the wealth accumulated renders the former the best customer of the latter.

England above every other country in the world, on account of her great commercial and shipping interests, on account of her continuing want of new markets for her goods, should welcome the progress of Russia and encourage her in the task of developing regions hitherto neglected, and which, perhaps, no other nation would have been able to colonise. The Siberian railway is the most important factor in this work, as it will bring to the sea the produce of regions hitherto entirely closed to the world, and the convenient terminus selected at Ta-lien-wan should meet with universal approval.

Russia needs peace and the friendly co-operation of the world in the great task of completing the work of Yermak and Muravioff, by the development of her great Asiatic dominion. The terrible climate has been hitherto the great obstacle to the progress of Siberia, but it will probably be overcome in the future; the experience of history has shown that a greater dominion over the forces of nature has enabled man to extend civilisation further north, in regions which seemed almost uninhabitable to the ancients. It is therefore a legitimate induction to suppose that in time even the most northern and desolate parts of Siberia may become the residence of a population able to develop its resources.

Siberia is now starting into a new life. She has gradually increased in importance and in general estimation : conquered by a few Volga pirates, for centuries she remained the land of convicts and exiles; then she attracted the attention of Muravioff, who foresaw her future value for Russia. But now Siberia has won the favour and interest of the sovereign; Nicholas II. has traversed the country and has learnt its wants and its future possibilities.

It was a great event for Siberia when the young prince, after inaugurating the work of the Siberian railway at Vladivostok, started on his homeward voyage across the country which Yermak had given to Ivan the Terrible, the last sovereign of the house of Ruric. The future will probably show that it is the most important event of modern Siberian history. The Siberians thoroughly realised its consequences. No sovereign of that house of Romanoff which had formed the greatness of Russia had ever visited the lone forsaken land, and the indifference of the Tsars had encouraged the neglect of officials.

The Siberians, though one in language, race, and customs with the great Russians, have acquired, like the Anglo-Saxons in America, some slight differences sufficient to base a conscious local pride, and they felt deeply this continued neglect. At last a young prince destined to ascend the throne was coming to visit Siberia, and he brought with him the promise of the great railway.

The whole country was thrilled by the news, as it had been over thirty years before when Muravioff announced his first navigation down the Amur. It is no exaggeration to state that never was the advent of a man hailed with such deep universal enthusiasm as the arrival of the young Tsesarievitch, now Nicholas II., in Siberia. Every town he passed through erected a triumphal arch to commemorate the occasion; Cossacks crowded on the cliffs of the Amur to shout hurrah as he passed. Lama monasteries have erected gigantic statues of Buddha to commemorate the auspicious event; in the single town of Chita there is a brass plate in the governor's palace to

CLIFF ON THE AMUR

Where the Cossacks cheered the Tsesarievitch as he passed

mark the spot where he slept, another in the school indicating where he received the children, and on a hill outside the town, a rough pillar erected by the Cossacks says, with its simple inscription : ' Here our chief [1] deigned to accept bread and salt.' [2]

These universal manifestations in a country so vast and barren, with such a scanty population, must have produced a deep impression on the young mind of the Tsesarievitch, for he has consistently made great sacrifices for the development of Siberia. Nicholas II. is the first Tsar that has had the opportunity of realising the vastness of his empire, of learning its real wants, and of understanding the true mission of his race.

His proposal to restrict the ever-growing armaments of Europe, which has puzzled public opinion, is probably ascribable to these motives acting unconsciously for years and unexpectedly bringing fruit. In his long monotonous voyage across the desert plains of Siberia, where, except in the few towns, it was impossible to gather a crowd even to see a future emperor, he must have perceived the great pacific work destined for Russia : the peopling of a vast territory, the cultivation of lands exposed to a rigorous climate, the transport of the hard-earned produce to an unfrozen sea. The thoughts of Tolstoi must then have hovered in his mind, and he must have felt, like his ancestors over a thousand years before, when they started from the Danube for the north-east, away from the war of races, that the mission of the Slavs is to struggle against the forces of nature and not against their fellow man.

[1] The heir-apparent is *ex officio* ataman or chief of all the Cossacks.

[2] The Russian symbols of welcome offered at the entrance of towns on official occasions.

APPENDIX

TREATY OF NERTCHINSK
August 27, 1689, O.S.

Sancti Sinarum Imperatoris mandato missi ad determinandos limites Magnates.

Som Go Tu Praetorianorum militum praefectus interioris palatii Palatinus, Imperii consiliarius etc.

Tum Que Cam interioris palatii palatinus, primi ordinis comes, Imperialis vexilli dominus, Imperatoris avunculus etc.

Lam Tan vnius etiam vexilli dominus

Pam Tarcha item vnius vexilli dominus

Sap so circa Sagalien Vla aliasque terras generalis exercituum praefectus

Ma La vnius vexilli praefectus

Wen Ta exterorum tribunalis alter praeses et caeteri una cum missis.

Dei gratia magnorum dominatorum Tzarum Magnorumque Ducum Ioannis Alexiewicz, Petri Alexiewicz totius magnae ac parvae, nec non albae Russiae Monarcharum, multorumque dominiorum ac terrarum Orientalium, Occidentalium ac Septemtrionalium, Prognatorum Haeredum, ac Successorum, dominatorum ac possessorum

Magnis ac plenipotentibus Suae Tzareae Majestatis Legatis Proximo Okolnitio ac locitenente Branski Theodoro Alexiewicz Golovin dapifero ac locitenente Iélatomski, Ioanne Eustahievicz Wlasoph Cancellario Simeone Cornitski

Anno Cam Hi 28·° crocei serpentis dicto 7·ae Lunae die 24 prope oppidum Nipchou congregati tum ad coercendam et reprimendam insolentiam eorum inferioris notae venatorum hominum, qui extra proprios limites, sive venabundi, sive se mutuo occidentes, sive depraedantes, sive perturbationes aut tumultus quoscumque commoventes pro suo arbitrio excurrunt,

tum ad limites inter utrumque Imperium Sinicum videlicet et
Ruthenicum claré ac perspicué determinandos ac constituendos,
tum denique ad pacem perpetuam stabiliendam aeternumque
foedus percutiendum, sequentia puncta ex mutuo consensu
statuimus ac determinavimus.

I

Rivulus nomine Kerbichi, qui rivo Chorna Tartaricé Vrum
dicto proximus adiacet et fluvium Sagalien Vla influit, limites
inter utrumque Imperium constituet.   Item a vertice rupis seu
montis lapidei, qui est supra dicti rivuli Kerbichi fontem et
originem et per ipsa huius montis cacumina usque ad mare,
utriusque Imperii ditionem ita dividet, ut omnes terrae et
fluvii sive parvi sive magni qui a meridionali huius montis parte
in fluvium Sagalien Vla influunt sint sub Imperii Sinici dominio,
omnes terrae vero et omnes rivi qui ex altera montis parte ad
Borealem plagam vergunt sub Ruthenici Imperii dominio
remaneant, ita tamen, ut quicunque fluvii in mare influunt et
quaecumque terrae sunt intermediae inter fluvium Vdi et
seriem montium pro limitibus designatam prointerim indeter-
minatae relinquantur.   De his autem post uniuscuiusque Imperii
legatorum in proprium regnum reditum rité examinatis et clare
cognitis vel per legatos vel per litteras postea determinabitur.
Item fluvius nomine Ergon qui etiam supra dictum fluvium
Sagalien Vla influit, limites ita constituet, ut omnes terrae quae
sunt ex parte meridionali ad Sinicum, quae vero sunt ex parte
boreali, ad Ruthenicum Imperium pertineant: et omnes aedes
quae ex parte dicti fluminis meridionali in faucibus fluvii
nomine Meyrelke extructae sunt ad littus boreale transferentur.

II

Arx seu fortalitia in loco nomine Yagsa a Russis extructa
funditus eruetur ac destruetur.   Omnesque illam incolentes
Rutheni Imperii subditi cum omnibus suis cuiuscumque generis
rebus in Russi Imperii terras deducentur.

Atque extra hos limites determinatos nullam ob causam
utriusque Imperii venatores transibunt.

Quod si unus aut duo inferioris notae homines extra hos
statutos limites vel venabundi, vel latrocinaturi divagabuntur,
statim in vincula coniecti ad illarum terrarum constitutos in
utroque Imperio Praefectos deducentur, qui cognitam illorum

culpam debitâ poenâ mulctabunt: Si vero ad decem aut quindecim simul congregati et armis instructi, aut venabuntur, aut alterius Imperii homines occident, aut depraedabuntur de hoc ad uniuscuiusque Imperii Imperatores referetur, omnesque huius criminis rei capitali poenâ mulctabuntur, nec bellum propter quoscumque particularium hominum excessus suscitabitur, aut sanguinis effusio procurabitur.

III

Quaecumque prius acta sunt, cuiuscumque generis sint, aeternâ oblivione sopiantur. Ab eo die quo inter utrumque Imperium haec aeterna pax iurata fuerit, nulli in posterum ex altero Imperio transfugae in alterum Imperium admittentur: sed in vincula coniecti statim reducentur.

IV

Quicumque veró Rutheni Imperii subditi in Sinico et quicumque Sinici Imperii in Ruthenico nunc sunt, in eodem statu relinquantur.

V

Propter nunc contractam amicitiam atque aeternum foedus stabilitum, cuiuscumque generis homines litteras patentes iteneris sui afferentes, licité accedent ad regna utriusque dominii, ibique vendent et ement quaecumque ipsis videbuntur necessaria mutuo commercio.

VI

Concilio inter utriusque Imperii legatos celebrato, et omnibus utriusque Regni limitum contentionibus diremptis, paceque stabilitâ, et aeterno amicitiae foedere percusso, si hae omnes determinatae conditiones rité observabuntur, nullus erit amplius perturbationi locus.

Ex utraque parte hujus foederis conditiones scripto mandabuntur, duplexque exemplar huic conforme sigillo munitum sibi invicem tradent magni utriusque Imperii legati.

Demum et iuxta hoc idem exemplar eaedem conditiones Sinico Ruthenico et latino idiomate lapidibus incidentur, qui lapides in utriusque Imperii limitibus in perpetuum ac aeternum monumentum erigentur.

Datum apud Nipchou anno Cam Hi 28·° 7·ae Lunae die 24.

CONVENTION OF AIGUN

MAY 16, 1858

LE grand empire de Russie, et de sa part le gouverneur général de la Sibérie orientale, l'aide de camp général de S. M. l'Empereur Alexandre Nicolaïévitch, le lieutenant général Nicolas Mouraview,—et le grand empire Ta-Tsing, et de sa part l'aide de camp général prince I-Chan, grand de la cour, commandant en chef sur l'Amour,—voulant établir une éternelle et plus intime amitié entre les deux empires, et dans l'intérêt des sujets respectifs, ont arrêté d'un commun accord :

I

La rive gauche du fleuve Amour, à partir de la rivière Argoun jusqu'à l'embouchure de l'Amour, appartiendra à l'empire de Russie, et sa rive droite, en aval jusqu'à la rivière Oussouri, appartiendra à l'empire Ta-Tsing ; les territoires et endroits situés entre la rivière Oussouri et la mer, comme jusqu'à présent, seront possédés en commun par l'empire Ta-Tsing et l'empire de Russie, en attendant que la frontière entre les deux Etats y soit réglée. La navigation de l'Amour, du Soungari et de l'Oussouri n'est permise qu'aux bâtiments des empires Ta-Tsing et de la Russie ; la navigation de ces rivières sera interdite aux bâtiments de tout autre Etat. Les habitants mantchous établis sur la rive gauche de l'Amour, depuis la rivière Zéia jusqu'au village de Hormoldzin au sud, conserveront à perpétuité les lieux de leurs anciens domiciles sous l'administration du gouvernement mantchou, et les habitants russes ne pourront leur faire aucune offense ni vexation.

II

Dans l'intérêt de la bonne intelligence mutuelle des sujets respectifs, il est permis aux habitants riverains de l'Oussouri, de l'Amour et du Soungari, sujets de l'un et de l'autre empire, de trafiquer entre eux, et les autorités doivent réciproquement protéger les commerçants sur les deux rives.

III

Les stipulations arrêtées d'un commun accord par le plénipotentiaire de l'empire de Russie, le gouverneur général Mouraview, et le commandant en chef sur l'Amour, I-Chan, et
plénipotentiaire de l'empire Ta-Tsing, seront exactement et
inviolablement exécutées à perpétuité ; à cet effet, le gouverneur
général Mouraview, pour l'empire de Russie, a remis un exemplaire du présent traité, écrit en langues russe et mantchoue,
entre les mains du commandant en chef prince I-Chan pour
l'empire Ta-Tsing, et le commandant en chef prince I-Chan,
pour l'empire Ta-Tsing, a remis un exemplaire du présent
traité en langues mantchoue et mongole, au gouverneur général
Mouraview pour l'empire de Russie. Toutes les stipulations
consignées dans la présente seront publiées pour l'information
des habitants limitrophes des deux empires.

Le 16 mai 1858, ville d'Aïghoun.

L'original est signé ainsi qu'il suit :

Nicolas Mouraview, aide de camp général de l'Empereur
et autocrate de Russie, mon très gracieux souverain, lieutenant
général, gouverneur général de la Sibérie orientale et chevalier
de plusieurs ordres ;

Pierre Peroffsky, conseiller d'Etat du ministère des affaires
étrangères, au service de S. M. I. l'Empereur et autocrate de
toutes les Russies ;

I-Chan, commandant en chef sur l'Amour ;

Dziraminga, adjoint du chef de division.

Contre-signé :

J. Schischmareff, secrétaire de gouvernment, interprète
attaché au gouverneur général de la Sibérie orientale ;

Aïjindaï, chef de compagnie.

PEKING CONVENTION

November 2, 1860

A la suite d'une révision et d'un examen attentifs des traités existants entre la Russie et la Chine, S. M. l'Empereur et Autocrate de toutes les Russies, et S. M. le Bogdokhan de l'empire Ta-Tsing, voulant resserrer encore davantage les liens d'amitié réciproque entre les deux empires, développer les relations commerciales et prévenir tout mésentendu, ont résolu de stipuler quelques articles additionnels, et, à cet effet, ont nommé pour leurs plénipotentiaires :

Pour l'empire de Russie, le général-major Nicolas Ignatiew, de la suite de Sa Majesté Impériale, et chevalier de plusieurs ordres ;

Pour l'empire Ta-Tsing, le prince Kong, prince de première classe, qui porte le nom d'Y-Sing.

Lesdits plénipotentiaires, après s'être communiqué leurs pleins-pouvoirs, trouvés suffisants, sont convenus de ce qui suit.

Article I

Pour corroborer et élucider l'article 1er du traité conclu dans la ville d'Aïgoun, le 16 mai 1858 (VIIIe année de Hien-Fong, 21e jour de la IVe lune), et en exécution de l'article 9 du traité conclu le 1er juin de la même année (3e jour de la Ve lune) dans la ville de Tien-Tsin, il est établi :

Désormais la frontière orientale entre les deux empires, à commencer du confluent des rivières Chilka et Argoun, descendra le cours de la rivière Amour jusqu'au confluent de la rivière Ousouri avec cette dernière. Les terres situées sur la rive gauche (au nord) de la rivière Amour appartiennent à l'empire de Russie, et les terres situées sur la rive droite (au sud), jusqu'au confluent de la rivière Ousouri, appartiennent à l'empire de Chine. Plus loin, depuis le confluent de la rivière Ousouri jusqu'au lac Hinkaï, la ligne frontière suit les rivières Ousouri et Son'gatcha. Les terres situées sur la rive orientale (droite) de ces rivières appartiennent à l'empire de Russie, et sur la rive occidentale (gauche) à l'empire de Chine. Plus loin, la ligne frontière entre les deux empires, depuis le point de sortie de la rivière Son'gatcha, coupe le lac Hinkaï, et se dirige sur la rivière Bélén-ho (Tour) ; depuis l'embouchure de cette rivière elle suit la crête des montagnes jusqu'à l'embouchure de la rivière Houpitou (Houptou), et de là, les montagnes situées entre la rivière Khoûn-tchoun et la mer jusqu'à la rivière Thou-men-kiang. Le long de cette ligne, également, les terres situées à l'est appartiennent à l'empire de Russie et celles à à l'ouest à l'empire de Chine. La ligne frontière s'appuie à la rivière Thou-men-kiang, à vingt verstes chinoises (li) au-dessus de son embouchure dans la mer.

De plus, en exécution du même article 9 du traité de Tien-Tsin est confirmée la carte dressée à cet effet, et sur laquelle, pour plus de clarté, la ligne frontière est tracée par un trait rouge et indiquée par les lettres de l'alphabet russe А. Б. В. Г. Д. Е. Ж. З. И. І. К. Л. М. Н. О. П. Р. С. Т. У. Cette carte est signée par les plénipotentiaires des deux empires et scellée de leurs sceaux.

Dans le cas où il existerait dans les lieux sus-indiqués des terrains colonisés par des sujets chinois, le gouvernement russe s'engage à y laisser les habitants et à leur permettre de se livrer comme par le passé à la chasse et à la pêche.

Après que les bornes-frontières auront été posées, la ligne de démarcation de la frontière devra rester à jamais invariable.

Article II

La ligne frontière à l'ouest, indéterminée jusqu'ici, doit désormais suivre la direction des montagnes, le cours des grandes rivières et la ligne actuellement existante des piquets chinois. A partir du dernier phare, nommé Chabin-dabaga, établi en 1728 (VIᵉ année de Young-Tching), après la conclusion du traité de Kiakhta, elle se dirigera vers le sud-ouest jusqu'au lac Dsaï-sang, et de là jusqu'aux montagnes situées au sud du lac Issyk-koul, et nommées Téngri-chan, ou Alatau des Kirghises, autrement dites encore Thian-chan-nan-lou (branches méridionales des montagnes Célestes), et le long de ces montagnes jusqu'aux possessions du Kokand.

Article III

Désormais toutes les questions de frontières qui pourront surgir ultérieurement seront réglées d'après les stipulations des articles 1ᵉʳ et 2 du présent traité, et, pour la pose des bornes-frontières, à l'orient, depuis le lac Hinkaï jusqu'à la rivière Thou-men-kiang ; et à l'occident, depuis le phare Chabin-dabaga jusqu'aux possessions du Kokand, les gouvernements russe et chinois nommeront des hommes de confiance (commissaires). Pour l'inspection des frontières orientales, les commissaires devront se réunir au confluent de la rivière Ousouri dans le courant du mois d'avril prochain (XIe année de Hien-Fong, troisième lune). Pour l'inspection de la frontière occidentale, la réunion des commissaires aura lieu à Tarbagataï, mais l'époque n'en est pas déterminée.

Sur les bases fixées par les articles 1er et 2 du présent traité, les fonctionnaires fondés de pouvoirs (commissaires) dresseront des cartes et des descriptions détaillées de la ligne frontière, en quatre exemplaires, dont deux en langue russe et deux en langue chinoise ou mantchoue. Ces cartes et descriptions seront signées et scellées par les commissaires, après quoi deux exemplaires, un en russe et l'autre en langue chinoise ou mantchoue, seront remis au gouvernement russe, et deux exemplaires semblables au gouvernement chinois, pour être conservés par eux.

Pour la remise des cartes et descriptions de la ligne frontière, il sera dressé un protocole corroboré par la signature et l'apposition des sceaux des commissaires, et qui sera considéré comme article additionnel au présent traité.

Article IV

Sur toute la ligne frontière établie par l'article 1er du présent traité, un commerce d'échange libre et franc de droits est autorisé entre les sujets des deux Etats. Les chefs locaux des frontières doivent accorder une protection particulière à ce commerce et à ceux qui l'exercent.

Sont en même temps confirmées par le présent les dispositions relatives au commerce établies par l'article 2 du traité d'Aïgoun.

Article V

Outre le commerce existant à Kiakhta, les marchands russes jouiront de leur ancien droit de se rendre de Kiakhta à Pékin pour affaires commerciales. Sur la route, il leur est également permis de commercer à Ourga et à Kalgan, sans être obligés toutefois d'y établir de commerce en gros. Le gouvernement russe aura le droit d'avoir à Ourga un consul (lin-tchi-khouan) accompagné de quelques personnes, et d'y construire à ses frais une habitation pour ce fonctionnaire. Quant à la concession d'un terrain pour cet édifice, au règlement des dimensions de ce dernier, comme aussi à la concession d'un pâturage, on devra s'entendre avec les gouverneurs d'Ourga.

Les marchands chinois sont également autorisés à se rendre en Russie pour y commercer, s'ils le désirent.

Les marchands russes ont le droit de voyager en Chine, en tout temps, pour affaires de commerce; seulement, il leur est interdit de se réunir simultanément en nombre de plus de *deux cents* dans le même lieu; de plus, ils doivent être munis de billets de l'autorité russe à la frontière, indiquant le nom du chef de la caravane, le nombre des hommes dont elle se compose et le lieu de sa destination. Pendant le voyage, ces marchands ont la faculté d'acheter et de vendre tout ce qui leur convient. Tous les frais de leur voyage sont à leur charge.

Article VI

A titre d'essai, le commerce est ouvert à Kachgar, sur les mêmes bases qu'à Ili et à Tarbagataï. A Kachgar, le gouvernement chinois cède un terrain suffisant pour la construction d'une factorerie avec tous les édifices nécessaires, tels que maisons d'habitation, magasins pour le dépôt des marchandises, église, etc., etc., ainsi qu'un terrain pour le cimetière et un pâturage, comme à Ili et à Tarbagataï. Les ordres seront donnés immédiatement au gouverneur du pays de Kachgar pour la concession desdits terrains.

Le gouvernement chinois ne répond pas du pillage des marchands russes commerçant à Kachgar, dans le cas où ce pillage aurait été commis par des gens venus d'au-delà des lignes des postes de garde chinois.

Article VII

Dans les lieux ouverts au commerce, les Russes en Chine, comme les sujets chinois en Russie, peuvent se livrer en pleine liberté aux affaires commerciales, sans aucune vexation de la part des autorités locales; fréquenter avec la même liberté et en tout temps les marchés, les boutiques, les maisons des marchands du pays; vendre et acheter diverses marchandises en gros et en détail, au comptant ou par échanges; les livrer et recevoir à crédit, selon leur confiance réciproque.

La durée du séjour des marchands dans les lieux où se fait le commerce n'est pas déterminée et dépend de leur libre arbitre.

Article VIII

Les marchands russes en Chine et les Chinois en Russie sont placés sous la protection spéciale des deux gouvernements. Pour surveiller les marchands et prévenir les malentendus qui pourraient survenir entre eux et les habitants du pays, il est loisible au gouvernement russe de nommer dès à présent des consuls à Kachgar et à Ourga, sur la base des règles adoptées pour Ili et Tarbagataï. Le gouvernement chinois peut également, s'il le désire, nommer des consuls dans les capitales et autres villes de l'empire de Russie.

Les consuls de l'une et de l'autre puissance sont logés dans des édifices construits aux frais de leurs gouvernements respectifs. Toutefois, il ne leur est pas défendu de louer, si cela leur convient, des logements chez les habitants du pays.

Dans leurs relations avec les autorités locales, les consuls des deux puissances observent une égalité parfaite, en exécution de l'article 2 du traité de Tien-Tsin. Toutes les affaires concernant les marchands de l'un et de l'autre empire sont examinées par eux de gré à gré ; les crimes et délits doivent être jugés, comme il est réglé par l'article 7 du traité de Tien-Tsin, d'après les lois de l'empire dont le coupable est sujet.

Les litiges, revendications et autres malentendus de même nature, survenant entre marchands à propos d'affaires commerciales, seront réglés par les marchands eux-mêmes, au moyen d'arbitres choisis parmi eux ; les consuls et les autorités locales doivent se borner à coopérer à l'arrangement à l'amiable, sans prendre aucune responsabilité relativement aux revendications.

Dans les lieux où le commerce est autorisé, les marchands de l'un et de l'autre empire peuvent contracter des engagements par écrit pour des commandes de marchandises, la location de boutiques, maisons, etc., etc., et les présenter à la légalisation du consulat et de l'administration locale. En cas de nonexécution d'un engagement écrit, le consul et le chef local prennent des mesures pour amener les parties à remplir exactement leurs obligations.

Les contestations qui ne se rapportent point à des affaires de commerce entre marchands, telles que litiges, plaintes, etc.,

etc., sont jugées de consentement mutuel par le consul et le chef local, et les délinquants sont punis d'après les lois de leur pays.

En cas de recel d'un sujet russe parmi les Chinois, ou de sa fuite dans l'intérieur du pays, l'autorité locale, aussitôt après en avoir été informée par le consul russe, prend immédiatement des mesures pour faire rechercher le fugitif, et aussitôt après l'avoir découvert le remet au consulat russe. La même marche doit également être observée relativement à tout sujet Chinois qui se cacherait chez des Russes ou se serait enfui en Russie.

Dans les cas de crimes graves, tels que meurtre, brigandage avec de graves blessures, attentat contre la vie, incendie prémédité, etc.; après enquête, si le coupable est Russe, il est envoyé en Russie pour être traité selon les lois de son pays, et s'il est Chinois, sa punition lui est infligée par l'autorité du lieu où le crime a été commis, ou bien, si les lois de l'Etat l'exigent, le coupable est envoyé dans une autre ville ou une autre province pour y recevoir son châtiment.

En cas de crime, quelle qu'en soit la gravité, le consul et le chef local ne peuvent prendre les mesures nécessaires que relativement au coupable appartenant à leur pays, et ni l'un ni l'autre n'a le droit d'incarcérer ni de juger séparément, et encore moins de châtier un individu non-sujet de son gouvernement.

Article IX

L'étendue que prennent actuellement les relations commerciales entre les sujets des deux puissances, et la fixation de la nouvelle ligne des frontières rendent désormais inapplicables les anciennes règles établies par les traités conclus à Nertchinsk et à Kiakhta, et par les conventions qui leur ont servi de compléments ; les relations des autorités des frontières entre elles et les règles établies pour l'examen des affaires de frontières ne répondent également plus aux circonstances actuelles. En conséquence, en remplacement de ces règles, il est établi ce qui suit :

Désormais, outre les relations qui existent à la frontière orientale, par Ourga et Kiakhta, entre le gouverneur de Kiakhta et les autorités d'Ourga, et à la frontière occidentale, entre le gouverneur général de la Sibérie occidentale et l'administration d'Ili, il y aura encore des relations de frontières entre les gouverneurs militaires de la province de l'Amour et de la province maritime et les tsiang-kiun (commandants en chef) de Hé-loung-kiang et de Kirin, et entre le commissaire des frontières de Kiakhta et le dzargoutcheï (pou-youèn), d'après le sens de l'article 8 du présent traité.

Conformément à l'article 2 du traité de Tien-Tsin, les gouverneurs militaires et commandants en chef (tsiang-kiun) ci-dessus nommés doivent observer une égalité parfaite dans leurs relations, et sont tenus de ne les entretenir que pour les affaires dans lesquelles leur administration est directement intéressée.

En cas d'affaires d'une importance particulière, le gouverneur général de la Sibérie orientale a le droit d'entretenir des relations par écrit, soit avec le conseil suprême (kiun-ki-tchou), soit avec la cour des relations extérieures (li-fan-youèn), comme principale autorité administrative dirigeant les relations et l'administration des frontières.

ARTICLE X

Dans l'instruction et la décision des affaires de frontières, de qu lque importance qu'elles soient, les chefs des frontières se conformeront aux règles énoncées en l'article 8 du présent traité ; quant aux enquêtes concernant les sujets de l'un et de l'autre empire, et aux châtiments à leur infliger, ils s'effectueront, ainsi qu'il est dit en l'article 7 du traité de Tien-Tsin, d'après les lois du pays auquel appartient le coupable.

En cas de passage, détournement ou enlèvement de bétail au-delà de la frontière, les autorités locales, aussitôt qu'elles en auront été informées et que les traces auront été indiquées au gardien du poste frontière le plus proche, enverront des hommes chargés de faire des recherches. Le bétail retrouvé sera immédiatement restitué, et s'il en manque quelques pièces, la répétition en sera exercée conformément aux lois ; mais dans ce cas l'indemnité à payer ne doit pas être élevée à plusieurs fois la valeur du bétail manquant (ainsi que cela se pratiquait auparavant).

En cas de fuite d'un individu au-delà des frontières, à la première nouvelle, des mesures sont immédiatement prises pour rechercher le transfuge. Le fugitif saisi est livré sans délai, avec tous les objets qui lui appartiennent, à l'autorité de la frontière ; l'examen des motifs de la fuite et le jugement de l'affaire elle-même s'effectuent par l'autorité locale du pays auquel appartient le transfuge, la plus rapprochée des frontières. Pendant tout le temps de son séjour au delà des frontières, depuis son arrestation jusqu'à son extradition, le transfuge est convenablement nourri et, en cas de besoin, vêtu ; la garde qui l'accompagne doit le traiter avec humanité et ne doit pas se permettre d'actes arbitraires à son égard. On devra en agir de même à l'égard du transfuge au sujet duquel il n'aurait été donné aucun avis.

Article XI

Les communications par écrit entre les autorités supérieures des frontières de l'un et de l'autre empire ont lieu par l'entremise des fonctionnaires les plus voisins de la frontière, à qui les dépêches expédiées sont remises contre récépissés.

Le gouverneur général de la Sibérie orientale et le gouverneur de Kiakhta envoient leurs dépêches au commissaire des frontières à Kiakhta, qui les remet au dzargoutcheï (pou-youèn) ; les gouverneurs d'Ourga expédient les leurs au dzargoutcheï (pou-youèn), qui les remet au commissaire des frontières à Kiakhta.

Le gouverneur militaire de la province de l'Amour envoie ses dépêches par l'adjoint (foudou-toun) du commandant en chef (tsiang-kiun) dans la ville d'Aïgoun, par l'entremise duquel les commandants en chef (tsiang-kiun) de Héloung-kiang et de Kirin transmettent les leurs au gouverneur militaire de la province de l'Amour.

Le gouverneur militaire de la province maritime et le commandant en chef (tsiang-kiun) de Kirin se transmettent réciproquement leurs dépêches par l'entremise de leurs chefs de postes frontières sur les rivières Ousouri et Khoùntchoun.

La transmission des correspondances entre le gouverneur général de la Sibérie occidentale et l'administration supérieure ou le commandant en chef (tsiang-kiun) d'Ili s'effectue par l'entremise du consul de Russie dans la ville d'Ili (Kouldja).

En cas d'affaire d'une importance particulière exigeant des explications verbales, les autorités supérieures des frontières de l'un et de l'autre empire peuvent s'expédier réciproquement leurs dépêches par des fonctionnaires russes de confiance.

Conformément aux dispositions de l'article 11 du traité de Tien-Tsin, les postes aux lettres et aux colis expédiées pour affaires de service de Kiakhta à Pékin, et retour, partiront aux époques ci-dessous, savoir : les *postes aux lettres, une fois chaque mois* de chacun des deux points, et les *postes aux colis, une fois tous les deux mois* de Kiakhta pour Pékin, et *une fois tous les trois mois* de Pékin pour Kiakhta.

Les postes aux lettres doivent arriver à leur destination en *vingt jours* au plus, et les postes aux colis en *quarante jours* au plus.

A chaque voyage, la poste aux colis ne doit pas être chargée de plus de *vingt caisses* ne pesant pas plus de *cent vingt livres* chinoises (ghin) ou *quatre pouds* chacune.

Les postes aux lettres doivent être expédiées le jour même où elles ont été remises, en cas de retard, il y aura une enquête et une punition sévère.

Le postillon expédié avec les postes aux lettres et aux colis doit se présenter au consulat de Russie à Ourga, y remettre les lettres et colis adressés aux personnes résidant en cette ville, et recevoir d'elles les lettres et colis qu'elles auraient à expédier.

A l'expédition des postes aux colis, les caisses dont elles sont chargées doivent être accompagnées de *lettres de voiture* (tsintan). De Kiakhta, les lettres de voiture, accompagnées d'un office, sont adressés au gouverneur d'Ourga, et de Pékin, également avec un office, à la cour des relations extérieures (li-fan-youèn).

Les lettres de voiture indiquent exactement la date de l'expédition, le nombre des caisses et leur poids total. Le poids spécial de chaque caisse doit être inscrit sur l'enveloppe même de la caisse, en chiffres russes, avec leur traduction en poids mongol ou chinois.

Si les marchands russes jugent nécessaire, pour les besoins de leurs affaires de commerce, d'établir à leurs frais un service de poste pour le transport de leurs lettres ou de leurs marchandises, la faculté leur en sera accordée, afin d'alléger le service de la poste de l'Etat. En cas d'établissement d'une communication postale, les marchands doivent simplement en prévenir l'autorité locale pour obtenir son assentiment.

Article XIII

Les correspondances ordinaires du ministre des affaires étrangères de Russie pour le conseil suprême (kiun-ki-tchou) de l'empire Ta-Tsing, et celles du gouverneur général de la Sibérie orientale pour le même conseil ou pour la cour des relations extérieures (li-fan-youèn) sont expédiées de la manière ordinaire par la poste, mais sans être astreintes aux époques fixées pour le départ de celle-ci ; en cas d'affaires d'une importance particulière, ces correspondances peuvent être expédiées par un courrier russe.

Pendant le séjour des envoyés russes à Pékin, les dépêches d'une importance spéciale peuvent également être expédiées par un fonctionnaire russe expressément désigné à cet effet.

Les courriers russes ne doivent être retenus nulle part en route ; ni par qui que ce soit.

Le courrier chargé de transporter des dépêches doit absolument être sujet russe.

L'expédition d'un courrier est annoncée vingt-quatre heures d'avance, à Kiakhta par le commissaire au dzargoutcheï (pou-youèn), et à Pékin par la mission russe à la cour militaire (ping-pou).

Article XIV

Si, ultérieurement, quelqu'une des stipulations relatives au commerce de terre arrêtées par le présent traité offre des inconvénients à l'une ou à l'autre partie, le gouverneur général de la Sibérie orientale est autorisé à s'entendre avec les autorités supérieures des frontières de l'empire Ta-Tsing et à conclure avec elles des conventions additionnelles, en se conformant dans tous les cas aux principes posés ci-dessus.

L'article 12 du traité de Tien-Tsin est en même temps confirmé et ne doit subir aucune altération.

Article XV

Ayant arrêté d'un commun accord les dispositions ci-dessus, les plénipotentiaires des empires de Russie et de Chine ont signé de leur main et scellé de leur sceau deux exemplaires du texte russe du traité et deux exemplaires de sa traduction en langue chinoise, et se sont réciproquement remis l'un à l'autre un exemplaire de l'un et de l'autre

Les articles du présent traité ont force légale à dater du jour de leur échange entre les plénipotentiaires de l'un et de l'autre empire, comme s'ils étaient insérés mot pour mot dans le traité de Tien-Tsin, et doivent être à toujours exécutés fidèlement et inviolablement.

Après avoir été ratifié par les souverains des deux empires, ce traité sera promulgué dans chacun des deux Etats, pour la connaissance et la gouverne de qui il appartiendra.

Conclu et signé dans la ville capitale de Pékin le deuxième (quatorzième) jour de novembre de l'an mil huit cent soixante de l'ère chrétienne, et la sixième année du règne de l'Empereur Alexandre II, et le deuxième jour de la dixième lune de la dixième année de Hien-Fong.

Signé :
Nicolas Ignatiew.
Kong.

PROTOCOL OF THE PEKING CONVENTION

Le 2 (14) novembre de l'an 1860, les hauts plénipotentiaires : pour l'empire de Russie, le général-major Ignatiew, de la suite de Sa Majesté Impériale et chevalier de plusieurs ordres ;—pour l'empire Ta-Tsing, le prince Kong, prince de première classe, suivis de leurs secrétaires et interprètes, se sont réunis à quatre heures après midi, dans une des salles du collège ecclésiastique russe, situé vers le sud, à l'effet de procéder à la signature et à l'échange du traité conclu aujourd'hui et devant servir de complément au traité de Tien-Tsin de l'année 1858.

En premier lieu il a été fait lecture de l'édit du Bogdokhan, dans lequel il est déclaré que Sa Majesté confirme mot pour mot le projet de traité additionnel, en *quinze* articles, soumis à sa ratification ; qu'elle promet de l'exécuter fidèlement et inviolablement, et ordonne à Kong-tsin-wang d'apposer le sceau et de signer le traité additionnel qui a été conclu. Kong-tsin-wang ayant ensuite déclaré qui cet édit suffit en tout point pour que la délimitation des deux empires et les autres articles du traité soient considérés comme définitivement ratifiés par le Bogdokhan, le plénipotentiaire de Russie a déclaré que, de son côté, il consentait à considérer le traité comme ratifié par le Bogdokhan, et qu'il était prêt à signer immédiatement le traité et à effectuer l'échange des exemplaires. En conséquence, les deux plénipotentiaires ont signé deux exemplaires du traité en langue russe et deux exemplaires en langue chinoise, et y ont fait apposer leurs sceaux. A la suite de quoi le général-major Ignatiew a remis entre les mains du prince de première classe Kong l'instrument du traité, transcrit dans les deux langues, et le prince de première classe Kong, ayant reçu le traité, a remis à son tour au plénipotentiaire de Russie l'instrument du traité également transcrit dans les deux langues.

L'échange des exemplaires du traité ayant été effectué, les plénipotentiaires ont signé le présent procès-verbal, en deux exemplaires, à Pekin, dans une des salles du collège ecclé-siastique russe, situé vers le sud.

Signé :

KONG.
NICOLAS IGNATIEW.

LEASE OF PORT ARTHUR AND TA-LIEN-WAN.

HIS MAJESTY THE EMPEROR OF CHINA, on the sixth day of the third moon of the twenty-fourth year of Kuang Hsü (March 27, 1898), appointed the Grand Secretary, Li Hung-chang, and the Senior Vice-President of the Board of Revenue, Chang Yin-husn, as Plenipotentiaries to arrange with M. Pavloff, Chargé d'Affaires and Plenipotentiary for Russia, all matters connected with the leasing and use by Russia of Port Arthur and Ta-lien-wan.

The treaty arranged between them in this connection is as follows :—

ARTICLE I

It being necessary for the due protection of her navy in the waters of North China that Russia should possess a station she can defend, the Emperor of China agrees to lease to Russia Port Arthur and Ta-lien-wan, together with the adjacent seas, but on the understanding that such lease shall not prejudice China's sovereignty over this territory.

ARTICLE II

The limits of the territory thus leased for the reasons above stated, as well as the extent of territory north of Ta-lien-wan necessary for the defence of that now leased, and what shall be allowed to be leased, shall be strictly defined, and all details necessary to the carrying out of this treaty be arranged at St. Petersburg with Hsü Ta-jên so soon as possible for the signature of the present treaty, and embodied in a separate treaty. Once these limits have been determined, all land held by Chinese within such limits, as well as the adjacent waters, shall be held by Russia alone on lease.

ARTICLE III

The duration of the lease shall be twenty-five years from the day this treaty is signed, but may be extended by mutual agreement between Russia and China.

Article IV

The control of all military forces in the territory eased by Russia, and of all naval forces in the adjacent seas, as well as of the civil officials in it, shall be vested in one high Russian official, who shall, however, be designated by some title other than Governor-General (Tsung-tu), or Governor (Hsün-fu). All Chinese military forces shall, without exception, be withdrawn from the territory, but it shall remain optional with the ordinary Chinese inhabitants either to remain or to go; and no coercion shall be used towards them in this matter. Should they remain, any Chinese charged with a criminal offence shall be handed over to the nearest Chinese official to be dealt with according to Article VIII. of the Russo-Chinese treaty of 1860.

Article V

To the north of the territory leased shall be a zone, the extent of which shall be arranged at St. Petersburg between Hsü Ta-jên and the Russian Foreign Office. Jurisdiction over this zone shall be vested in China, but China may not quarter troops in it except with the previous consent of Russia.

Article VI

The two nations agree that Port Arthur shall be a naval port for the sole use of Russian and Chinese men-of-war, and be considered as an unopened port so far as the naval and mercantile vessels of other nations are concerned. As regards Ta-lien-wan, one portion of the harbour shall be reserved exclusively for Russian and Chinese men-of-war, just like Port Arthur, but the remainder shall be a commercial port freely open to the merchant vessels of all countries.

Article VII

Port Arthur and Ta-lien-wan are the points in the territory leased most important for Russian military purposes. Russia shall, therefore, be at liberty to erect, at her own expense, forts, and build barracks and provide defences, at such places as she desires.

ARTICLE VIII

China agrees that the procedure sanctioned in 1896 regarding the construction of railroads by the Board of the Eastern China Railway shall, from the date of the signature of this treaty, be extended so as to include the construction of a branch line to Ta-lien-wan, or, if necessary, in view of the interests involved, of a branch line to the most suitable point on the coast between Newchwang and the Yalu river. Further, the agreement entered into in September 1896 between the Chinese Government and the Russo-Chinese Bank shall apply with equal strength to this branch line. The direction of this branch and the places it shall touch shall be arranged between Hsü Ta-jên and the Board of the Eastern Railroads. The construction of this line shall never, however, be made a ground for encroaching on the sovereignty or integrity of China.

ARTICLE IX

This treaty shall take full force and effect from the date it is signed, but the ratifications shall be exchanged in St. Petersburg.

Signed March 27, 1898.

INDEX

PRINTED BY
SPOTTISWOODE AND CO., NEW-STREET SQUARE
LONDON